Air Power in the Age of Total War

AIR POWER IN THE AGE OF TOTAL WAR

John Buckley

Indiana University Press
Bloomington and Indianapolis

Published in the United Kingdom by
UCL Press Limited, 1 Gunpowder Square, London E4A 3DE, England

and in North America by
Indiana University Press, 601 North Morton Street, Bloomington,
Indiana 47404

Manufactured in the United Kingdom

Library of Congress Cataloging-in-Publication Data
A catalog record for this book is available from the Library of
Congress.

ISBN 0–253–33557–4 (cloth)
ISBN 0–253–21324–X (paper)

1   2   3   4   5   03   02   01   00   99

Contents

List of tables

Acknowledgements

In the preparation of this book I have received assistance from many parties and it is my pleasure to acknowledge them here. First, I must thank my colleagues in the Department of History and War Studies at the University of Wolverhampton for allowing me the time away from teaching to prepare this work. Additionally, I must thank those students who have undertaken *HS1000: Bomber Offensive* over the last few years and have asked many searching and pertinent questions, and who have surely taught me as much as I them. I am also very grateful to Steven Gerrard and Aisling Ryan for their patience and understanding and to Jeremy Black, general editor of the *Warfare and History* series.

For comment and advice, thanks are due to John Gooch, Simon Ball, Michael Paris, Peter Caddick-Adams, Peter MacDonald, Toby McLeod, Mark Howells, Steve Mills, Charles Singleton, Paul Ruewell and two anonymous readers. All have given up valuable time in reading drafts, offering direction and indicating errors. Finally to friends and family, who have suffered unflinchingly the burden of my writing this book, I offer a great vote of thanks for their patience and understanding.

John Buckley
Department of History and War Studies
University of Wolverhampton
May 1998

Glossary

AA	Anti-aircraft
ACTS	Air Corps Tactical School
Armee de l'Air	French Air Force
Asdic	Early name for sonar
Blitzkrieg	Lightning war
BuAer	Bureau of Aeronautics (US Navy)
CAS	Chief of the Air Staff
CID	Committee of Imperial Defence
CinC	Commander in Chief
Enigma	German encryption system
Flak	Anti-aircraft fire
FOFA	Follow-on forces attack
ICBM	Intercontinental ballistic missile
IJN	Imperial Japanese Navy
Luftwaffe	German Air Force
MAD	Mutually Assured Destruction
MIRV	Multiple independently targetable re-entry vehicles
NATO	North Atlantic Treaty Organisation
NSC	National Security Council
RAF	British Royal Air Force
Regia Aeronautica	Italian Air Force
RFC	Royal Flying Corps
RN	Royal Navy
RNAS	Royal Naval Air Service
SAC	Strategic Air Command
SAM	Surface to air missile
SLBM	Submarine launched ballistic missile

ULTRA	Allied intelligence gained from breaking Enigma codes
USAAC	United States Army Air Corps
USAAF	United States Army Air Force
USAF	United States Air Force
USN	United States Navy
USSBS	United States Strategic Bombing Survey
USSR	Union of Soviet Socialist Republics
V/STOL	Vertical or short take-off and landing
VVS	*Voyenno-voznushnyye sily* (Soviet Air Force)
Window	Metal foil strips designed to blind German radar systems

Chapter One

Air power in the age of total war

There have been many changes in the nature and conduct of war in the twentieth century, but perhaps that which has had the greatest impact, both in revolutionizing the battlefield and in expanding the scale and scope of war, has been the advent of air power. In the space of a little over 40 years, aircraft progressed from the Wrights' first faltering flights in the Kill Devil Hills in 1903 to the mass destruction of Dresden, Tokyo and, most poignantly, Hiroshima and Nagasaki in 1945. The air raids of the Second World War, in particular those which to this day evoke bitter feelings of resentment and guilt, were the culmination of a revolution in warfare which saw aircraft do more than any other weapon to bring in the era of total war.

Air power was to prove radically different from any other arm in the history of war. In the 5,000 years or so of recorded history, stretching from the nascent cities of Sumer to the end of the nineteenth century, war had been essentially two dimensional. Enemy fleets and armies could be avoided, even defeated, by means other than direct combat but ultimately ground forces of infantry and cavalry and their supports were the final arbiters of victory or defeat. Enemy forces, for the most part, could be kept at arm's length by effective military activity whereas cities and rear zones could be protected by high walls and fortifications, thus minimizing the impact of enemy raids. The destructive zone of war was always limited to where the enemy could deploy their land or naval forces, whether it was in armed combat or in the prosecution of a siege or blockade. The impact of such war was consequently restricted to the damage done by the armed forces themselves, with little, if any, immediate consequence for the civilian populations not directly in their path. Economically, politically and culturally the war may have had significant consequences, but physical destruction was more often than not confined to the combatants and those unlucky enough to be too close to the fighting.

Aircraft changed this natural order of things. The effective utilization of air power added, for the first time in history, a third dimension to war: a dimension which allowed direct attack on enemy rear zones, cities, economies and, perhaps most importantly, civilian populations. Moreover, the zone of conflict was extended by aircraft from the immediate battlefield to the rear zones of armies. Supply routes were open to attack and soldiers were given little respite from the front. Just as importantly, air power offered the means with which to gather intelligence and information on the enemy army's movements and aircraft rapidly developed the ability to intervene in a direct and offensive manner on the battlefield itself. Nevertheless, the impact of air power on military campaigns, while it was eventually to become crucial and at times pivotal to success, was only one facet of the significance of air power. In addition to tactical or operational air power came strategic air power: that is the use of air forces to attack the enemy state, its centres of population, and its economy directly. This facet of air power was instrumental in shaping the attitude of human civilization towards war, culminating as it did in the atomic bombings of Japan in 1945.

Strategic air power and total war

The twentieth century saw the advent of so-called "total war", and aircraft were to play a significant role in developing the totality of conflict. In the past, long drawn-out wars had had devastating effects on societies, causing massive upheaval and even mass migration of dislocated populations. However, these conflicts had only rarely resulted in direct and sustained attack on the people themselves. That had changed by the time of the Second World War in particular. Air power provided the means with which to attack enemy populations directly, creating huge ethical and moral problems. Was targeting civilians a justifiable or legitimate stratagem simply because the capability now existed? If they were working in factories producing tanks and guns, were they not as culpable as the men in uniforms who represented them? In the age of total war, was it not true that whole societies rather than elites were, for the first time in the modern era, in conflict with each other and consequently open to attack?

There is a widespread perception that war and human society has somehow degenerated into a new barbarism in the twentieth century and that the emergence of total war and all its attendant excesses has been the principal result.[1] However, compared with the wholesale destruction of civilizations and cultures in the ancient and medieval world, the desire in the twentieth century to use extreme methods in war is nothing new. It is spurious to confuse inability with unwillingness or restraint in the prosecution of war. What air power contributed to the development of a more total war than the Mongol conquests, or the destruction of the indigenous civilizations of the Americas, was the means with which to prosecute a greater degree of war, both in terms of destruction and in the perceptions of societies. Many civilizations have used whatever methods were available to prosecute war, often with few restraints, and air power was in reality nothing more than a further, if highly significant, step in this particular direction.

However, it is clear that in many ways the thought of aerial attack on civilians, particularly massed strategic bombing, has coloured our perceptions of air war in the first half of the twentieth century. Although popular images such as the Great War's knights of the air, Biggles and victory rolls over Biggin Hill still pervade our thinking, the starkest images we have of air war are those of Hamburg, Dresden, Hiroshima and Nagasaki. Generally, studies of air power in the broadest sense have concentrated closely on the relative merits or failings of strategic bombing. From the very earliest days of controlled air flight, and indeed even before, the advocates of air power claimed that aerial bombing attack would prove to be the most decisive form of warfare, bringing enemies to the point of capitulation in a very short space of time. Despite the fact that they had little impact on air force development themselves, air power advocates such as Guilio Douhet, Billy Mitchell and Alexander de Seversky did much to publicize the notion that air power alone could be decisive in wars. Their claims proved to be the yardstick by which the bombing offensives of World War II would be measured, and ultimately be seen to fail.

However, this perceived failure, coupled with the shocking imagery of Dresden and Hiroshima, has distorted the picture of air power. Strategic bombing was a failure only by the standards of its arch-proponents. Clearly, bombing did not win World War II by itself, nor was it ever likely to. But it did contribute greatly to the economic collapse of the Axis powers, not only in terms of direct destruction but also in the restraining impact it had on production and in destroying the *Luftwaffe* in the last two years of the war.[2] It is not enough to argue, as some have, that the considerable expansion of the German economy from the middle of 1942 was evidence for the failure of the bombing offensive.[3] It is indicative, however, of what Albert Speer might have achieved if he had not had to take into account the repeated aerial pummelling of Germany for the last three years of the war.

Nevertheless, despite its achievements, the bombing offensive of World War II still raises many questions. The resources allocated to the campaign by the Allies, especially the British, were huge and, it has been argued, they were denied many other possible strategic options. The continued prosecution of the offensive on a vast scale when the Germans seemed to be taking it in their stride and suffering only limited losses – though of course they were suffering in many hidden ways – only becomes shrewd when viewed with the benefit of hindsight. Moreover, the heaviest destruction inflicted by the bomber fleets came in the last year of the war when, many have argued, German and Japanese defences were already starting to crumble. The importance of the bombing offensive to the outcome of World War II remains a hotly disputed issue and, if the moral and ethical aspects of the campaign are also considered, it is clear that the debate will continue to dominate perceptions of air power.

Ethics and air war

The expansion of war into the air resulted in significant changes to perceptions of what was acceptable in wartime conditions. Targeting cities and industrial centres certainly appeared to make good strategic sense, but clearly there was far more to this issue than mere military expediency. Bombing urban centres, on whatever pretext, meant killing civilians and to many this was an unwelcome and immoral escalation of the already brutal activity of war. Yet, arguably, the conduct of war throughout history has been influenced less by morality and more by military capability, balanced by political acceptability. This in turn has been shaped by the objectives for which a society was fighting. In total war environments, both the stakes and the military capability have been high, resulting in the use of previously unparalleled methods of waging war. Ultimately, the key factor for the legitimacy of a stratagem has been its effectiveness. Would it allow you to win and bring the war to a speedy conclusion?

Aerial bombing clearly offered the greatest challenge to those who sought to limit war to military personnel. However, even before 1914, the distinction between combatant and non-combatant had become blurred and the scale of mass industrial war was often to render such notions worthless. Attempts to outlaw or limit the effects of bombing ultimately came to very little and, as has often been the case in war, technical capability and political need have usually dictated the level of violence in conflicts. Even at a theoretical stage, the emergence of air power served to cause debate at the

1899 and 1907 Hague Conferences which were set up to offer guidelines to moderate the conduct of war. There were immediate ambiguities as attacks on *undefended* urban centres, by whatever means, were not allowed, but naval bombardment of a military target was, even if in the vicinity of the civilian population.[4] Moreover, history is replete with examples of civilians being deliberately targeted in war, especially in sieges and times of blockade. Was indiscriminate starvation any better than indiscriminate bombardment?

Deep ethical and moral issues emerged from the growth in capability and theory concerning aerial bombardment and industrial war. Attacks on military centres, even if this resulted in "collateral civilian casualties", were acceptable, but crossing the Rubicon came when the notion of targeting civilians themselves was developed. During the First World War, bombing strategy, although primarily aimed at military areas, also accepted that inaccurate bombs would hit and kill civilians and this was acceptable because it would damage enemy morale. Deliberate targeting of civilians declined as a strategy in the 1930s but re-emerged during the Second World War in the RAF once it proved impossible to bomb anything accurately. Although the Allied governments never admitted it openly, from early 1942 onwards first the Royal Air Force and then latterly the United States Army Air Force (USAAF) pursued a policy of area bombing. In effect this was a policy of deliberately destroying urban centres and their populations in an effort to cause disruption and chaos in the enemy state and thus undermine their war effort. This proved to be a less effective way of damaging the enemy state than precision bombing (as undertaken by the USAAF over Europe) but until 1944 it was the only method with which the RAF, flying at night to keep their losses under control, could achieve anything.

The rationale in military terms made sense *if* it could be proven to be effective. Despite continuing claims to the contrary, strategic bombing in World War II – area bombing included – did make a major contribution to the defeat of the Axis powers (see Chapter Six), but is this in itself enough? Acceptable behaviour in war is largely determined by contemporary attitudes within both the belligerent and neutral societies. The fact that controversy still surrounds the firebombing of Dresden and Tokyo, to say nothing of the atomic bombings of Hiroshima and Nagasaki, implies that western civilization was and is uncomfortable with such actions. In part this may be connected with the persisting belief that area bombing did not work and was unnecessary to defeat Germany and Japan. But it is surely also wrapped up with notions of civilians being non-combatants and therefore not being legitimate targets in war.

However, in large scale industrial war, and the Second World War in particular, such distinctions become very blurred. Why would those organizing and supporting the war effort in Germany be less of a legitimate target than soldiers fighting at the front, especially in an age when most soldiers are conscripts and may have been indifferent supporters of or even hostile to the Nazi regime? Moreover, are those who build and manufacture the weapons of total war any less culpable than those who use them? The argument that such workers are "undefended" surely collapses with the development of anti-aircraft guns, high performance interceptors, night-fighters and radar.

Ultimately, the ethical problems of strategic bombing vary in proportion to perceptions of effectiveness. If it contributed significantly to the defeat of the Axis powers, then it becomes more acceptable; if it did not, then area bombing in particular becomes indefensible. Those states which used such strategies realized that they were travelling a dangerous and perilous moral path. The fact that they sought to conceal the scale and nature of their actions from their own populations reveals much about their self-doubt and how much stomach they believed their own people had for such tactics.[5]

Tactical and operational air power

The emphasis on strategic bombing in the past 50 years has to a degree concealed the impact of air power on the conduct of war in other areas, many of which shaped the outcome of war as much if not more so than strategic bombing. The importance of ground support operations was considerable. Without aerial control, or at least the denial of such power to an enemy, land operations became at the very least hazardous and at worst untenable. The impact of German air power in leading the so-called *blitzkrieg* of World War II was impressive, as was Soviet and most notably Allied domination of the air over the battlefield in the latter stages of the war. In both world wars, where logistical support was crucial, the surrendering of airspace to the enemy usually led to the interdiction of rear zones, loss of initiative and the curtailment of resupply. Additionally, aerial intelligence gathering and artillery spotting were important elements of ground support that offered considerable advantage, especially if simultaneously denied to the enemy.

The value of airborne troops should also be considered, for although they often played a supportive role to the main ground forces, they were also useful in seizing important areas or denying them to the enemy. The surprise element of such forces was often the key, as in the German offensives on Belgium and the Netherlands in 1940 and the assault on Crete in the following year. The Allies did much the same in Normandy in 1944, and in the failed Rhine crossing, *Operation Market Garden*. However, the value of such operations was often partial and could only produce a small operational advantage. This was because such forces were lacking in heavy equipment and could not hope to prevail against traditional land forces. Nevertheless, the nature of operations had been changed by the advent of such flexible forces.

Air power was also a key factor in the development of clandestine operations. Resistance groups, intelligence agents and whole guerrilla armies could continue their activities behind enemy lines thanks to resupply from the air. To Tito's partisans in Yugoslavia, and for British strategy between the middle of 1940 and late 1941, the use of air power to foster underground armies was significant, although in the latter case it was never an entirely realistic means of prosecuting the war.

In maritime operations the impact of air power was perhaps even more notable. Even in the First World War the role of aircraft in providing air cover to convoys was crucial. In the Second World War it was essential. The provision of air escort to merchant shipping across the whole Atlantic by 1943 ended the U-boat offensive. It could have done so much earlier and the debate as to why this did not occur continues.[6] Naval support in the shape of reconnaissance and gunnery direction was already being developed in the 1914–18 conflict but was to be replaced in importance during the interwar years by direct aerial attack on naval and merchant shipping. The world's navies fought a rearguard action against air power that was commendable, if ultimately doomed, and which for the most part revolved around the question of whether aircraft could sink modern capital ships. Although many navies claimed that modern battleships were safe from aerial attack, by the Second World War they could only rarely operate without air cover. The *Bismarck* was crippled and doomed by air attack, the *Prince of Wales* and the *Repulse* were helpless in the face of concerted aerial bombing and the two greatest battleships ever built, the Japanese *Yamato* and *Musashi*, were sunk by single-engined US naval bombers in the last months of the war.

The importance of air power to the conduct of maritime operations was emphatically demonstrated in the campaigns against Japan. In this theatre, between 1941 and 1945, offensive strategy was effectively dominated by the aeroplane. The island-hopping operations were only viable when air superiority was attained, either by land based or carrier-borne air power. In addition, the projection of force in the Pacific was dictated by aircraft carrier battle groups which rapidly supplanted the battleship as the capital vessel in naval warfare.

7

Air power and national strategy

Ultimately, the strategic or tactical value and use of air power to any given state relied on a number of crucial factors. In particular, it is essential to note that the development of air power within states was linked to national strategies, although at times the connections seemed to be inappropriate. The creation of state air power was not an end but a means, a method, of prosecuting national policy. Too often historians and others have criticized planners for not having appropriate air policies, the obvious examples being those states which did not develop strategic bombing forces in the 1930s, and those which did not create independent air forces like the RAF. The reality is of course, that the strategic requirements of states dictated their air power needs: what was right for one power was not necessarily appropriate for another.

For example, nations such as Japan and Germany did not develop strategic bombers prior to World War II for a number of reasons, one of which was that such a policy did not suit developing national strategy. There were many other reasons, such as technical difficulties and lack of industrial resources, which resulted in strategic bombing being repeatedly marginalized once the war was underway and Germany seemed to be winning without having to resort to the kind of long and attritional conflict in which heavy city bombing might have played a significant role. Likewise, in World War I on the Western Front, although the Allies sought to maintain the offensive they also aimed to take the air war to German lines and rear zones in an aggressive and usually costly manner. In contrast, the Germans more often preferred to adopt a reactive and defensive doctrine that was better suited to their largely defensive posture for much of the war on the Western Front.

In addition, many powers had only finite resources available and, for the continental states, armies and ground forces were the primary concern. For France in the interwar era, a large army and its much vaunted *Maginot Line* were of more importance than strategic air forces in keeping the *Wehrmacht* at bay. Indeed, it may well have been the case that the dabbling of the French air force with the theories of Douhet and its own struggle for independence contributed to the disaster of 1940, though this is by no means clear.[7] Likewise, the Soviet Union, embroiled as it was with internal and border affairs, had only a limited role for strategic air power in national strategy. This, along with the experience of the Spanish Civil War, and because of the purges in the late 1930s, resulted in the end of heavy bomber forces in the USSR. Too often the question of national air strategies has been posed incorrectly – it was not a question of why the rest of the world did not adopt strategic bombing, but why Britain and the USA persevered with it?[8] In both cases strategic bombing fitted neatly into national strategy. For Britain, it was an excellent way of trying to avoid having to fight on the continent as they had in World War I. Whereas in the past the British Royal Navy had provided the means of avoiding the continental commitment, so now the prospect of bringing wars to dramatic finales within weeks of beginning strategic air campaigns seemed to offer the way of evading the creation of great armies of the sort that had been ultimately necessary to defeat Napoleon and also Imperial Germany in World War I. For the USA, bombing of industrial centres was a vital precursor to ground operations in Europe and the Far East. The USA's productivist approach to war, which symbolized total war more than any other, recognized the need to disable the enemy's industrial output prior to, or in conjunction with, ground assault.

However, while British and US air power strategy may have converged on aerial bombing, they differed radically on the value of an independent air force. For the USA, like Japan, tactical maritime air power was crucial to the conduct of operations in the Pacific and for this a specific naval air arm was considered essential. For Britain, carrier operations were not of the same order of importance. Although the navy viewed its interwar imperial duties very seriously, national strategic requirements resulted in the subjugating of dedicated maritime air power to the needs of the RAF: first in its land based imperial policing duties and secondly in its independent strategic bombing role. Ultimately, this policy resulted in Britain being unprepared to defend its overseas trade routes with maritime aircraft in the Second World War. This would have been essential for victory in the Battle of the Atlantic. In this respect, national strategy was undermined by not applying air power in trade defence.

Japan also failed to use air power resources effectively in the field of trade defence, contributing greatly to the disastrous loss of merchant shipping in the later stages of World War II.[9] Even the Imperial Japanese Navy's much vaunted carrier fleet was arguably not as central to national strategy as it should have been. The Imperial Navy still clung to the notion that the Pacific war would be decided by a large scale surface fleet showdown: they considered that their carrier fleet would be a useful arm in the early stages of the war, when Japan was on the offensive, but would only play a limited supporting role in the closing stages of the war.[10] In contrast, the USA placed carrier doctrine at the centre of its strategy, albeit because of limited alternatives, and deliberately avoided surface confrontations with the Japanese. The US forces rapidly realized that concentrated and mobile air power was the key to operations in the Pacific. This was something that the Japanese never fully accepted.

Therefore, it can be seen that nations chose the mix of air power forces necessary for them to prosecute certain policies and that no state's requirements were the same. Where inappropriate choices were made, failure often followed. It is also worth noting that defeat in war did not necessarily mean that air power strategy had been wrong. For Germany in World War II, general operational support of land campaigns was essential and their decision to relegate strategic bombing in the interwar era was entirely correct. For Britain, inadequate maritime air power was the price that had to be paid to support independent air strategy, which was more crucial to British survival than carrier aviation.

Limitations of air power

Even when effective air power choices were made, there were many limitations on the impact that aircraft could have on the conduct of war. For all the successes and advantages of air power, there were many disasters and shortcomings and there is an all too frequent temptation to overstate the value of aircraft to the conduct of war. Certainly, before World War II the nature of air power was largely supportive to land and sea operations. Air power in World War I was by 1918 an important aid to ground offensives and to protecting sea routes, but the gaining of air superiority, or indeed total air supremacy, was not in itself decisive.

By World War II, the impact aircraft could have on operations was far greater, but in order to press home the advantage of air power control of airspace had become essential. In short, for aircraft to intervene decisively in ground or sea operations over a protracted period, air supremacy was required and this was extremely difficult to attain. Short term air superiority was common, where a concentration of air forces could gain effective freedom to intervene for a short time in a restricted area. However, enemy response was rapid and, once air superiority was being contested, the ability of aircraft to act decisively against ground forces fell away markedly.

Even in the 1950s when air power in the nuclear world had gained a position unparalleled in the history of conflict it could not be that effective in the tactical or operational sense because of many political, ethical and moral restraints. Moreover, the value of strategic nuclear forces was largely limited to their deterrent effect, it being discovered that power of that magnitude was unusable in anything other than superpower confrontations. Indeed, the ability of air forces to destroy whole cities is only power if it is perceived that the arm will be used and, as was ably demonstrated in the

Korean War, few in authority had the stomach for such mass slaughter. The post-war world has illustrated that air power is a weapon of total war and, when restraint has to be shown, its significance falls away dramatically.

Gaining air supremacy was the key to using air power to its full potential but such control was rarely attained. In part this was because the advantage lay with the defender in any air superiority battle. Offensive air battles often took place over enemy territory where fighters and bombers would aim to neutralize the enemy air forces and thus win at least air superiority. Once such control was achieved and air forces had the ability to intervene in land operations at will, the effectiveness of air power to be decisive increased dramatically. However, it proved much easier in both world wars to prevent the enemy from gaining such air superiority for any length of time, thus denying them air supremacy. By fighting defensive air battles over friendly territory, damaged aircraft had a much greater chance of returning to base, thus saving equipment and, more importantly, pilots and aircrew. For example, during the Battle of Britain, RAF personnel could be recovered whereas *Luftwaffe* crew were taken prisoner and their aircraft lost. Unlike land battles where successful offensives forced the enemy to retreat and allowed the recovery of tanks, equipment and casualties, air battles, even when successful, resulted in high levels of attrition. These largely unrecoverable losses could be disastrous, for training investment in air personnel was much higher than in other armed forces.

In comparison, defending against air attack proved to be much cheaper, and smaller defensive forces could often hold tactical and operational advantages. In winning air superiority over Europe, the Allies were forced to invest far greater resources than it cost the Germans to defend their air space. Ultimately, the Axis air forces were defeated in long battles of attrition and the Allies were successful because they could absorb the losses whereas the Germans could not. Thus, the ability to contest air superiority was the key to preventing the enemy from using air power to its full potential and it was the key to allowing friendly aircraft to intervene in the operations of hostile forces. However, once air power capability was lost in a large scale war it was almost impossible to re-enter the battle in the air with any purpose. Thus, there was a fine line between maintaining a minimum but vital level of air effort, and total disaster.

However, even when air power could be used to the full, it could only function within certain parameters. In the age of total war there was only so much that either strategic or tactical air forces could do to influence the outcome of the war. Indeed, the Allies won air supremacy over Germany by the spring of 1944, long before the war came to an end; and in the Pacific, Japanese air power was effectively extinguished in June 1944, at the Battle of the Philippine Sea. Moreover, Japan was never able to mount a serious air defence against the US strategic bombing offensive which was to devastate their cities. However, they were still prepared to fight in August of the following year. It took the atomic bombings and the Soviet declaration of war to push Japan towards surrender terms that were acceptable to the USA.

Allied aircraft were able to roam over both Germany and Japan virtually unmolested for almost a year before the war was brought to an end. However, it was a combined arms offensive which ultimately secured victory against the Axis powers. It is clear that many operations crucial to the Allied victory could not have taken place without air superiority – the Normandy landings and the subsequent breakout being a case in point – but it is also true that many battles and campaigns were won when air power played only a marginal or at least only a supportive role. The great "turning point" battles of the Eastern Front, such as Stalingrad and Kursk, were contested without air power proving decisive either way.

Air power was arguably most significant in maritime operations. This was certainly true in the Pacific, but again the US forces still had to win costly and bloody land battles against stubborn and determined Japanese forces who were for the most part unsupported by aircraft. Additionally, the projected Allied losses (approximately 30,000) for *Operation Olympic*, the invasion of Japan in November 1945, were still considered high enough that whatever air power had hitherto achieved it was not in itself enough, until Hiroshima, to force a successful conclusion to the war.

The totality of war

Important and crucial as air forces proved to be in winning wars, the direct effect on operations and campaigns was only part of the impact of air power on war. There were many broader and deeper aspects to the new age of air oriented war than the ability of aircraft to win battles, the most important being air power's role and place in the development of total war. As a concept, total war is widely used when referring to the two world wars, though it remains a loose and imprecise term. Although it was used by Ludendorff, Goebbels and Churchill at various times, the term really became established with the work of the historian Arthur Marwick in the 1960s. He argued that total war could be gauged by the use of a four tier model. For Marwick, total war caused mass destruction and devastation; caused great strain on social and political structures within societies; called for the mobilization of previously disadvantaged groups in war production; and had a profound psychological impact on state and society. More controversially, Marwick argued that total war provoked significant and long-lasting social change. The latter point in particular has been seriously questioned by many historians. But in defining what total war may or may not be, or indeed in analyzing whether or not it ever occurred, Marwick's model provides a rough starting point. The role of air power in shaping the development of total war was crucial and perhaps was the most significant weapon in this process.[11]

There are perhaps two main themes to the wider implications of air power in the age of total war. First, air power clearly exhibits many of the aspects that Marwick indicated, and that we have come to regard, as illustrating total war – targeting civilians, bringing the war to the home front, the fear of air attack and the apocalyptic vision of air power that predated the fear of nuclear holocaust by a generation. Air power was therefore a clear and direct cause of total war in a physically destructive sense. Secondly, air power was a measure of total war, for more than any other weapon the aircraft was a product of industrial warfare and the modern era. No other weapon required the economic investment and technological know-how required by modern war than aircraft. In many ways air war was the epitome of total war, an icon of a specific age in warfare and human civilization.

The impact of air power on society was a crucial factor in the creation of the new style of war. As has been stated, aircraft provided the means with which to take war itself directly to the home front: to the civilian populations of the belligerent powers. The effects of war had been felt by noncombatants since human civilization had first emerged; through siege, blockade and occasional acts of genocide. But the aeroplane added a completely new dimension to this interaction. For many states, especially those in Europe which existed in close proximity to each other, the threat of direct attack on their cities from the air was a very real one. As Uri Bialer demonstrated, by the 1930s Europe was living in the shadow of the bomber. It was a new experience for the masses of the modern world to endure, and one that we of the nuclear age and its "four-minute warning" have come to accept and place at the back of our consciousness.[12] Even in the USA, far removed from most of this process until the advent of intercontinental ballistic missiles in the 1960s, the fear of air attack grew to incredible proportions in the interwar era. The possibility of Japanese carrier-borne air attack from the Pacific, or German air assault from bases acquired in South America, however far-fetched and remote were considered actual strategic threats.[13]

In many ways it could be argued that air power globalized war for the first time; a process from which few were immune.[14] Whole societies became engendered with the notion of Armageddon from the air, long before

13

it became a reality. The roots of this process can be traced back to the first air war novels of the late nineteenth and early twentieth centuries. Jules Verne and H.G. Wells, the most famous of these novelists, both described how air power would revolutionize world civilization, rendering age old structures of societies redundant. H.G. Wells' *The war in the air* (1908) described great air battles between European airship fleets in which the USA itself ultimately became embroiled. By the 1930s, filmic depictions of the end of the world order brought about by massive air wars – Wells' *Things to come* – combined with the First World War panics about how societies could survive air attack, to produce major concerns within states about the apocalyptic nature of air war. Baldwin's famous statement that "the bomber will always get through" epitomized better than any other the real concerns of interwar peoples about their vulnerability to air attack.

In Britain, more than any other state, these concerns took root. The Zeppelin and heavy-bomber raids of World War I did cause a considerable public outcry, resulting in the creation of the world's first independent air force, the RAF. The real concerns of the British government centred on how much direct attack their society could sustain. Why should the mass of the population suffer to sustain a war fought for public elites? During the 1914–18 conflict the true horror of war had been hidden away from the British public in France and Belgium, with the public image being carefully managed by the government. Consequently, the war, though greater than any before, was still essentially out-of-sight and out-of-mind. However, when the whole of society was confronted with death and destruction from the air, surely the "great lie" would be exposed and revolution would follow? The breakdown in law and order had been noted by the government during 1917, when German air raids, although quite limited in scale, caused a good deal of social and moral panic. With the advent in the 1930s of the modern heavy-bomber, coupled with the potential use of poison gas, the fear of air attack provoking the collapse of society was very real in British politics. Such was the concern that national strategy in the years leading up to the Second World War was for a time based upon the notion that other states were equally intimidated by the threat of the bomber. British policy centred on air deterrence: by matching or surpassing levels of air power in potential enemy states – Germany – the status quo in Europe could be maintained. Unfortunately, the policy was seriously flawed because other powers were not as fearful of air attack as the British, although it was a cause of serious concern.[15] The British case was an extreme example of the fear of the bomber, but it is a clear indication of the level of air mindedness in interwar society.

Although not everyone shared Britain's excessive concerns, significant measures were taken before and during the war to save society from collapse by providing defence against air attack. The evidence of the new totality of war, precipitated by air attack, was there for all to see. Gas masks, air raid shelters, evacuation of children from cities, air raid wardens, blackout proced-ures, anti–aircraft gun batteries, barrage balloons, searchlights, air raid sirens, bomb damage, clear-up duties and many other measures were forced upon society by air attacks, or even the threat of such assaults. There was even an Air Raid Protection Institute set up in London with an attendant journal to disseminate all the latest thinking on equipment, gadgets and civil defence. The impact of air power on society during and even before the advent of the war was considerable and far reaching.

However, far from causing the collapse of society as many argued it would, air attack actually forced the many strata and groups within even the most divided of communities to pull together in the interests of mutual survival. Indeed, air bombardment helped to consolidate opinions against enemies during war. Far from wanting to surrender or overthrow govern-ments civilian populations demanded that their armed forces "give as good as they got". To a degree, resentment caused by bombing was focused on the enemy rather than on home governments. Indeed, some historians even go as far as to state that bombing of cities was counterproductive in that it hardened the resolve of populations and persuaded them to go on fighting.[16]

It is clear that, far from fracturing societies and causing revolutions, air bombardment often pushed the bulk of the population together, at least superficially. Modern research has been presented that argues that too much has been made of this resilience of societies under air attack. This resilience supposedly cut across class boundaries but the notion of classes all being in the same boat was and has been exaggerated. However, at the very least the worst forecasts of the interwar theorists proved to be ill-founded.[17] Despite the total experience of war society did not collapse, even when subjected to mass area bombings on the scale of Hamburg, Dresden and Tokyo. It has been argued that Germany and Japan were able to resist air bombardment on such a huge scale because of the nature of their regimes – authoritarian, regimented and conditioned by excessive propaganda. However, before the Second World War, similar analysts claimed that totalitarian dictatorships were brittle and especially prone to morale-sapping air raids, saddled as they were with alien and unnatural forms of government which evoked little deep-rooted support.[18] Conversely, liberal democracies could endure the excesses of total war, as had been proved by the First World War, thanks to their greater bases of national support. This is of course a simplistic approach, for there were many other factors which dictated whether a state could or could not survive aerial attack, such as the nature of its industrial base, the distribution of its population and geographical factors. However, both lines of reasoning may be correct for it is just as possible that despite all the upheavals and destruction of air bombardment, the fear of air attack far outweighed the reality. Air power was simply not capable of bringing about the destruction of whole modern societies in the manner envisaged in the interwar era – that potential did not emerge until the nuclear age.

The measure of total war

As well as being a direct cause of total war, air power was also an indirect measure of the new age of industrial warfare. The aeroplane was the supreme embodiment of all that total war stood for: it was more dependent on economic and technological factors than any other weapon; it required vast investment in an effort merely to remain viable as obsolescence overcame aircraft more rapidly than any other arm; and air power was arguably the most wasteful weapon of war, frittering away the nation's resources in a highly profligate manner. Air power was in essence a yardstick by which a state's total war capability could be measured. Both the breadth and depth of effort required by a state to enter and stay in the air power "club" meant that membership was only open to the most advanced technological nations. The exponential rise in defence spending in the twentieth century has come about due to the rise in both the amount and the sophistication of equipment required to remain a top level power. As the century has moved on, so some states have been forced out of the top league.

Only the great powers of the early part of the century had the capability to develop and maintain first-rate air fleets. The aeroplane was yet another factor in the acceleration of western states down the road to total or modern industrial war and away from the conflicts hitherto witnessed in the wider world and in the West. The gap between those states with industrial might and technological know-how grew enormously in the late nineteenth and early twentieth centuries, but the rise of air power was perhaps the most significant development in the ever widening gulf between the great military powers and the rest.[19] It is inconceivable that Britain would have suffered the same failures and disasters as it did in the Second Boer War (1899–1902) if it had had an effective air power capability.

Non-industrial states such as Transvaal and Orange Free State would no longer have been able to compete in open, traditional, military conflict with air power equipped armies, such as Britain's. Nor could they aim to match or even begin to contest air power status with large western powers because they had no industrial base to create the support structures needed for a major air power effort. Whereas armies could be raised quite easily and equipped to a limited degree, perhaps from abroad, and still be able to compete, air forces could not. Such was the cost, and so high were the attritional rates, of maintaining air power that only the richest and strongest nations could participate in a meaningful way.

The success of western style powers when using air forces against the nations of the wider world was significant: notably the Italians in Abyssinia, the Spanish and French in Morocco and the British in Iraq and Somaliland. Indeed, the divide between the West and the rest of the world had grown so large by the post-World War II period, that new styles of warfare had to be sought, a search that was eventually to lead to people's war, which was demonstrated so graphically in Vietnam and Afghanistan.

In many ways, the abandonment of traditional forms of war by the wider world when confronted by western power, or at least its unwillingness and inability to come to terms with the West's annihilatory Clausewitzian view of conflict, is a testament to the impact of industrial war, of which air power was the most significant factor. Air power was the final step along a path which resulted in the West winning military dominance over the world to such an extent that the other states had to abandon the idea of trying to play the same game.

However, although industrial states could develop air power (as they had previously developed sea power) and thus gain significant advantages over states which could not, they themselves had to be able to match, or at least be able to compete with, their own industrial rivals or face the consequences. Clearly, military and political rivalry was nothing new, but the demands of maintaining air power were such that the effort required to match other states grew rapidly and was soon beyond the means of a number of nations. Only a limited number of industrial powers were able to develop the component technologies to support first rate air fleets, and thus another division had been created in the military pecking order. By the time of the Second World War, only a handful of states were able to count themselves as first rate air powers, and by the post-war era only the USA, a declining Britain, and a burgeoning USSR were left. While air power was only one factor in the decline of the old world order and the arrival of the bi-polar Cold War world, it was one of the most significant factors in separating the new superpowers from the great powers they replaced.

The pressures on governments to meet the demands of air power were significant throughout the period and unlike the demands of navies and armies, the threat of air power was direct and immediate and could not be ignored. Unfortunately, the nature of air power was such that not only were there problems of mass-production of equipment to arm the air force, but

17

there were also crucial issues concerning technological capability. More than in any other armed force, technology was absolutely essential to air power effectiveness. Not even the tank was as thoroughly dependent on scientific innovation and advancement as the aeroplane and its attendant supports. Air power saw the first significant linking of the scientific community and the military in an effort to forge productive and technological advantages that might confer success in battle and war. Because air power had thrown up so many new problems of navigation, accuracy, aerial firepower, location and so on, problems quite different to those of the past, so the drive to solve them had to rely heavily on scientific investigation and reasoning. Trial and error by the military was no longer enough and the more successful air powers were those who linked science and technology with the requirements of the military.

In the First World War, the development of aircraft technology was impressive. In the early stages of the conflict, aircrews shot at each other with revolvers and rifles and dropped bombs by hand, more by guesswork than anything else. The innovations of forward firing machine guns and bomb aiming and delivery devices were such that if one side had them and the other did not, loss of control of airspace was a real possibility. The need to counter such technological advances was therefore essential. By the time of the Second World War the technological race had become even more pronounced, with radar and radio-assisted bombing becoming crucial to success or failure. Radar was a key advantage for the British in 1940 and the lack of it was a direct cause of Japan's catastrophic defeat at Midway in 1942. In the same way, the technological side of the strategic bombing campaign was pivotal to success and failure. Increasingly more sophisticated and better equipped aircraft were produced in an attempt to win operational advantages. New innovations could win significant coups for one side or the other: the introduction of *x-verhafen* radio beams by the Germans resulted in the heavy damage to Coventry in 1940; the use of "window" by the Allies in 1943 aided in the destruction of Hamburg; the advent of the long-range Mustang escort-fighter in 1944 brought about the winning of air supremacy by the Allies; and of course technology ultimately resulted in the atomic bombings of Japan. During the post-war period, even without military conflict, the respective adversaries worked slavishly to maintain parity in air power and nuclear technology. Not to do so may have unhinged the delicate balancing act that the superpowers had saddled themselves with. Rarely had history witnessed such military based paranoia and never with such stakes at risk.

The introduction of new types of aircraft, more effective electronic devices and, just as importantly, the development of doctrine and trained personnel to use this new equipment, were in themselves indicative of the technological face of air war. Although the resulting advantages were often not decisive in themselves, they did indicate the relative position of the belligerents and the manner in which they were coping with the stresses and exigencies of total war. For the most part it was the Allies in the Second World War who were able to manage the technological input into the air forces better than their Axis enemies. Initially, the German and the Japanese air forces held both qualitative and quantitative advantages over their opponents, particularly over the smaller powers such as Poland, Belgium, The Netherlands and the Balkan states, again emphasizing that only the very rich could now compete in air power confrontations. Nevertheless, and in spite of the many early victories, the *Luftwaffe* and the Japanese air forces began to fall behind the Allies in the implementation of new technology and personnel investment. They were quite capable of designing equally and often more advanced aircraft at an experimental and development stage, but the ability to produce enough of them efficiently and quickly was beyond them. The Germans developed a whole generation of advanced jet aircraft in the closing stages of the Second World War, most famously illustrated by the Messerschmitt Me 262. However, for political as well as economic reasons they could not produce enough of them to make a difference. Even the Japanese had designed a number of excellent aircraft, quite capable of matching the US Navy's Hellcats, Corsairs and Avengers, but again they were unable to mass-produce them. In both cases they were crippled still further by their inability to train enough pilots to fly the aircraft they had. It should be remembered that it was the inability to train and invest in aircrew as much as anything that undermined Axis air power efforts in World War II.

The standard historical belief that the Allies' "mediocre many" simply swamped the Axis powers' "superior few" is therefore inaccurate. By the end of the war, Allied air power not only greatly outnumbered that of its enemies, it also largely outclassed it. This was not so much in the area of design and theory, but in what was readily available, in mass-production, and had aircrew to fly it. The ability to mass-produce effective equipment and train sufficient personnel was the cornerstone of Allied success in World War II, and a clear measure of the manner in which the respective approaches to total war differed between the belligerents. The Allies, with their sophisticated and responsive industries, were able to meet the needs of their armed forces and generate technological development and advancement internally in a manner that the Germans had never thought possible in a capitalist economy. For example, Goering had stated that the US economy was fit only for producing refrigerators and automobiles. Conversely, the Soviet economy was suited to total war by its strictly centralized and managed industries, and it was this single-minded approach to the war that resulted in part in the recovery of Soviet air power. As the Axis economies floundered in a morass of confusion, rivalry and dissipated effort, the authoritarian and pragmatic Soviet economy proved remarkably suited to the type of modern industrial war thrust upon it.

Whereas the Allies coped with and embraced the dictums of modern air war, the authoritarian yet disorganized and disparate Axis dictatorships struggled. Their air power development was continually hindered by an interfering political/military leadership which did not understand the requirements of mass-production, and by a decentralized non-integrated economy used neither to political management nor to the necessary adaptability of modern capitalist models. Repeated design changes and shifting specifications saw new aircraft types put back months and eventually produced in a hotchpotch fashion, often resulting in poor reliability and service back-up. In consequence, the *Luftwaffe* had virtually disappeared from the skies by the middle of 1944 and the last vestiges of real Japanese air strength were frittered away in a series of fruitless attritional battles in 1942–3 and then gunned down over the Philippine Sea in June 1944 during the so-called "Great Marianas Turkey Shoot".

A clear measure of the Axis powers' inability to sustain their air power effort was their failure to train adequate numbers of replacements. The Japanese naval air arm suffered heavy casualties at Midway in 1942, when its carriers were sunk from beneath it, and later around the Solomons. It was never able to fully recover. Even two years later, the Imperial Japanese Navy was unable to field properly trained replacement aircrew whereas the Americans turned out huge numbers of both high quality aircraft and well trained aircrew. Post-war analysis of German flying accident rates in 1944–5 seemed to indicate surprisingly low levels, until it was noted that German pilots were being shot down faster than they could crash. As has been stated, the degree of training investment in pilots and aircrew per head was much higher than in the other armed forces. It was an investment only the Allies with their vast resources and more capable organization, in both World Wars, could afford to keep making.

The depth of adjustment and management of the economy was a clear indication of the demands of total war, and air power was, arguably, a key indicator as to how well a particular economy had adapted to the new style of war. Whereas the Allies were able to meet the demands total war air power made of their economies, their enemies were not, and this perhaps tells us a great deal about why victory came to the Allies in World War I and II.

Conclusion

Air power more than any other arm in the twentieth century epitomized total war. It brought the realities of war home to the civilian population for the first time, resulting in the mass militarization of society on a scale unknown in the modern world. The needs of defence against air attack were huge, both materially and psychologically. Hitler foresaw a time when every family in Germany would have an anti-aircraft gun in their back garden both as a real and a symbolic statement of the desire to fight on. Although it never quite came to that, the impact of air power on society was deep and lingering. The fear of air attack in the 1930s shaped defence and even foreign policy and though the real impact of air power in the Second World War was nothing like as dreadful as some had predicted, it was still enough to trouble the conscience of western civilization in the post-war period. This led to what some have curiously and inaccurately described as "total peace". Nevertheless, images of Dresden and Hiroshima, however distorted by the debates of the passing years, still weaken the perception of Allied success for many people.

Yet perhaps such air power, the most vivid facet of total war, was an essential part of victory. The new totality of war made heavy demands on economies and societies, demands that ultimately only the Allies in the world wars could meet. By using air power to batter and drain Germany and Japan of material and technological resources, the Allies were able to gain significant advantages. The fascist dictatorships were not particularly suited to the demands of total war, and ultimately it was the responsibility of the Allies to use such a form of war to win. Paradoxically, the most effective exponents of air war in the first stages of World War II were the Axis powers themselves, but they sought to use it, along with other new arms, as a way of evading the kind of total war that the Great War had portended. In reality, what they were perhaps demonstrating so vividly was that air power was not sufficient to avoid industrial wars, and indeed was actually a prime accelerating factor in the deepening and widening of total war.

Chapter Two

The birth of air power

It is often assumed that the beginnings of air power rest with the first controlled, powered flight of the Wright brothers in the Kill Devil Hills, near Kitty Hawk, Carolina in December 1903. While the achievement of the Wrights in propelling the first true aircraft into the air was remarkable, especially considering their background and their lack of formal scientific and academic training, in reality aviation had been around for quite some time in a variety of guises. Additionally, the notion that air power would or could be decisive in war situations, on a level far surpassing all other forms of conflict, had also taken root well before Orville Wright guided the "flyer" into the air for its inaugural 120-foot, 12-second flight.[1] Indeed, the singular lack of impact of the Wrights' breakthrough, though partly of their own doing, was symptomatic of the already long standing, world wide fascination with flight, of which the events at the Kill Devil Hills formed only a part. It was not until the Wrights went public with their "flyers" in 1908 that the significance of their contribution became clear.

The conquest of the skies had been a preoccupation of human civilization for centuries and stories abound of the earliest attempts at flight. The famous legend of Daedalus and Icarus is told in many languages and many early cultures revered deities who were imagined to have mastered flight. Strangely, the Graeco-Roman cultures, the founders of scientific and secular based western civilization, have few such tales and only the story of Archytas of Tarentum has made an impression from those times. He apparently constructed a wooden dove that was supposedly powered by a jet of steam.[2]

The first military use of aerial devices came not from the West but with the Chinese invention of the kite around 300 BC and it appears that the Chinese began to use kites to lift men into the air to spot enemy armies and to follow their movements some three centuries later. With the Chinese invention of gunpowder in approximately AD 800 came the rocket, probably the first example of powered flight. They were used with sporadic success to bombard enemy positions and in siege situations. By the time of the wars against the Mongols in the thirteenth century the rockets may well have been stabilized by fins to provide stability in flight and to aid accuracy.[3] In Europe and the Middle East, recorded attempts at flight in the Middle Ages usually involved some hapless individuals throwing themselves off towers or mountains and attempting to flap furiously or glide using cloaks. These ended in predictable failure, but in the thirteenth century there were recorded considerations of flying machines and balloon type devices which might conquer the air. However, although the principle of flight was noted, the practicalities remained beyond even wild speculation.

Beyond a children's toy helicopter device which appeared in the four-teenth century, and Leonardo da Vinci's innovative and curious designs for a clockwork ornithopter a century or so later, the first practical steps in the direction of flight came in the eighteenth century. It had already been established a century before that man-powered flight would require some form of mechanical assistance as Giovanni Borelli and Robert Hooke had noted that human muscles alone were not sufficient to lift men into the air. Despite the fact that it was in Britain that the avidly read experiments of Henry Cavendish and Joseph Priestly into the properties of gases were conducted in the 1760s and 1770s, it was in France that hot air and hydrogen balloon development began.

The balloon – the first means of flight

It was Joseph and Etienne Montgolfier who stumbled on the fact that hot air rises and produced the first true flying device – a hot-air balloon. The first public flight famously carried a sheep, cockerel and duck in September 1783. The Montgolfiers immediately saw military potential and Joseph supposedly claimed that the hot-air balloon experiments might lead to an aerial assault on Gibraltar being possible.[4] The first hydrogen balloons were in operation soon after and by the end of 1783, for the first time in history, practical flight had been achieved. As early as November 1783 a British pamphlet entitled *The air balloon: or a treatise on the aerostatic globe, lately invented by the celebrated Mons. Montgolfier of Paris* had been published. However, British attitudes to ballooning were dismissive and it was in France that the early pioneering work was undertaken.[5]

The military application of such technology soon followed in the French Revolutionary and Napoleonic Wars. On the outbreak of war in 1793 the *Commission Scientifique* called for balloons to be delivered to the army for military use, and a formal "Aerostat Company" was established in 1794.[6] Importantly, considering the future heavy demands of air power on skills and technical training within a society, the *Compagnie d'Aerostiers* required a very high proportion of skilled tradesmen. However, the arm had limited success and many practical problems remained. The Aerostat Company travelled with Napoleon's army to Egypt but was abandoned when the campaign failed and Napoleon disbanded the balloonists on his return in 1799.[7] Nevertheless, the military application of an air arm for observation purposes had been established.

Balloons were first used aggressively in war in 1849 when the Austrians tried to bomb Venice, but although around 200 hot-air balloons may have been used, they had little effect.[8] Balloons were employed by the Union armies in the US Civil War (1861–5) and they even utilized the latest telegraph technology to transmit battle reports directly from the air to the ground. Nevertheless, the balloons were still crude and notoriously unstable in any conditions other than dead calm and the Union balloons were abandoned in 1863. Notably, after Gettysburg a Confederate general commented on the defensive and cautious influence balloon observation had on his forces. Extra care had to be taken to try and avoid being spotted from the air, and delays were caused, giving an advantage to the Unionist forces.[9] Attempts by Captain F. Beaumont, who had been attached to the Unionist balloon forces, and Lieutenant G.E. Grover to persuade the British Army to adopt balloons for observation duties met with scepticism and it was well into the 1870s before Britain started to take an interest.

Indeed, it was the Franco–Prussian War (1870–71) that provoked real European interest in military air forces. Although only limited numbers of balloons were used in the war, balloon mail was employed by the French during the siege of Paris, as was the dropping of propaganda leaflets over Prussian lines.[10] Over the next two decades, French, British, German, Italian, American, Austrian and Russian balloon forces were established. Both the British and Italians even used balloons in imperial roles in the late nineteenth century.

The airship – the arrival of controlled flight

The next major step in the development of air power was the dirigible airship: effectively a powered balloon capable of flying in any direction with little thought to the wind direction, which had thus far dictated the manner of balloon flight. As early as 1852, the Frenchman Henri Giffard had built and flown a form of steam powered airship with limited directional capabilities. The arrival of the gas engine in the 1860s resulted in new airship designs, but it was in the 1870s that airship development began in earnest. In 1872, the French government procured a large non-rigid airship (basically a semi-directional balloon) designed by Stanislas Dupoy de Lome. An airship designed by Paul Haenlein later that year achieved an airspeed of 9 mph. By 1888 the Germans Gottlieb Daimler and Dr Karl Wolfert introduced a petrol fired engine to power their airship, and this soon attracted the interest of the Kaiser. In 1897 Wolfert demonstrated his latest airship, but the display ended in disaster when the airship exploded killing both occupants. The use of a petrol fired engine close to a huge pocket of highly volatile hydrogen was to remain, unsurprisingly, a major concern of airship designers.

The first rigid airship (where the hydrogen envelope was supported and protected by an aluminium frame) was designed by the Austrian David Schwartz. The inaugural flight of this aircraft ended in destruction too, although this was probably due to poor handling and inappropriate weather conditions. Nevertheless, the Schwartz rigid airship design inspired Count Ferdinand von Zeppelin to pursue its development in order to create a new weapon for Germany. Despite many setbacks and failures, by 1909, long after the Wrights had flown the first true aircraft, Zeppelin was operating commercial airships to fund his military activities and to make the German people more air-conscious. The success of Zeppelin's airships caused some concern in Britain and France, and attempts to copy the German success subsequently followed.

Clearly with the advent of true dirigible airships in the first few years of the twentieth century, air power had arrived. Before the Wrights proved to the world that heavier-than-air craft could fly, balloons were being used in warfare, as the British had most recently demonstrated in the Second Boer War (1899–1902), and the airship appeared to be the way ahead for offensive military air power.

The Wrights and the arrival of powered flight

The scientific investigation into heavier-than-air flight had already been pursued in the nineteenth century by, among others, William Henson and John Stringfellow who carried out experiments on powered models.[11] However, the first real advocate of heavier-than-air flight was the Scarborough-based

British enthusiast Sir George Cayley. Between 1796 and 1853 he proposed helicopter designs and, importantly, the use of fixed wing gliders which he eventually constructed and had flown. The problem of powering the flight was still effectively beyond prevailing technology, but the basic founding principles of fully directional powered flight were there. Others followed Cayley's example. William Henson patented an "Aerial Steam Carriage" in the 1840s, and the Frenchman Felix du Temple de la Croix designed and built a hot-air or steam-powered monoplane which briefly flew in 1874. In October 1890 another Frenchman, Clement Ader, built a steam-powered aircraft which took off and flew for 54 yards. However, despite his claims, little further progress was made. The American, Hiram Maxim, attempted to construct a steam-powered device which would lift straight off the ground in 1894, and the US government sponsored Samuel Langley to the tune of $50,000 to build a man-lifting aircraft. Both were failures and in fact it was the German Otto Lilienthal who did most to foster development of fixed-wing powered flight with a series of some 2,000 glider flights before he was killed in 1896. The results of Lilienthal's experiments were picked up by Percy Pilcher in Britain and in 1896 he patented an aircraft design which was basically a glider powered by a petrol engine. Pilcher may have beaten the Wright brothers to the goal of controlled powered flight, but he was killed in a glider crash in 1899.

In Dayton, Ohio, the Wright brothers, Wilbur and Orville, were also encouraged and inspired by the work of Lilienthal.[12] After a period of self-taught design they achieved powered flight in December 1903, and followed up the success with further developments and experimentation. News of their earlier efforts and publications had already spread and in 1902 the Briton P.Y. Alexander met them in the USA, and led Wilbur Wright to suspect that he was working for the British government.[13] In 1904 Colonel Capper was despatched from Britain to find out what the Wrights had achieved, but the brothers were not yet willing to open negotiations.[14]

The immediate impact of the Wrights' work is often overstated for although they had achieved what many had thought impossible, it was some time before it became clear to the world that the breakthrough had been made. Curiously, the first published eye-witness account appeared in the journal *Gleanings in Bee Culture*. The brothers perceived that their creation had important military possibilities and might even prevent wars by creating "an awesome military deterrent".[15] The Wrights attempted to sell their invention and its patent for $200,000, but after the Langley fiasco the US administration was wary. The British, German and French governments also missed the opportunity to take the lead in aerial development by purchasing the Wright "flyer". Unwilling to risk having their invention compromised, the Wrights packed up their fledgling aircraft and did not fly between October 1905 and May 1908. It was only when they began demonstrating their aircraft in the USA and Europe in 1908 that interest really started to blossom.

The growth of "air-mindedness"

Perceptions of air power in the western world were to develop rapidly once it had become clear that air travel, and therefore air conflict, had become a reality. It is indeed strange in the late twentieth century to discuss the growth of "air-mindedness", but ultimately it became a serious concern of western peoples, perhaps in a similar vein to modern notions of space travel. In the same way that there was little other than scientific speculation prior to the 1960s upon which to base assumptions about space exploration, so the world of the 1900s had to rely on what amounted to, in many cases, science fiction. The roots of air-mindedness lie well in the past, long before powered flight was a practicality. Jonathan Swift referred to aerial bombardment from a flying island in *Gulliver's travels* (1726), while Robert Paltock described flying people in *The life and adventures of Peter Wilkins* (1751). There were many other works which alluded to or were based around flight. Curiously, much of the speculation concerning aerial battles between balloons in the French Revolutionary and Napoleonic Wars was pictorial rather than literature based, as I.F. Clarke has argued in his study of war predictions.[16] In 1810, Julian von Voss published *Ini: a romance of the twenty-first century* in which he wrote of great airships vying for control of the air in an effort to gather information on enemy armies.

As Michael Paris has argued, the growth in air literature was halted by the prevailing post-1815 political climate in which major wars seemed to have been eradicated. It was not until the middle of the century that new perceptions of war again began to emerge. Herrman Lang's *The air battle* (1859) created the most vivid image of great air fleets battling it out in the skies, once the armies and navies had been eliminated. He saw such sky wars as being akin to Napoleonic battle, but curiously did not foresee air-fleets attacking cities directly. The first groundbreaking future war novel, *The battle of Dorking* written by Sir George Chesney appeared in 1871, and it precipitated a period of widespread writing on the subject.

However, it was the French novelist Jules Verne who became most associated with aerial warfare books. As early as 1863, Verne was marrying scientific fact and speculation with adventure stories to great effect. He wrote a number of tales concerning ballooning, but it was in the 1880s that Verne published *The clipper of the clouds* which was the first major speculative air power work. Verne's story centres on an electrically powered airship, the "Albatross", not too far removed from the scientific realities of the 1880s, and this was perhaps one of the reasons for the book's popularity. Additionally, Verne illustrated the destructive side of technological innovation, reflecting his growing doubts over the future of civilization. Verne repeated the formula in the 1904 novel *The master of the world*, in which the world's powers attempted to secure the use of a highly advanced aerial vessel against which there was no defence.[17]

Others followed Verne's lead and books such as Tom Greer's *A modern Daedalus* (1885) and Harry Collingwood's *Log of the flying fish* (1887) and *With airship and submarine* (1908) generally pursued the aerial theme. Verne's stories inspired many to aerial achievements such as Santos Dumont who became the first pilot in Europe. Early pioneer aviators such as Geoffrey de Havilland, Philip Joubert de la Ferte and even Billy Mitchell claimed to have been influenced by Verne's books.[18]

In the 1890s, partly inspired by the London based American air power enthusiast/inventor, Hiram Maxim, Graham Moffat and John White wrote *What's the world coming to?*, in which, by the twenty-first century, air fleets dominate the world and have put an end to ground armies. Indeed, the use of aircraft to attack cities and towns directly started to emerge, in books such as George Griffiths' *The outlaws of the air* (1895) and Douglas Fawcett's *Hartmann the anarchist* (1895). It has been argued that these novels helped to bring home to society the fear of aerial attack and went on to shape the myths and excesses of air power.[19]

However, by far the most famous literary influence came from the British writer H.G. Wells, already renowned for his science fiction works such as *The time machine* (1895) and *The war of the worlds* (1898). His first important air power work came in 1902, entitled *Anticipations*. Wells wrote of air forces being crucial to warfare in the next few decades, and also discussed the notion that "command of the air" was an essential precursor to the effective use of air power. Undoubtedly, however, it was the famous novel *The war in the air* (1908) that proved to be his most enduring aerial work, describing as it did a major air war between the great powers of the world: New York is laid waste, and after a series of fruitless battles, civilization regresses. The book again picked up certain elements that later found their way into air power strategy. Wells argued that the initial "knockout blow" was crucial, and that "command of the air" was vital to the delivery of such attacks. The superiority of air forces over land and naval arms was clearly stated, as was

the inherent hostility and conservatism of the traditional armed forces towards air power.

The influence of Wells' works is of course difficult to gauge accurately,
but he was widely read by the young especially and he was friends with Leo
Amery, who became a parliamentary spokesman for aerial matters in 1911.
Indeed, the first British officer to fly, Lieutenant J.W. Dunne, was an ac-
quaintance of Wells, and Captain Jean Ferber, the French airman, also indicated the influence of Wells' work on him.[20]

Literature from the era leading up to World War I did help to foster "air
mindedness" and with the growth in aerial activity, and media attention
given to it, air power became a subject of debate, and in certain circles
provoked consternation. Generally, the future war novels predicted that air
power would be a crucial, and perhaps pivotal, aspect of modern war with
roles ranging from reconnaissance to artillery-spotting prevailing, although
references to aerial bombing were also made. Initially, concerns over the
ethical aspects of aerial bombing resulted in the novels only portraying mad
scientists or megalomaniacs using such tactics, but by the years leading up to
the Great War, with tension and nationalism flourishing, such reticence was
diminishing. The view often portrayed in the literature was of society buck-
ling under aerial attack, with panic and chaos rapidly following bombing of
cities. Superficially at least, this view was to be reinforced by the events of
World War I, leading to the strategic theorizing of the interwar era.[21]

The air power revolution, 1908–9

Aerial activity in Europe and the USA prior to 1908 was patchy and sporadic, despite the efforts of some within the press to boost interest. It was in
France that most work was carried out with a powered glide, similar to the
Wrights' first effort of 1903, taking place at Meudon in 1905. By that year,
the French had the most powerful aero-engine then in existence, surpassing
even the Wrights' designs, thanks to the pioneering work of Leon Lavavasseur.
By 1908, the leading French aviator was Henri Farman who had managed to
stay aloft for 30 minutes. However, the arrival of Wilbur Wright in August
of that year shattered the illusions of the Europeans, as the "flyer" easily
outperformed the best that the French had and, despite the claims of the
official French history of military aviation, it was the Wrights who provoked
the dramatic upturn in the interest in aerial matters.[22] Wilbur Wright made
over 100 flights in France in 1908, including one flight of three hours which

covered 80 miles. One member of the Aero Club de France claimed that "compared with the Wrights we are as children".[23]

In October of 1908 Henri Farman flew from Bouy to Reims, approximately 30 kilometres, but the real importance was that he had taken off without having to return to the lift-off field, thus adding greatly to the practical military use of aircraft. The Germans took note, with the General Staff pushing for the development of German aeroplanes, against a wary War Ministry which wanted private enterprise to deliver aircraft first. By the end of the year, ten German companies were endeavouring to build aircraft, but the airships of Count Zeppelin still led the way in German air power development.[24] In Britain individuals and small groupings such as the Short brothers, pursued aeroplane development and the War Ministry saw fit to issue specifications for a desired aircraft, demonstrating their interest in aerial matters.[25] However, it was the ceaseless efforts of Lord Northcliffe, the newspaper baron, which really pushed air power in Britain. In the USA, foreign interest in the Wrights prompted further government investigation into flight and in 1907 an aeronautical division was set up in the Signal Corps. Procurement of an aeroplane and an airship followed. Unsurprisingly, the Wrights won the contract for the aircraft, although a crash in 1908 at Fort Myer, Virginia, which injured Orville Wright and killed a passenger caused delay. The US Army did not receive its first aeroplane until the following year.[26]

In Austria–Hungary air power development was taking its first faltering steps with the War Ministry in Vienna wanting to pursue a deal with the Wrights. However, this collapsed due to the cost involved.[27] In Italy, the War Ministry set up a centre for flying in 1908 and was considering buying a "flyer" from the Wrights, despite certain reservations that aircraft were not yet suitable for military operations. Even in Russia steps were being taken to keep up with the West, partly at the behest of newspaper pressure. By 1909 the Russians had developed a dirigible airship, and as the news of the Wrights spread, a newly formed Imperial All-Russian Aero Club began to raise funds to promote aerial activity.[28]

It was clear that despite popular perceptions of the reactionary and conservative attitudes of the armed forces, most were not averse to investigating the possibilities of air power, following the revelations of the Wrights. Certainly, public pressure grew and was fuelled by the nationalistic fervour then prevalent in Europe. The notion that a rival power might take a military leap forward, and thus change the balance of power, was an important factor in the rise of air leagues, aero-clubs and pro-aerial pressure groups. The influence of the Zeppelin, the "flyers" of the Wrights and the literature of writers such as Wells and the burgeoning aviation press is undeniable.

However, although the potential and fear of air power had taken root, the armed forces of the West had to take a more pragmatic view. With ever increasing arms expenditure swallowing up huge proportions of national spending, and with militarism rife, any expenditure on new weapons had to be very carefully considered. Moreover, the actual capabilities of aircraft in war were unproven and doubtful in light of the prevailing technology. Yet the pressure and interest was such that in the five or so years up to the First World War, military air power began to develop into a useful, though still most definitely ancillary, arm.

Military aviation before the Great War

France

By the eve of the First World War, France was the leading European aeroplane developer, surpassed only by Germany's strength of mainly airships. The years after the Wrights saw French pioneers endeavouring to equal and then surpass the achievements of the Americans. The foundations of the French aircraft industry were layed by devotees such as Louis Bleriot, Alfred de Nieuport and Robert Esnault-Pelterie who effectively hand built their aircraft in a manner akin to craftsmen. Without a serious market there was no other way.

However, the French had a major advantage in the shape of their aero-engine manufacturing, which surpassed all competitors including the Wrights. In particular, early success was based on the so-called "Gnome" engine, which was much lighter than, and thus superior to, its rivals. Bleriot crossed the English Channel in 1909 and at the famous Reims airshow 250,000 spectators and enthusiasts attended to see the aviators of the day. Other such shows fuelled military interest and the French army acquired a series of aeroplanes for the engineers and artillery, who were already contemplating the aircraft's use in spotting and observation. Although interest in aircraft was growing, the division of air power in France between the engineers and the artillery was to prove disruptive.[29]

In September 1910 the French air arm's aeroplanes proved their worth to the War Minister and to General Roques in a series of army field manoeuvres, the first to involve aircraft. Notably, the airships available for the manoeuvres were unable to fly owing to the weather conditions, contributing to their fall from favour within the French military. The fact that Imperial Germany, France's arch-rival, was viewed as the chief exponent of

31

the airship also did little to aid the airship's case. Roques was to claim afterwards that aircraft were now indispensable to military operations.[30] He went on to head the Inspectorate of Military Aviation established in October 1910 to oversee all aerial matters in the French military. By 1912 he was arguing that the development of offensive aerial weaponry was the next crucial stage, as air combat and bombing would be of importance in a future war. Consequently he ordered special tests to investigate the use of bombing aircraft against troop formations. His successor Colonel Hirschauer presided over a series of manoeuvres involving 60 aircraft in 1912 and the General Staff's conclusions stated that aircraft were suitable for a wide variety of battlefield roles, though low level operations might be hazardous.

Although its aviation lead was maintained, the French air arm suffered from a number of distractions in 1913 and 1914 that served to weaken its superiority. Hirschauer was involved in a controversy in 1913 centred upon the role and nature of air power and which eventually led to his replacement.[31] Thus, control of air forces in France once again became the subject of debate with arguments for more central direction of air power aligned against those who argued for more autonomy.

The state of the French aeroplane industry was a key factor in the debate. As in Britain, moves were afoot to bring aircraft production under central control thanks to the general inefficiency of French producers. However, this inefficiency was a product of the nature of a nascent industry, although the French military's policy of concentrating its orders with certain favoured firms helped to restrict the growth of the industry.

In response to concerns over low level bombing, artillery aviation officers pushed for armoured aircraft to provide protection against ground fire. However, such a leap was beyond the current aviation technology and merely served as another distraction for an already overstretched industry. Nevertheless, the fear of heavy losses to ground fire when on low level missions was to be proved well-founded by the events of the Great War.

However, in April 1914 aerial development had reached such a level that a Directorate of Military Aeronautics was established with General Barnard as head. Additionally, further investigations into bombing and aerial combat were undertaken at the behest of the General Staff, who were now beginning to see real value in air power, albeit still on a limited scale. An annual bombing competition took place and tests involving aircraft mounted cannon were carried out, but the military high command remained convinced that reconnaissance was the key role of aircraft, and on the eve of war in 1914 this was almost certainly accurate. However, even France possessed reactionary and conservative attitudes towards air power within its military ranks, such as General Foch who saw no value in aircraft whatsoever. In war, he claimed about aviation's value, ". . . c'est zero".[32]

On the outbreak of war, France still held aerial superiority in certain areas, but the lead was nowhere near as significant as it might have been. The aircraft and aero-engine industry was the strongest in Europe, but time and effort had been wasted and the lead of 1912 had been frittered away in internecine squabbles and ill-fated development initiatives. Indeed, by August 1914 the French air arm only had 141 aircraft available which did not compare favourably with Germany's 245 aeroplanes and ten airships.

Germany

German air power followed a different line to that of France in the years leading up to World War I. The airships of Count Zeppelin were to be, in some ways, the most significant aspect of air power development and, in a broader sense, more symbolic of Imperial German power. Certainly, the Zeppelin was the most sophisticated and advanced airship of the era, but crashes and problems in 1909 had led to military contracts being withheld and the Zeppelin was forced to rely on its new civilian airline and public support. It also had in the aeroplane a rival which was beginning to develop at a pace.

The controversy over whether Germany should concentrate on aeroplanes or airships continued in the lead up to the Great War. The General Staff plumped for aeroplanes on grounds of cost and ease of operation, while the War Ministry preferred airships for reconnaissance duties and for broader strategic reasons. Supporters of the Zeppelin repeatedly played the nationalism card, on at least one occasion recruiting the Kaiser to support them, whereas the aeroplane was portrayed as a French weapon and one to be eschewed by Imperial Germany. Consequently, the German aeroplane industry struggled to assert itself and was overshadowed by foreign competitors and hampered by technical failings. Military contracts were small and only 130,000 marks were allocated to aeroplane procurement in 1910. The situation was not aided by the lack of a civilian market for aircraft. By April 1914 the army still only had ten airships though improvements in performance had led to high expectations of the Zeppelin. General Moltke and others were even considering knockout bombing blows akin to those later envisaged in the interwar era. However, the reality of the pre-World War I period was somewhat different as Zeppelins were prone to handling difficulties in anything other than good weather conditions. They were also extravagantly expensive to build and maintain. The Z9 of 1914 cost the equivalent of 34 biplanes.[33] Aircraft development continued with support again from air enthusiast Moltke and the General Staff, although the pace of improvement was steady rather than remarkable. Aircraft production was hindered, however, by stuttering aero-engine development which at the behest of the army had emphasized reliability rather than higher performance, and was to lead to serious short-comings in the war.

Popular support for air power was fostered in Germany by the influence of the army, even in the field of civilian aircraft.[34] A National Aviation Fund set up in 1912 raised 7.2 million marks which had financed the purchase of 62 aircraft and the training of 162 pilots by August 1914.[35] The level of importance given to air power in Germany was considerable in comparison with many other powers, but the War Ministry, like its counterparts else-where, remained unconvinced by the zealous claims of certain air power enthusiasts. Nevertheless, the Zeppelin retained an almost mythical aura, which it clearly did not deserve. For example, although the navy was more pragmatic about the airship – it had only one in 1914 – it still retained dreams of using an expanded Zeppelin force for maritime reconnaissance and bombing missions.

Britain

In 1909 Louis Bleriot crossed the English Channel by aircraft and thus at a stroke rendered that narrow strip of sea, which had for so long protected Britain, potentially worthless. "England is no longer an island", proclaimed Lord Northcliffe after the news of powered flight reached British shores. Indeed, on the face of it, Britain's entire national strategy, based as it was around naval supremacy, had been compromised by the arrival of air power. Germany's airships and France's lead in aeroplane development caused con-siderable consternation in British circles. In fact, although the potential of aircraft was significant, in the years leading up to World War I, air power was decidedly embryonic and even in World War II the importance of naval supremacy and the English Channel was reaffirmed. Nevertheless, rivalry with Germany and long term military considerations meant that Britain could not stand by and let others dictate air power development. However, it took a concerted campaign by air minded groups and individuals, such as Lord Northcliffe, to push aerial development along. In 1909 the Committee of Imperial Defence (CID) decided that air attack on Britain was not possible, partly because no civilized nation would resort to such barbarity, and thus spending on aerial development should be strictly limited. Aircraft design and construction was effectively left to private enterprises, such as Geoffrey de Havilland, Frederick Handley-Page and the Short brothers.

Northcliffe, recently a visitor to the Reims airshow, was not satisfied. He published widely on the subject of air attack and vigorously supported the creation of the Aerial League of the British Empire in 1909. Further Zeppelin scares prompted the creation of a parliamentary committee on aeronautics but little was done until 1911. By that time, four aerodromes were in operation and both the army and the navy were beginning to take an active interest in air power. The army developed their Balloon School into an air battalion with 13 aircraft and three airships. Naval air power suffered a setback when a large airship was wrecked before flying, but then received a boost with the appointment of Winston Churchill, an ardent advocate of air power, as First Lord of the Admiralty.

Under growing pressure to do more, the government instructed the CID to investigate the role of air power in military and naval operations again. The aviation budget had risen from £9,000 in 1909 to £131,000 in 1911 and by 1913 it had reached £500,000.[36] In 1912 both the army and the navy set up air services which were to expand steadily in the years leading up to war. Already involved were names who would later shape and influence the growth of air power on an international scale, men such as future RAF Chiefs of the Air Staff, Frederick Sykes and Hugh Trenchard. The Royal Flying Corps, established by the army, attempted to formulate doctrine and press ahead with aircraft procurement. Unlike their European competitors, the British attempted to control aircraft development through the Royal Aircraft Factory at Farnborough, a policy which came close to destroying private aeroplane development. The policy aroused considerable consternation and to a degree demonstrated that the British had not yet come to terms with the growing link between the military and industrial enterprise and innovation, especially in new technological areas such as air power.

The naval air wing did not become properly independent until it was developed into the Royal Naval Air Service (RNAS) in 1914, but its procurement policy was different to the army air wing in that it relied on private aircraft manufacturers for its supply of aeroplanes. The naval air wing was initially instructed to abandon the development of the airship on grounds of cost, until another Zeppelin scare forced a change of policy. However, the cost of airship development was prohibitive and at the outbreak of war in August 1914 British airship strength did not compare favourably with that of Germany. Nevertheless, naval air power development had led to the testing of a cruiser acting as a seaplane tender and in September 1914 a fully fledged seaplane carrier, HMS *Ark Royal*, was launched.

Generally, Britain's aircraft industry was small and unprepared for the outbreak of war. Although certain high quality designs were under development, the poor state of British aero-engine production was a serious problem and the Royal Flying Corps (RFC – the army air wing) and the RNAS were largely dependent on French engines. Aware of the gap between Britain and Europe, Frederick Sykes (later Chief of the Air Staff) and others fostered close links with the press in an effort to raise the profile of the RFC, with some success. However, attitudes to air power varied. Some were far sighted and sanguine such as Frederick Lanchester, whilst others, Douglas Haig included, saw little prospect of aircraft being of any value in the war, though contrary to popular belief he was later to change his opinion. The majority however, recognized that aircraft, especially in the field of reconnaissance, would be of some value. Certainly, on the outbreak of war Britain lagged some way behind both France and Germany in air power development.

United States of America

Paradoxically, in spite of the achievements of the Wrights, the USA took longer to embrace air power than the Europeans. Away from the volatile pressure of European militarism and nationalism, the USA lacked the impetus to develop what the Wrights had delivered to them. Quite simply there was no strategic need for major investment. There was no cash for development until 1911 and the army had only one Wright flyer and one pilot. The Wrights and Glenn Curtiss, another leading airman, were forced to work long and hard to boost interest in aviation in America, setting up, for example, a series of airshows and circuses where aircraft would perform for sizeable crowds.

Slowly, the US armed forces began to take an interest setting up a flight school and allocating $125,000 for aviation in 1912, although in contrast with Europe this was a small investment and little of substance was done. Nevertheless, US aircraft were involved in operations at Vera Cruz against Mexican forces and in pursuit of Pancho Villa in the years leading up to entry into the Great War in 1917. Despite this, and paradoxically in view of the USA's industrial potential, US air power in 1917 was distinctly embryonic.[37]

Austria–Hungary

The aeroplane took longer to establish itself in Austria–Hungary as a potential aid to military operations, and took even longer to become integrated into the Austrian economy. Lacking industrial and technological sophistication, Austria–Hungary was always, like Russia, likely to struggle to meet the challenge of air power development. As a measure of the growing importance of economics in war air power was a test that the largely agrarian and ramshackle empire was ultimately unable to meet. Interest in air power on the part of the army, as in most other powers, did take root quite early, however. The War Ministry took note of aircraft improvements at the Budapest Air Week of 1910 and subsequently argued for the expansion of the civil air industry to support future military development. The industry was reliant on foreign designs such as, for example, the German Taube.

Austro-Hungarian air power was boosted by the appointment of General von Auffenberg, who was an air power advocate. However, although hopes for the use of air power, and aerial culture in general flourished in Austria–Hungary, the restraining factor was to remain the indigenous aero-industry, which struggled to survive. The failings of home companies resulted in German firms such as DFW and Albatross moving in. Certainly, a lack of investment on the part of a conservative and parsimonious War Ministry was a contributory factor in the stunted growth of the home aircraft industry, but with war looming Austria, perhaps more than any other state, had to concentrate its meagre resources on tried and tested military necessities. In the years leading up to 1914 this arguably did not include air power.

On the outbreak of war, the Austro-Hungarian army could muster 40 aircraft and the navy approximately 15. Under the strain of industrial war, Austria was to struggle more than any other great power to maintain and expand its air forces.[38]

Italy

As in many countries, Italian air power originated in the army engineers, where a number of airships were built between 1908 and 1909. An aviation school soon followed with a grant of 10 million lira in 1910 based around home produced dirigible airships and foreign purchased aeroplanes. Guilio Douhet, later to become a leading air power advocate, was already writing about the potential future value of air power in *La Preparazione*. Douhet, who eventually became head of the Italian air force, pressed hard for economic support for the aircraft industry, although with limited effect. One success was the construction of the world's first true bomber aircraft in 1913 by Gianni Caproni who was himself a fervent believer in Douhet's developing air power ideas.

Indeed, it was Italy's air service which was the first to be used in anger in operations in Libya against Turkish forces, the reports of which helped the British decide to set up the RFC. These reports were also examined closely by other nascent air powers.[39] The African campaigns certainly pushed air power into the limelight in Italy, with a major fund raising campaign for the air fleet resulting by 1912/13 in the first aircraft factory being set up, albeit with French support. Nevertheless, in 1914 Italian air power was small and underdeveloped compared to France and Germany. It was also reliant on overseas designs and technology, although the War Ministry was attempting to alleviate this problem by encouraging home design and production. In the long term however, Italy was constrained by the limited scale of its industrial base, though not to the same degree as Austria–Hungary.[40]

Imperial Russia

Russia's first dabblings with air power effectively came with the founding of a fixed balloon observation service which saw service in the otherwise disastrous Russo-Japanese war of 1904–5. Fear of western Europe's developing air mindedness prompted further action in Russia. Again, newspaper pressure from 1907 onwards was a major impetus to action, with airship development similar to the other great powers considered essential. By 1909 Russia was testing its first home produced dirigible, assisted by government funding. However, the emergence of heavier-than-air powered flight radically altered the situation. By 1908 aeroclubs were springing up in Moscow, Kiev and most importantly at the Imperial All-Russian Aero Club in St Petersburg.

As in other cases, air power received support from a number of high placed individuals and in Russia the Grand Admiral, Grand Duke Alexander Mikhailovich, became one of its leading advocates. He was in France when Bleriot crossed the English Channel and he immediately set about purchasing French aircraft. By 1910 Russia was holding airshows similar to those being held elsewhere in Europe, and the aeroplane was rapidly supplanting the airship. More military interest followed and in 1912 aviation was taken over directly by the General Staff. Russian pilots even gained combat experience in the Balkan Wars of 1912–13.

However, Russia's biggest problem, similar to Austria–Hungary, was its lack of a sophisticated and technologically advanced economic base to support its fledgling aircraft industry. Debate raged as to whether better aircraft should be purchased from abroad or whether Russia should persevere with cruder home produced designs to foster better long-term development. Visiting French officers mocked Russian designs, but logically if Russia was to develop as an air power, native designs and production had to be persevered with. However, with an industrial base such as Russia's this was going to prove exceptionally difficult.

On the outbreak of war, Russia's front line air force was considerable – 244 aircraft. However, many were already obsolete, and the support services for this size of air force were decidedly lacking. Orders had been placed for another 400 aircraft, including ten Sikorsky four-engine heavy-bombers, but again the likelihood of Russian industry being able to meet this demand and to meet the attendant logistical support requirements was very low.[41]

Conclusions

In the years leading up to World War I a number of factors shaped and influenced the nature and speed of air power development. The growth of air mindedness was certainly important, and the pressure brought to bear on governments as a result of burgeoning public interest and excitement in the conquest of the air from 1909–12 was also a significant influence. Indeed, there were many other peripheral factors, but the two most significant in supporting air power development were the involvement of the military, and economic provision. In some cases, the latter was lacking, and in the case of the USA it was the former.

Contrary to popular perceptions, the armed forces of Europe in particular considered it essential to keep abreast of air power innovations. Their essentially pragmatic enthusiasm was no doubt fuelled by military rivalry and nationalistic fervour, and any involvement was linked to the possible use of aircraft in any future major war, which by 1912 seemed to be a probability rather than a possibility. Without military involvement, aeroplane and airship development would have floundered once the initial public interest over the achievements of the Wrights and subsequent aviators had subsided. Only in Germany with the Zeppelin, and in France, had aerial development really begun before the events of 1908–9.

Civilian aviators were at the forefront of aircraft technology and experimentation but the founding of true aero-industries was almost entirely dependent on military and government backing. The kind of air league fundraising activities that helped to save the Zeppelin programme in Germany were merely short-term measures and could not go on indefinitely. Private companies who for the most part supplied the military with aircraft lived or died by military contracts.

The methods and policies of the military establishments also shaped the nature of aircraft development. In an era of experimentation and haphazard design initiatives, the attempts of the British to centralize aircraft development under the aegis of the Royal Aircraft Factory served merely to stifle initiative and to starve private companies of contracts necessary for survival. The French and Germans, who were by 1914 the world's leading air powers relied more heavily on private adventures for their aircraft, but again sought to control their respective industries via the issuing or otherwise of contracts.

The second crucial factor which shaped air power prior to World War I was economic development, both in the field of industrial capacity and technological sophistication. Both were essential prerequisites for a healthy air power. Russia, Austria–Hungary and, to a lesser extent, Italy were all hampered by the inability of their industrial bases to provide the capacity for continued air power growth. This was coupled with technological deficiencies that restricted sustained experimentation and innovation and fused with industrial shortcomings to preclude the founding of long-term major air power status. Military interest existed and doctrinal and theoretical innovations were already taking root, but membership of the first rate air power club was already being restricted to the highly developed economic states of northern Europe and the USA.

Although military interest in aircraft development was essential to founding aero-industries, it did not necessarily lead onward and upward. The military establishments up to 1914 saw only limited roles for aircraft in war – essentially reconnaissance and artillery spotting. The chasm between what the military considered was technically feasible and what the air power advocates claimed would emerge after serious development of air power was vast. The aspirations of the latter group however, simply could not be realized by the technology of the day, and armed forces had to deal with the realities of a Europe cascading towards war. However, by relying so heavily on military funding, aero-industries encountered problems, in particular the smothering of innovation. Aeroplane firms were in essence dictated to by the armed forces and their particular vision of air power in any future war, perspicacious or myopic as it may be. Armies tended to emphasize reliability, ruggedness and stability. Aircraft manufacturers had to meet their demands or face rejection and bankruptcy. This relationship could have damaging effects. For example, in Germany aircraft development had been stunted by the army's demands for certain kinds of aircraft, often developed at the expense of experimentation. German aircraft in 1914 were reliable and steady, thus making them useful reconnaissance aircraft, but investigation into larger and more powerful engines had been marginalized. It was a problem that was to plague German aircraft development and production throughout the Great War. The link between military requirements and industrial productive innovation was still some way off and indeed, it was never to be properly established in some countries.

On the outbreak of war in 1914 French and German air power was the most developed. The level of reliance of their partners on their aero-industries as the war progressed was testament to this. French superioriy in aeroplane technology was to prove a more important and longlasting advantage than Germany's lead in airships, but in 1914 this was by no means obvious. Indeed, in numbers of available aircraft Germany also seemed to have a significant advantage in 1914 – 245 to France's 141. In airframe design, Germany was to excel as the war progressed, but failings in engine design and production were to remain considerable hindrances, and the roots of this can, in part, be traced back to the pre-war years. France's advantages lay in its superior aero-engine industry and in the depth of its aircraft production expertise and support services, not to mention its significantly higher proportions of reserves. Military enthusiasm for air power in 1914 was still mixed. For many it was a distraction from the proper job of fighting, but most accepted the need not to be compromised in the future by the enemy gaining a serious aerial advantage, should it become technologically feasible. Few believed air power would be a decisive factor in 1914 or in the foreseeable future, but most agreed that aircraft may become a necessary part of military operations.

Chapter Three

The First World War, 1914–18

More than any other period in the history of air warfare, the First World War is popularly viewed as an era of fighter aces, chivalry and heroism, in stark contrast to perceptions of the suffering and carnage below in the trenches. Moreover, while popular images of air combat in World War II are based around great battles or campaigns with few heroes, the literature and films of the Great War extol the virtues of heroism and the actions of "aces". During and after the First World War, where the role of the individual was swamped by the deeds of the masses, writers sought out heroes for their respective populations to focus upon, and the "knights of the air" offered one of the few viable options. Lloyd-George referred to them as the "cavalry of the clouds".[1] Manfred von Richthofen (the Red Baron), Oswald Boelcke and Eddie Rickenbacker, for example, all became famous heroes largely because of the perceived nature of aerial fighting between 1914–18, which supposedly offered an older, honourable and more gallant approach to war than the bloodletting of the Somme and Verdun. Indeed, in the post-First World War era a flood of new air adventure literature emerged: books such as *The Red Baron* and *King of the air fighters* and magazines such as *Battle aces* and *War birds*.[2] Laurence Goldstein has likened the memoirs of the aces to the age old tales of knights and heroes, all fired with a strong moral purpose.[3] The enduring image of air conflict in the First World War had already been cast.

The reality was of course somewhat different. For example, loss rates among pilots and aircrew greatly exceeded those of other armed forces and was to remain a serious problem for the duration of the war. The demand for new airmen was such that many of a nation's most able men were rushed into action, sent aloft with inadequate training and preparation, and promptly frittered away. The BBC comedy series *Blackadder goes forth* humorously depicted the life expectancy of new pilots, once airborne, as being 20 minutes. The truth was not too far removed. A single day's losses on hazardous low level operations could be almost a quarter and aircraft replacement rates often ran at over 50 per cent. In view of the fact that aerial forces used in the Great War were not large until the last 18 months or so, the casualty figure of over 50,000 airmen is an indication of the high attritional rates incurred by air forces. Indeed, the casualty rates ran at somewhere approaching 50 per cent, especially in the British air forces which pursued a distinctly offensive and aggressive aerial strategy for much of the war. Death rates were also alarming, with 15 per cent of airmen trained by the French being killed, while the British and Germans may have suffered even higher levels.[4] The fact that many aircrew were lost in landing and as a result of basic flying accidents underlines the inadequacies of training.[5] Tragically, more British pilots were killed in training than in combat.[6]

Moreover, the notion that the famous airmen of the Great War were in some way chivalrous is also largely exaggerated and steeped in mythology. The age of the individual ace of the air was a relatively short one because, by 1917, air forces had grown to such sizes that tactics and operations were dominated by large formations and combined effort rather than singular heroism. Nevertheless, many "heroes" did emerge to dominate the attentions of contemporary and post-war air combat writing. Their "knightly" and heroic image however, is open to debate, not least because it was largely a product of wartime propaganda. Success in aerial combat was often linked with technological advantage, and had little to do with prowess or chivalry. The German airmen Boelcke and Immelmann dominated the air in 1915 thanks to the superiority of their Fokker Eindekker monoplane, and Albert Ball likewise later gained fame thanks to his Nieuport aircraft. Even Richthofen's success was, to a degree, based on the technical attributes of the Albatross.

Nevertheless, although technological advantage did offer success, only a few men were able to seize the opportunity. Even so, despite the popular image, the key to survival and long-lasting fame was neither chivalry nor camaraderie. The air aces were ruthless and efficient exponents of their art, and the belief that they were paladins of the air is simply not sustained by the evidence. Richthofen preyed on slow reconnaissance aircraft, William Bishop possibly invented the incident which earned him his Victoria Cross and Mick Mannock apparently enjoyed seeing his German adversaries die in the air.[7]

Yet the heroic image of Great War air fighting persists, clouding discussion and debate on the impact of air power on World War I. In many libraries, whereas air power selections on the Second World War often include a number of high quality analytical works on a variety of aspects of the air war, the same can rarely be said of the Great War where books on air power are still largely dominated by the traditional "aces of the air" approach.

The First World War marked the beginning of modern air power in many ways, and the crucial aerial events of the Second World War were rooted in the 1914–18 experience. The first air superiority campaigns, ground-attack operations and strategic bombing offensives were all undertaken in the Great War and the impact of air cover on convoys was a crucial factor in the defeat of the U-boat menace in 1917–18. On a wider scale, the impact of aerial bombing and combat profoundly altered perceptions of war, deepening the already marked move towards total war involving civilian populations and whole economies. Air power with high wastage and attrition rates proved to be a major drain on national resources, and more importantly on particular areas of economies – the most expensive and technologically-based sectors. The pressures of production, technical superiority and training put enormous strains on emerging aero-industries and few were able to maintain significant effort in the field for the duration of the war. The wider and deeper aspects of the air war of 1914–18 tell us a great deal more about the impact of air power in this critical and formative period than do the much repeated tales of the air aces and their individual acts of heroism.

The air war and national strategy

The conduct of the air war by all sides followed certain strategic axioms that rapidly became apparent as the war became established. However, it is fair to say that air policy mirrored or suited specific national strategies more obviously in some cases than others. The air strategies adopted were most clearly influenced by geostrategy in that the major continental powers, notably the French and the Germans, placed great emphasis on aerial observation and reconnaissance aeroplanes to support their armies, which were crucial to their national strategies. Conversely, the British developed maritime air power to support their navy, which again was their defensive linchpin.

After the failure of the Schlieffen plan to bring about the desired rapid victory, Imperial Germany was forced to adopt a largely defensive posture for much of the war on the Western Front. In part, this was in recognition of marked quantitative inferiority. Consequently, German air strategy was for the duration of the war essentially defensive, aimed at denying operational advantage to the Allies. German air power sought to drive Allied air power out of German skies by making such offensive operations cripplingly wasteful. The German air forces were able to maintain this policy almost until the end of the war when they started to be overrun by weight of numbers and to be undermined by ever increasing supply problems. However, this is not to say that German air strategy was negative. When it was required, offensive duties were undertaken and often gained local air superiority for significant periods of time, over Verdun in 1916 for example. Elsewhere, German air power supported the strategic aim of knocking Britain out of the war in 1917 by a combination of U-boat blockade and heavy bomber raids. The probable effects of aerial bombing could only be guessed at but the linking of air power to national strategy was clear: it had become apparent that unless France could be isolated and defeated on land the war would not be won by Germany. Although the air offensive eventually failed, and unrestricted submarine warfare resulted in the USA declaring war in 1917, the crucial point to note is that air power was linked directly to national strategy in an effort to achieve certain political aims. For most of the war the British and the French pursued an aggressive and offensive strategy against Germany, resulting in the flawed attempts at decisive battles on the Western Front, for example at Ypres, the Somme and Passchendaele. Again, air strategy reflected this with a high level of air superiority fighters deployed by the British (55 per cent of the air force by 1918) and a growing interest in aerial bombing, though this was partly prompted by the desire for reprisal raids following German air raids on Britain.[8]

Of the other powers, only the Italians were able to mobilize their air forces to meet strategic aims, and then only with any effect by 1918 when Austrian defences were starting to crumble. The adoption of aerial bombing reflected Italy's geographical position *vis-à-vis* its opponent and demonstrated that a stronger industrial base, properly organized, could offer considerable air power advantages over a state not so well equipped.[9] Austria–Hungary suffered throughout the war from the lack of a sound industrial base and, despite competent design work, continued to be heavily reliant on Germany, providing yet another drain on her senior partner's already over-stretched resources. Russia, despite beginning the war with a considerable air fleet, was never able to maintain it effectively and, like Austria, suffered from industrial shortcomings. The Russians were heavily reliant on French support to maintain their air fleet, but the inability of the home economy to support the expansion of the nascent aero-industry under the pressures of war, and fundamental failings in logistical support, led to the marked disintegration of Russia's air forces. As early as September 1914, the frontline air strength had dropped by 40 per cent and replacements were exceptionally difficult to procure at home, principally because of aero-engine

Table 3.1 – Air force composition, August 1918

Source: Morrow, *The great war in the air*, p. 346.

shortcomings. The implication was clear: an unsophisticated and technologically deficient economy such as Russia could not adequately sustain a major air power effort.[10]

Reconnaissance and aerial observation

The first and perhaps the most crucial duty of the belligerent air forces in 1914, and indeed for much of the war, was that of reconnaissance and observation. Armies for centuries had been effectively two-dimensional in their intelligence-gathering, relying on scouting cavalry, fast moving light-infantry or espionage. The advent of air power, even in the relatively primitive form of aerial balloons, added greatly to the ability of armies to keep each other under observation and the later arrival of the aeroplane dramatically increased this ability. Paradoxically, this new method of gathering information, highly effective as it was, became a severe braking and hindering influence on offensive ground operations. Much of military activity, especially offensive operations, relies heavily on surprise and continuing momentum, often gained by concealing intent until the moment of impact. In the age before air power this task was easier to accomplish, but the arrival of the observation balloon and then the reconnaissance aircraft severely curtailed the ability of armies in the First World War to catch their enemies unawares. The build-up for the big push was invariably kept under observation from the air and the defenders were able to prepare in good time. For example, the build up for the Somme offensive was already being noted in February 1916 by German aircraft, contributing to the Germans' defensive preparations which were to thwart Haig's attempted breakthrough.[11] If anything, air power hindered offensive capability unless the enemy's reconnaissance aircraft could be driven from the skies.

The importance of aerial observation was further, and perhaps crucially, emphasized by its contribution to the pivotal role of artillery fire in the war. The First World War saw artillery play the key battlefield role, replacing small arms fire as the chief weapon. Contrary to popular belief it was massed and concentrated artillery fire that brought about the deaths of more combatants in the First World War than any other weapon. Technology had moved on rapidly in the later stages of the nineteenth century and the destructive power of modern artillery had by 1914 not been fully appreciated. However, it soon became clear that artillery was the most destructive force on the battlefield, surpassing both the machine gun and rifle as the key weapon. Aircraft, both balloons and aeroplanes, became the principal directors of artillery fire and it was their observation and spotting duties which considerably improved the accuracy and effectiveness of shell-fire. Again, therefore, air power greatly contributed to the defensive nature of the war, for although artillery was an excellent means of breaking up enemy attacks, it was never able to provide the key to the breakthrough. This was to remain a product of all arms co-ordination, a doctrine arguably unattainable until 1918.[12] In the interim, artillery directed by aircraft, proved to be a major stumbling block to fighting the "decisive" battle so eagerly sought by the respective general staffs. Arguably, the aircraft was instrumental in bringing about the stalemate of the First World War battlefield and although it was eventually to prove a factor in solving the problem, during the 1914–18 period it was a smothering and constraining force, hardly the dynamic panacea envisaged by many pre-war novelists. Reconnaissance and artillery spotting were the key roles played by air power in the Great War. All other aerial duties either attempted to deny use of aerial observation to the enemy by use of fighter aircraft, or as in the case of strategic bombing, were of little real importance in deciding the outcome of the war.

The importance of observation really started to become clear when the initial war of movement on the Western Front had ground to a halt in the autumn of 1914, although prior to this the value of aerial observation of enemy movements had been indicated at the time of the Battle of the Marne, where aeroplanes had kept the respective armies informed of the enemy's positions.[13] However, once the front had settled down to the archetypal trench warfare that we have come to associate with the Great War, the use of balloons as a means of keeping the enemy under everyday surveillance came to the fore.

Before World War I, reservations about the aerial balloon were being voiced in light of the combustibility of its hydrogen and the fact that it was expected that the war would be a short, fluid and mobile conflict, in which the static balloon would be of little value. The French even went as far as abolishing the bulk of their balloon units prior to the war. However, as the war developed, one of the most noticeable, though subsequently less famous, sights of the battlefield was to be the array of observation balloons which lined the front, variously christened "sausages" by the French and "*das Mädchen's traum*" (the maiden's dream) by the Germans in recognition of the observation balloons' rather phallic shape.[14] It was a sight only really associated with the Great War as the advent of more mobile warfare in the interwar era and the Second World War meant that the value of the static balloon to armies was considerably reduced. Moreover, even as the First World War progressed and aeroplane technology improved, the balloon became more vulnerable to air attack while the reconnaissance aeroplane grew increasingly more flexible.

Nevertheless, for much of the war the aerial balloon proved to be the ideal platform for artillery spotting and observation. At a height of 4,000 feet and in favourable conditions, a balloon observer could see 15 miles into the enemy rear zone, offering valuable information on the activities of the opposing army. In some ways the balloon was superior to the moving aircraft, as high-powered binoculars could only be used effectively from a steady and static position.[15] Observation was an important part of the balloon's duties, but the key role proved to be artillery spotting and direction: such was the state of the new technology that gunners in World War I rarely, if ever, saw the enemy and soon became heavily reliant on information fed back to them from the air. This role, coupled with the highly destructive power of modern artillery, made balloons key weapons in the war. Increasingly sophisticated techniques were introduced for linking aerial observation with artillery fire, and it soon became clear that the importance of the balloon was making it a target for enemy aircraft or of artillery fire itself. The balloon observer was effectively a sitting duck and safety measures were crude. Although parachutes were provided should the observer need to escape, they occasionally failed to work, and in any case offered little chance of survival should the hydrogen filled balloon explode above and come crashing down on the hapless observer.[16] Efforts to offer better protection to balloons, such as attendant anti-aircraft guns, were partially successful but did not mask the fact that the balloon, despite certain inherent advantages was not a viable long-term option for army reconnaissance work. Balloons were often targeted by the enemy in an attempt to deny their artillery appropriate guidance, and increasingly as the war went on balloons fell foul of deliberate enemy action. Unlike reconnaissance aeroplanes which had to be actively hunted, balloons could not escape, and if the enemy was inclined they could blind a sector's artillery fire for a length of time by attacking and destroying the balloons, which of course they could locate quite easily.[17]

The reconnaissance aeroplane had already proved its worth during the short period of mobility in the summer of 1914. However, it took some time for armies to establish firm and reliable lines of communication between airmen and staff headquarters, and many valuable reports and pieces of information went astray, or were ignored in the near chaos of the first summer of the war. Nevertheless, aeroplanes played a significant role on the Eastern Front where the war continued to show a degree of mobility, when the war on the Western Front had degenerated into a muddy stalemate. Indeed, Field Marshal von Hindenburg was especially grateful for the information provided by German airmen prior to the crushing victory over the Imperial Russian forces at Tannenburg.[18] The value of aerial reports was also noted by Joffre in the lead up to the Marne, and by the British at Mons, and consequently led to a re-evaluation of the role of aircraft. The experience of the summer of 1914 convinced many ground force commanders of the value of aerial observers and they clamoured for more aircraft to be attached to their units. Expansion programmes followed and a greater emphasis was placed on aircraft types suitable for reconnaissance and observation.

The value of aircraft in artillery direction began to be emphasized once the war had ground to a halt in the autumn of 1914, and new codes of practice were rapidly developed and introduced. The importance of artillery operations can be gauged by Joffre's decision in September 1914 to switch the emphasis of air duties from reconnaissance to artillery spotting and direction, and for the rest of the war this remained the aircraft's primary function.[19] Initially, there were many technical problems, for it proved very difficult to relay information back to the artillery units themselves from a moving aeroplane, again emphasizing the advantage of a fixed balloon with its physical tie to the ground. However, technological advances were made ranging from smoke signals, to lamps, to cumbersome wireless transmitters which until quite late in the war could only send messages and not receive them. The development of aerial photography should also be noted for the valuable information it gave to planners and staff officers. In 1914, the use of airborne cameras had been around for some time and many of the major powers had investigated their value on the outbreak of war. The Germans were the most advanced in his field and went to war in 1914 with 100 aerial cameras. By the end of hostilities photographic technology had improved considerably and images could be taken from as high as 15,000 feet.[20] Photographs were rapidly distributed down the chain of command, even to the trenches, and complex and detailed plans could be drawn up of enemy positions and fortifications. During the war the Germans apparently took enough photographs to cover the area of Germany six times over.[21]

The age of armies marching blindly around Europe was gone for good, and the aeroplane was the reason for this change. However, aircraft had once again contributed to the strategic stalemate by providing so much information that the element of surprise was largely lost, that is until more sophisticated techniques at concealment, infiltration and faster preparation could be developed.

The emergence of air combat and the search for air superiority

Although the first, and arguably most important duty of aircraft in the First World War was reconnaissance and observation, so the interception and destruction of such aircraft was likewise to become a crucial factor. If enemy reconnaissance aircraft could be driven from the skies, then an important operational advantage would be obtained. As has been noted, the gathering of information on army preparations, movements and artillery direction was an important factor in stifling offensive enemy activity and preparing friendly attacks. If information could be denied to the enemy while simultaneously maintaining friendly reconnaissance operations, the potential for offensive action to be successful could be increased, perhaps dramatically so. The need to shoot down or drive away enemy observation aircraft therefore soon became recognized as an important activity of air forces, again underlining the importance attributed to reconnaissance operations.

Even before the war broke out, there had been contemplation of the nature of aerial combat and its importance to ground operations. Such terms as "air superiority", "air supremacy" and "mastery of the air" were bandied about, usually then as now, in an interchangeable fashion. Yet again the importance of reconnaissance duties was emphasized. Major Frederick Sykes, later to be the RAF's second Chief of Air Staff (1918–19), commented in 1913 that gaining command of the air was an essential precursor to ground operations.[22] This would have to be achieved through aerial combat, though the obstacle of how such actions could be fought remained. Until the advent of the Lewis and Hotchkiss machine guns in 1911/12 which weighed considerably less than rival heavier machine guns, there were no viable aerial anti-aircraft weapons. By the outbreak of war the linking of machine guns with aircraft was still in its infancy and there were no true fighter aircraft until 1915. Indeed, in the early stages of the war, combat between aircraft was frowned upon to a degree and such fighting as there was relied on individual initiative. Additionally, it should be remembered that the aircraft of 1914/15 were still technologically primitive. British BEs could manage speeds of only 60 mph and with an operational ceiling of 3,000 feet it was enormously difficult to catch, let alone attack, enemy aircraft. Moreover, many single-engined aircraft had "tractor" type engine arrangements where the propeller was fixed on the front of the aircraft and pulled the aircraft, as opposed to the "pushers" which had the propeller to the rear of the engine/wing assembly and thrust the aeroplane. The former arrangement proved to be most efficient in the long-term but also naturally prevented the use of forward firing machine guns, as pilots still had to fire their guns manually at this time.

Initially, it was the French who were the first to advance the role of the fighter aircraft. In 1915 they introduced a policy of throwing up an aerial barrage of aircraft across the front to deny the Germans access to French airspace. The French single-seater Morane-Saulnier monoplane of 1914 and the British two-seater Vickers FB5, which appeared in the spring of 1915 and mounted a forward firing machine gun (it was a pusher engined aircraft), gave the German pilots some cause for disgruntlement, armed as they still were with pistols and rifles. Nevertheless, it was clear that in aerial performance terms, the two-seater aircraft was no match for the single-seater, although the latter suffered in that the pilot could not fire accurately and fly at the same time.

The problem was to be solved in 1915. First, a French aviator, Roland Garros, developed metal deflectors which encased part of the wooden propeller and literally knocked the bullets out of the way. However, this caused efficiency and safety problems as aircraft could still destroy their own propellers with the device. It was the introduction of interrupter gears which synchronized the engine with the machine gun and prevented the gun from firing when the propeller was in the line of fire that was the real break-through in the development of the true fighter/interceptor aircraft. This advance is usually attributed to Anthony Fokker, a Dutch aircraft designer working for the Germans, but there is evidence to suggest that the idea dated back to 1913 and the work of a German engineer, Franz Schneider.[23]

More importantly, it was the Germans who were the first to marry the synchronized forward firing machine gun to a fast and manoeuvrable single-engined aircraft in the Fokker Eindekker, which started to arrive at the front in the middle of 1915. This was the first real example of technology providing one side in the air war with a distinct tactical and operational advantage over the other. The Allies were forced to respond, and the technological aspect of the air superiority war was to swing back and forth for the next three years.

The Eindekker was soon to have an impact by ending French bombing raids when losses inflicted by the new fighter grew too high. By the end of 1915, the Germans began inflicting heavier losses on Allied aircraft over the frontline, the Royal Flying Corps attributing the loss of 20 aircraft between November 7 and January 12 to the new "Fokker scourge" as it was christened.[24] Armed with the Eindekkers, the Germans attempted the first co-ordinated air superiority campaign over Verdun in 1916, where they used fighters both to deny French reconnaissance aircraft access to German airspace and to escort German reconnaissance aircraft when they flew over French territory. New aggressive German fighter tactics as pioneered by Oswald Boelcke and Max Immelmann had immediate impact and the unprepared French air forces were rapidly swept from the skies.[25]

The French were forced to hit back in this first struggle for air superior-ity, and Joffre appointed Major Tricornot de Rose to re-establish control of French airspace. He put together a high quality force of 15 *escadrilles* (French air groups) to contest the air over Verdun, adopting offensive patrols with the avowed intent of fighting German aircraft and driving them from the skies.[26] The air campaign swung back and forth with ever larger concentra-tions of aircraft (French *groupes de chasse* and German *Jagdstaffeln*) being deployed. Ultimately, the French emerged victorious and German artillery fire became progressively less effective once their reconnaissance aircraft were being driven from French airspace on all but rare occasions. As Lee Kennett has argued, the Verdun air campaign was the first to demonstrate the value of winning air superiority, or at least of denying it to the enemy, and of the pivotal role of fighter aircraft in such operations.[27] Moreover, just as the war on the ground and at sea had become campaigns of attrition so too did the war in the air when fought on the scale of Verdun, and sub-sequently over the Somme. The Allies were successful because they could feed in more resources than the Germans, and by mid-to-late 1916 the technological battle had swung back in the favour of the Allies who also now had fighters equipped with synchronized forward firing machine guns.

The Germans responded with a major reorganization of their air forces into specific fighter, bomber and reconnaissance units. New and more advanced fighters were introduced such as the Albatross D-1. By the winter of 1916/17, the air superiority war had tilted back to the Germans, especially as the French were rebuilding after the losses at Verdun and the British were doing likewise after the Somme. Indeed, although the RFC could deploy 550 aircraft by the spring of 1917, they lost 140 of them to the newly invigorated German air forces.[28] However, by the middle of 1917, again aptly demonstrating the new technological aspect of war, the advantage had swung back to the Allies with the introduction of Sopwith Camels, SE-5s and latterly the SPAD and Nieuport 28s which gained and then maintained the lead on both technological and numerical grounds. The formula was to be repeated against both major Axis powers in World War II, when once again the technological battle for air superiority swung to and fro and was eventually decided by weight and effective allocation of resources.

No other theatre of operations saw such a concerted effort to seize and then maintain air superiority as the Western Front, but paradoxically the value of total air supremacy was demonstrated most effectively elsewhere. Aerial ground support operations in Palestine showed what could be achieved, but the Turks had no real means of contesting air superiority, and for the Germans in the West, merely challenging Allied air superiority over the front was an effective use of resources in itself. Simply denying air supremacy to the Allies was crucial, and the German air forces, heavily outnumbered as they were by 1918, especially in light of the ever increasing flow of equipment and men from the USA, never totally lost control of their airspace.

Ground support operations

The value of artillery observation and reconnaissance has already been noted, but from the first air superiority operations grew the opportunity for aircraft to intervene directly in the ground war – what later became called ground-attack duties. Aircraft were to hold a marked psychological advantage over ground troops, even when the land based forces became used to air attacks and were able to develop counter-measures. The initial impact of concerted air attack on ground forces was notable therefore for the panic it created. The Germans were suitably impressed by the Allies' use of ground-attack aircraft over the Somme in 1916 to begin closer investigations themselves.[29]

It was the Allies who pressed the development of ground-attack aircraft as a logical progression of their air superiority campaign. If the Allies were able to gain control of German airspace for periods of time, what were they to do with it? The British and French, who were actively pursuing an offensive and aggressive air war strategy, developed the idea of using their air superiority fighters as ground-attack aircraft, thus making them multipurpose. Allied fighters began to be equipped with bombs and were detailed to attack trenches and the rear zones of the German lines. Almost immediately, ground support operations split into two distinct halves: close air support, directly attacking enemy front-line troops to gain advantages for friendly ground forces; and battlefield interdiction, disrupting enemy rear zones, supply lines and support units.[30] Essentially, ground support operations have remained so divided ever since, with the former duty considered to be the most dangerous activity undertaken by aircraft and aircrew. Loss rates on close-air support operations were always high, never less than 30 per cent in fact, and with threats coming from both enemy interceptors who would be awaiting them, and ground fire with the increasing introduction of anti-aircraft gunnery, many pilots preferred aerial combat and all its inherent dangers to the exigencies of ground support operations.[31]

German policy was quite different to the Allied approach, and reflected national strategy. The German air forces in World War I were essentially defensive in nature, and aimed to deny the Allies the freedom to roam German airspace. They did not attempt to engage the Allies too often in drawn out battles for air superiority, preferring to wait for the enemy to cross German lines where they would be attacked by dedicated fighter interceptors. Nevertheless, it quickly became apparent that ground-attack operations were effective, if costly. However, German development originated in the need for rugged two-seater escort aircraft to provide protection for the more vulnerable reconnaissance aircraft. These escorts then began to double as ground-attack aircraft, for which their sturdy construction made them well-suited.[32] Thus, German designs tended to be twin-seater aircraft with greater ground-attack capability, whereas the Allies modified single-seater fighter aircraft to carry out these duties.

Both ideas had advantages and disadvantages. The German model led to superior ground-attack aircraft, which would be more vulnerable to enemy fighter-attack, while the Allied plan resulted in more flexible but less capable ground-attack aircraft. Which strategy was most effective is rather difficult to gauge, as Richard Hallion has argued, because the Allies had general air superiority in the later stages of the war and the performance of superior German ground-attack aircraft such as the Junkers J1 "Furniture Van" could not be properly analyzed. Nevertheless, where ground-attack aircraft could be deployed they had a considerable impact, especially when air superiority, or even air supremacy, could be attained.

It was in 1917, during the Passchendaele campaign, that the British first used ground-attack aircraft in a predetermined and organized manner to disrupt German ground forces, although the organization was still rather *ad hoc*.[33] By the Cambrai offensive of 1917, both sides were using ground-attack aircraft with some effect, as it was considered that aircraft could prevent stalemates from developing and were able to maintain momentum in an attack, predating aspects of *blitzkrieg* by a little over 20 years. The importance of aircraft in co-operation with the tank also came to the fore in the Cambrai offensive as it rapidly emerged that the biggest threat to tanks was anti-tank gunfire, in this early stage of armoured warfare usually provided by direct firing artillery. However, aircraft were able to maintain the tank's offensive capability by neutralizing enemy gun batteries. Although problems were to persist in co-ordinating such aircraft/tank operations, the axiom of all arms co-ordination being the key to breaking the stalemate on the Western Front was beginning to be realized.[34] It was clear that aircraft could add an offensive dimension to ground operations. This was particularly evident on the Western Front in 1918 when the Germans attempted to end the war with a final knockout blow.

The Germans had developed an effective doctrine for the use of aircraft in supporting the new "stormtrooper" tactics.[35] Indeed, 38 ground-attack squadrons were deployed by the Germans for the offensive.[36] General Ludendorff was especially impressed by the contribution of the German air forces to the breakthrough, noting the value of combined arms co-ordination to the near success. The numbers of aircraft and the size of formations involved rose dramatically as the importance of aircraft increased, with over 600 aeroplanes being used by the French to lead a counter-attack against German forces between Courcelle and Wargemoulin on 11 June 1918. Air superiority was initially gained and German observation aeroplanes were driven from the skies, before French aircraft attacked enemy positions and allowed French forces to defeat the German attack.[37]

Subsequent offensives in 1918, in particular St Miheil in September, demonstrated the continuing need for air superiority before aircraft could really begin to influence ground operations. Despite the advantage of numbers gained by the Allies around St Miheil – they were able to muster 1,481 aircraft of which 701 were directed to attain air superiority and to carry out ground-attack missions – the Germans were still able to contest control of the air space and carry out a number of aggressive ground support missions of their own.

Ultimately, unless air superiority could be maintained at a level akin to air supremacy, aircraft could not be decisive, even if they were technologically capable of being so against a modern well-equipped enemy, which in 1918 was still far from proven. Nevertheless, tactics for neutralizing German anti-tank guns were developed, principally using smoke to screen advancing British tanks, but once again close air support operations took a heavy toll, influencing post-war RAF perceptions of the value of such duties.[38] However, if the correct circumstances could be manufactured, the potential for aircraft to influence ground operations was evident. It was doubly true if modern air forces were deployed to support operations against enemies who could not contest air superiority effectively, as was demonstrated in campaigns against the Turks and Bulgarians, although this could hardly be expected in modern war against significant powers.[39]

By the end of hostilities, ground support operations had become an integral part of the mix of modern forces required to conduct campaigns. Many problems in the use of aircraft in these roles were being overcome, such as communications with the ground and other aircraft, and close co-operation with mobile land forces, which now included tanks in significant numbers. Whereas air forces flinched from the heavy loss rates on close air support, the foundations had, nevertheless, been laid for the creation of *blitzkrieg*.

Maritime aviation

On the outbreak of war, naval aviation was still embryonic, even more so than its land based cousin. Although experimentation and development was taking place, there were many different attitudes to the future of maritime air power and the lack of uniformity in views of the future illustrated the confusion. Unsurprisingly, airships were favoured by Germany, and for a time by Britain, and indeed they seemed to have the features required for maritime operations: endurance and lifting/carrying capacity.[40] Aeroplane development followed a number of routes, although in the early stages the debate centred on the relative advantages and failings of seaplanes and flying boats. The former were land-planes with floats fitted to replace the under-carriage, while the latter had amphibious hulls and were purpose designed for operating from water. Seaplanes were smaller, handier and cheaper, while flying boats were longer-ranged but more expensive to build and operate. By 1914, aircraft were already capable of operating from ships, though these seaplane tenders tended to be converted vessels and not always entirely suitable. Nevertheless, all the major powers had some form of maritime air capability on the outbreak of war, although the realities of trying to operate aircraft in the generally hostile environment of the sea proved to be a major stumbling block. Moreover, few forces had any clearly defined doctrine for the employment of their charges, despite trials and battle manoeuvres involving aircraft in 1913. The most important contribution to the maritime war made by air power was in the anti-submarine campaigns around the British Isles and in the eastern Atlantic. Although air power was to continue to develop in other areas, reconnaissance and gunnery direction for example, it was in combating the U-boat that maritime air forces played their most influential role in the Great War.

The U-boat had already caused a good deal of consternation and soul searching in pre-World War I navies, largely because they were forcing a radical and generally unpalatable re-evaluation of the nature of modern naval warfare. The cornerstone of naval supremacy had always been the ship of the line, or the battleship. In order to be able to use the sea for operations, at least for any length of time, control of the surrounding waters had to be exercised by warships. The supreme embodiment of this was, by 1914, the big-gun battleship. If a power wanted to be taken seriously in naval terms it was measured by the number of modern battleships it could send to sea.

The U-boat, and indeed ultimately the aircraft, threatened this *status quo*. They both allowed a nation to project a potent form of maritime strength without having to build battleships, which was rather frustrating for the British and Germans, who had spent the previous 15 years or so in a ruinous naval arms race. For Britain in particular, the threat of the U-boat had to be taken seriously, because submarines could directly attack sea-borne trade routes on which the British economy, more than any other, was heavily dependent.

The Germans were forced to concede by 1916, despite the tactical success of Jutland, that their expensive surface fleet, still heavily outnumbered as it was, was unable to tackle Britain's Grand Fleet with any real chance of success, and thus greater reliance was placed on the U-boat fleet. Although the use of submarines to sink merchant shipping without warning would give Imperial Germany an unfavourable press and might antagonize the USA, it was considered that an all out U-boat offensive could swing the war in Germany's favour by forcing Britain to sue for peace.[41]

Initially, the U-boat offensive was highly successful, with Admiral Jellicoe at one point claiming that Britain could not go on with the war if such high losses continued. Indeed, if Britain came close to being forced out of the war, it was as a result of the U-boat campaign. The turning point came when the British introduced escorted convoying, rather than sailing their merchantmen individually. However, the use of airships, seaplanes, flying boats, and, latterly, land based aircraft made convoys virtually invulnerable to submarine attack and consequently eliminated the U-boat as a threat to British security. The U-boat's only advantage lay in its ability to submerge for short periods to avoid detection. However, once underwater its speed fell away dramatically and the submarine was effectively unable to locate or attack enemy shipping. The crucial role aircraft played in this campaign was in surrounding convoys with air cover, consequently driving U-boats away from the merchant ships even though such cover was extremely unlikely to inflict damage on submarines. This was the role Allied aircraft were to play in the Battle of the Atlantic in World War II, ultimately with the same result.[42] Elsewhere, maritime air power had little effect on the war, although the potential was clear. Naval reconnaissance and gunnery direction clearly benefited from air support but, Jutland aside, there was precious little in the way of action to test what was and was not feasible in wartime. Moreover, the ability of aircraft to attack or destroy naval shipping was never really tested, despite the continuing development of bombers and torpedo-bombers.[43]

The airship enjoyed something of a renaissance for a time in maritime duties. As a weapon of war, faith in the hydrogen filled dirigible airship was shattered by a series of disasters and catastrophes in the early stages of the conflict, and its vulnerability to anti-aircraft fire and fighter aircraft was repeatedly proven. However, the airship's superior endurance and bomb load capacity indicated that it could be effective on naval operations. Despite this, poor weather over the North Sea was the bane of the airship's life, even preventing Zeppelins from intervening in the Battle of Jutland. Subsequently, when battles for air superiority, similar to those over land, began over the sea the airship was again driven from the skies. Everywhere, that is, apart from the western approaches to Britain where the airship was able to operate outside the range of German fighters and provided excellent air cover to convoys.

By the end of the war, British maritime air power, which was by some distance the most developed, amounted to some 3,000 aircraft, 55,000 men and 12 aircraft handling ships. Much had been done to indicate what the future might hold with the first naval air reconnaissance, bombing and anti-submarine operations all having taken place by 1918.[44] The basics of maritime air power were evident but the aircraft had certainly not been able to convince conservative naval elements of their value, and the majority of the world's fleets continued to remain sceptical about the potential of air power well into the interwar period.

The birth of strategic bombing

Despite the impact of tactical air power on the conduct of World War I, both on land and at sea, the epitome of air strength in total war still remained the bomber and the pre-war idealists, in spite of the state of prevailing technology in 1914, supported the creation of a massed bomber force to deliver great destructive blows against the enemy. Initially, this was represented by the Zeppelin fleet of Germany, and Allied newspapers warned their readers of the threat of bombing raids as soon as war broke out.[45] The apocalyptic vision was of course wholly unrealistic, and the majority of airmen were well aware of the aircraft's limitations, but the enthusiasts had, in the years before the war, glossed over what was and was not possible. More than anything it was the prospect of demoralizing the enemy with aerial bombing which sold the idea to politicians and military observers, and the repeated outbreaks of "Zeppelinitis" in newspapers increased the pressure on those in power still further. The airship was therefore seen by many to be the key to successful aerial bombing. Planning for air raids to be undertaken in the early stages of a future war was being considered seriously by the Germans and French by 1914.[46] Targeting was already developing and the idea of deliberately attacking enemy morale as well as industrial and administrative centres was under consideration.

However, when war broke out difficulties started to emerge. Problems of navigation, endurance and bombing accuracy had all been conveniently passed over by the bombing enthusiasts prior to the war, and when the defenders started to organize themselves, and even dared to shoot back at the bomber aircraft, the realities of long-range bombing began to cause serious misgivings. Airships proved to be a profound disappointment. They began to fall foul of ground fire and the weather. The much vaunted Zeppelin raids on Britain achieved very little in the way of substantive physical damage, although in the aftermath of a raid in 1915, that paragon of Victorian Englishness, the cricketer W.G. Grace, was a much mourned casualty. In total there were 54 German airship raids on Britain, the last as late as 1918, but the campaign was effectively brought to a halt in 1916 when airship losses grew too great. As defences improved, especially with the development of interceptor fighters, the Zeppelin became an expensive and vulnerable behemoth. By 1916 it had been replaced by long-range bomber aircraft. Indeed, it has been calculated that German airship crews suffered the highest casualty rates of any part of the German army.[47] Other powers rapidly came to the same conclusion about the value of airships as the Germans: the Italians notably lost two airships on night-time bombing raids in 1915,[48] while the French mirrored the Germans in abandoning their army airships by 1917.[49]

The successor to the airship proved to be the large, multi-engined bomber, developed by a number of powers both before and as the war progressed. The Germans produced a number of such aircraft, notably the Friedrichshafen GIII, the Gotha V and the Zeppelin Staaken RVI. These heavy-bombers were intended to deliver a joint knockout blow to Britain in conjunction with the launch of unrestricted submarine warfare. However, although they were more successful than their airship predecessors, they too were eventually forced to abandon daylight raids in order to keep losses down, as they were beginning to suffer at the hands of concentrated anti-aircraft fire and better organized fighter defences. Moreover, large aircraft of this type were still relatively new and lacked an effective gestation period. German development went back only to the RGO1 programme of late 1914 and successive designs encountered many problems, most notably the Gotha, which suffered from structural weaknesses to such an extent that more aircraft of this type were lost in flying accidents than on combat duty.[50]

Notably, a trend was established that was to be followed many times in attempted strategic bombing campaigns. Daylight raids by Zeppelins in 1915–16 and heavy bombers in 1917–18 proved to be too dangerous and were replaced by night-time operations to keep losses down. This, however, seriously affected bombing accuracy, ultimately did not provide the protection desired and eventually led to the abandonment of bombing operations. Physical destruction from both Zeppelins and heavy-bombers was minimal in World War I with total damage amounting to less than one per cent of that caused by rats.[51] However, the psychological impact of bombing was to be far more profound and was markedly to influence perceptions in the post-war world.

Early French daylight efforts were suspended when German Fokker Eindekker fighters started to take a significant toll of the bombers and, like the Germans, they switched in 1916 to night operations. The Allies were unable and unwilling to undertake a serious long-range bombing campaign until much later in the war when, with the influx of US equipment and the gradual diminution of German defences, the prospects for bombing offensives against targets as far away as Berlin looked fair. However, practical difficulties remained and the RAF, under Sir Hugh Trenchard, lacking the resources to do much else, largely carried out a series of interdiction raids in an effort to disrupt the zone behind the German lines. Trenchard was heavily criticized by his great rival Sir Frederick Sykes for not adopting a more systematic and strategic approach to the bombing campaign, but anything more was technically beyond the Independent Air Force and losses were still heavy. For 543 tons of bombs dropped on Germany, of which a considerable percentage were dropped on "non-strategic" targets, the RAF suffered 352 aircraft lost or damaged. The bombing campaign of 1918 resulted in such little physical damage that post-war analyzers, searching for something to acclaim, emphasized the effect bombing had on morale even though this was difficult to quantify. The roots of the RAF's interwar *raison d'être* were being firmly planted in 1918.[52]

In Italy some of the more important developmental work was undertaken by the Italian air forces against the Austrians. Three-engined Caproni bombers had been under development prior to Italy's entry into the war in 1915 and the Austrians countered with Gothas supplied by the Germans. However, despite a series of raids on Adriatic ports, neither side was able to mount a serious offensive until the Italians mustered some 50 bombers by the end of 1918, by which time the war was grinding to a conclusion.[53]

Debate continued on all sides throughout the closing stages of the war as to whether long-range bombing was an effective use of resources. Many believed that air power should be used to support the land battles and that attacks on cities or enemy industries were merely distractions. Hugh Trenchard, later an arch-proponent of strategic bombing, argued in 1918 that air forces should be used to aid the army, although he and others were to change their views as a result of the impact of bombing on the population of London and its environs. The real impact that the summer of 1917 had on the development of strategic bombing was the influence that the scenes and reports of panic and consternation had in London as the German bombers roamed overhead, apparently at will. Although death and damage was limited, the image of a city close to the point of collapse into anarchy, grossly exaggerated as this may have been, went on to be used by advocates of strategic bombing in the years after the war. In an effort to allay fears that Britain was helpless and at the mercy of the Germans, the British government, following the findings of the Smuts Committee, established the RAF in April 1918 as the first independent air force. As well as helping to bring to an end a series of duplication of effort fiascos between the RFC and the RNAS, the RAF was charged with defeating the air raids and underpinning public confidence in Britain's air defences. Additionally, one of the more overlooked motives was that of revenge: Lloyd-George announced that Britain would strike back at Germany, not necessarily for sound strategic reasons but for public consumption.[54]

It was clear that bombing of civilian populations aroused great feelings quite out of proportion to the deaths and damage incurred: only 300 tons of bombs were dropped on Britain by German aircraft, killing 1,400 people, a tiny fraction of the carnage of the Western Front.[55] Yet the disruption caused in London, whether by bombing or by fear and terror, made strategic air offensives look viable and indeed possibly very effective. Certainly, the Italian air power advocate, Guilio Douhet, took notice of the situation in London and in other cities subjected to aerial bombing. Paradoxically, similar attention was not paid to the problems encountered by the strategic bombers themselves, not least the heavy losses suffered once the defenders had properly organized themselves. Moreover, the initial panic soon faded when it became clear that defence was viable and that life could go on. It was to remain a serious failing of the air power advocates that they were rather selective in the information they relied upon to prove their arguments.

Nevertheless, strategic bombing had become firmly embedded in air power consciousness as a result of the Great War, even though there was little of real substance to support some of the wild claims that were subsequently made. It was as much the political impact of the raids on London that laid the foundations for the often slavish beliefs of the RAF in the interwar era. Although national air power strategies were based as much on strategic requirements and necessity after 1918 than service ideals and experiences, it is worth noting that the British suffered more than most from aerial bombing and, along with the USA, they never truly encountered the difficulties of mounting such operations as endured by the Germans and French. To a degree, the pattern of the interwar era had been formed by 1918 and largely as a result of the various powers' experiences of the Great War.

The economics of air power

The expansion of the aero-industries in the First World War was remarkable by any standards and was a clear indication of the importance of economic mobilization to modern war. Once it became obvious that the war was not going to be over by Christmas 1914 and the demands for ever larger armed forces grew, so it was that the utilization of a state's energies was required to continue to prosecute the war. For the first time, whole populations became embroiled in war, even if indirectly, and with conscription and mass-production factory work, including female labour, the nature and scale of war had taken an exponential leap forward. The demands of air power on home industries and economies were arguably more pronounced than any other aspect of war production. Not only did air power require ever increasing output but it also made heavy demands on a nation's technological base. The need to marry military requirement, industrial mass-production and scientific advancement was a test that few states were able to meet effectively,

Table 3.2 – World War I frontline strengths

Source: Angelucci, *Military aircraft*, p. 29.

and certainly over any length of time the smaller and less advanced industrial powers began to suffer.

The scale of expansion is certainly worth noting. On the outbreak of war in 1914 the British air forces (RFC and RNAS) numbered a little over 2,000 men, but had reached 291,000 by November 1918, making the RAF the largest air force.[56] The French had grown from 3,500 to 90,000 in the same period[57] while, remarkably, the US Air Service, which had joined the war only in 1917, had expanded from 1,395 to 195,000 by the armistice.[58] Even the Italian air forces numbered around 100,000 in November 1918.[59]

In terms of engine and airframe production all the major combatants increased their output dramatically as the war progressed. In 1914 such levels were measured in hundreds at best but by 1918 monthly airframe output was reaching levels of 3,000 in Britain, 2,700 in France and even in Germany, where the stresses of the blockade and being heavily outnumbered were beginning to tell, 2,200 airframes per month were being produced. In engine production, France led the way at 4,000 per month while the British and Germans were at half that level. Throughout the war France produced

63

52,000 aircraft, Germany 48,000 and Britain 43,000. French aero-engine production at 88,000 doubled the output of Germany and Britain. If the war had gone on into 1919, the USA was ready to surpass the Europeans in engine production thanks to the Liberty model, but was still reliant on European airframe technology. Like many other aspects of the rise of air power, 1919 appeared to be the year in which the aircraft and its attendant industries would come of age. The other powers' production levels were dwarfed by the big three.[60] Austria–Hungary managed a mere 4,346 engines between 1914–18 and Russia was heavily dependent on France for its air power requirements. The methods and policies adopted by the belligerents in the war give a fair indication of the demands of air power on economies and societies. There was a marked contrast between the approaches of Germany and Britain to production and industry organization. Germany managed to mobilize its aircraft industry quite adequately, but not always as effectively as it might have. Moreover, there was a marked split between the front-line and the home front and, as was also the case in Austria–Hungary, the Germans suffered from bureaucratic wrangling and petty squabbling. Efforts by the military to control the situation did not help as they were preoccupied with aircraft technology and capabilities rather than the organization and standardization of the industry, thus adding significantly to their supply problems. Indeed, any aircraft which met ministry requirements was adopted by the air force and consequently introduced into service. Once again, supply problems ensued as each aircraft type required its own spare parts and logistical support structure.

However, the most significant problem to confront the Germans was that of aero-engine production and development which was hindered by two poor decisions taken by the aviation inspectorate, which curiously did not contain aero-engine experts. In 1914 it was decided that development of engines of over 150 hp would be suspended so as not to interfere with engine production, just at the time when the Allies were pressing ahead with such development. This strangled development and led to German aircraft manufacturers having to work with low-powered engines for much of the war. Secondly, in 1915 the inspectorate decided not to pursue the procurement of a Benz 240 hp engine, later only to order 500–600 hp engines for the R-plane bombers. By the end of the war, Allied engines ranged from 300–450 hp types while the Germans were still labouring with 185–250 hp models.[61] Paradoxically, the decision to stick to tried and tested engine technology to keep up engine output succeeded in hindering technological innovation, whereas the lack of central planning and control in airframe development produced sophisticated aircraft designs, often superior to Allied models, but not in high enough quantities or with adequate support.

The complicated and non-standardized production techniques of the German aero-industries also created drawbacks in contrast to the British. The latter power was able to expand its productive base considerably in the later stages of the war by adopting a number of policies which could be identified more closely with the demands of industrial war. The British aero-industry grew from 60,000 workers in August 1916 to 347,000 by November 1918, almost twice the size of the French industry (180,000). However, as has been noted the respective outputs of the two industries, and indeed the German industry too, were not reflective of the disparity in size of workforce. Britain relied heavily on labour dilution with the replacement of skilled labour by unskilled workers, usually women. In August 1916 this level had stood at 31.7 per cent, but by October 1918 had been increased to 46.1 per cent. This resulted in a much higher ratio of workers to aircraft produced – about one aircraft per month per 120 workers – but allowed an easier expansion of the industry than was possible in Germany where the lack of skilled labour was a key factor in hindering increased production. [62]

German aircraft were relatively complicated and sophisticated in comparison with Allied designs, mostly in an effort to make up for engine and numerical deficiencies. But in the final two years of the war such an approach fused with increasing administrative chaos, faltering transportation and shortages of materials and labour to cause many problems. As John Morrow has argued, it was becoming clear to the German high command that a modern economy could not be ordered about like an army.[63]

The French were able to meet the challenge of modern war by careful management and procurement policy decisions and, thanks to the adoption of a standardization plan as early as October 1914, they were able to maintain their lead for much of the war. The policy of standardization was also pursued by the British, but their industry was less well developed and thus had to rely more on labour dilution to keep up with the increasingly excessive demands of the war. Standardization resulted in France producing 264 prototypes for 38 service models, Britain 309 for 73, while Germany constructed 610 prototypes for 72 service models. This policy allowed the French to harness an already well developed aero-industry while at the same time maintaining a significant lead in engine production, where independent initiative was encouraged. In stark contrast with Germany, where engine production was stifled and restricted to two main producers, France's aero-engine industry was allowed to flourish and thus their lead was maintained throughout the war.[64]

By 1918, France and Britain, along with increasing support from the USA, were threatening to swamp the German air forces. The Germans were no longer able to keep up, nor had they any further reserves to call upon and the prospects for 1919 were bleak indeed. The Germans' most significant failing was their inability to manage their air industries effectively. While the French adopted perspicacious procurement policies from the off and the British greatly expanded their aero-industry base with unskilled labour, the Germans failed to adopt standardization until 1917 (when arguably it was too late), and were unable to take a firm grip of the entire production system, being too liberal with airframe output and too narrow and restrictive over engine production.[65]

However, one can be too critical over these failings, and it must be noted that the Germans were forced into a defensive air strategy by a combination of numerical inferiority and increasing material deficiencies. In contrast, the Allies could be more aggressive and profligate with their uses of air power, safe in the knowledge that replacements would probably be forthcoming. Technological superiority was crucial to the Germans to make good their deficiencies in numbers, but they were increasingly unable to translate this into any battlefront advantage. In the closing stages of the war the Germans were ahead in aircraft technology, with the innovative work of Hugo Junkers resulting in the J.10, the first all metal, low wing, cantilever aircraft,[66] and the Fokker D7. However, the simpler Allied designs were effective enough and much easier to mass-produce. The greater realization by the Allies that efficient mass-produced aircraft were the key to success in modern war was borne out by the events in the closing two years of the conflict and the lessons were to be used 20 years or so later in World War II. What is also worth noting is that mass-production did not result in poor quality aircraft. Although the Germans had superior airframe designs, the overall techno-logical aspect of the air war had swung decisively towards the Allies by late 1917, as a result of a combination of effective qualitative superiority in key areas, notably engine design, and considerable quantitative advantages across the board.

Conclusions

Historians have tended to polarize in their estimations of the impact of air power on World War I, tending to claim that air power contributed either a great deal or, conversely, very little. Moreover, too much attention has been paid to the impact of the war on the development of air power in light of what came later. Consequently, there has been something of an over-estimation of the importance of strategic bombing and perhaps too little consideration given to the impact of air power on the Great War itself.

This in part has come about thanks to the more excessive claims of the air power enthusiasts who consistently exaggerated the possible impact of the aerial weapon on the conduct of the war, despite the realities which often confronted them. However, as some historians have argued, the air power advocates were not wrong so much as they were unrealistic: much of what was being claimed about air power both before and during the Great War was, in the long term, to come true. As one historian has put it, "the aviators envisaged and promised great things, but their aircraft continually let them down".[67]

It is clear that air power was in some fields an important and occasionally crucial influence on the First World War, but in no particular area can it be viewed as decisive. Although many military leaders recognized that air power had become an integral part of armed forces, it was not in itself the arbiter of success or failure. There were some crucial aspects, such as aerial reconnaissance and artillery direction, which were the most significant parts played by air power, but it could not in itself decide the outcome of a campaign.

Nevertheless, the Great War did see the beginnings of most of the future facets of air power. The concept of air superiority emerged and with it the fighter battles that represent a most striking image of air power. Maritime air power was born and the arguments over the extent to which the aircraft would revolutionize naval warfare began in earnest, though the most significant role of the aircraft at sea, convoy protection, was strangely overlooked. There was even the first hint of the use of airborne troops when the American air power enthusiast, Billy Mitchell, argued in 1918 for the dropping of an entire division behind German lines. Perhaps the area which attracted most attention was that of strategic bombing. This was the one way in which air power might be able to decide the outcome of a war. Indeed, despite all the problems encountered by the French and the Germans, Allied plans for strategic bombing in 1919 were ambitious indeed. The fact that they went untested was perhaps a contributing factor to the unquestioned slavish beliefs that persisted in some air forces throughout the interwar years. The divide between the arch air power proponents and the heads of the older services was increasing by the end of the war and was to continue to cause disagreements for much of the 1918–39 era.

The degree of technical advancement in aircraft design in the Great War remains unclear. Contemporary views included Hugo Junkers, who stated prior to the war that a conflict would certainly boost aerial development,[68] while his compatriot Ernst Heinkel believed that the war had moved on aero-technology by six years in the space of four-and-a-half.[69] Extreme views included French Air Chief, General Duval, who claimed that the war had accelerated aerial development some 50 years,[70] to the German historian

Gerhard Wissmann who believed that because of the profiteering nature of capitalist systems and the demands of mass-production, the war had actually retarded development.[71]

John Morrow takes a more balanced view stating that, while the demands of war had hindered careful examination of advances made and some development had been haphazard, in general, aircraft of 1918 were much superior to those of 1914 and the level of co-ordinated effort on the part of government, industry and science was such that progress of a similar level could not have been contemplated in peacetime. In particular, German airframe technology had advanced dramatically between 1914 and 1918 in an effort to make good the deficiencies of German aero-engines. Conversely, the Allies' superior engines had allowed them to standardize and simplify airframe production, but the engines themselves were more powerful and reliable in 1918 than in 1914 by a factor four to five.[72] It is also worth noting that in the post-war years a number of military aeroplane designs were used to begin the first organized and widespread air passenger services, something unfeasible in 1914.

It is clear that the war did accelerate aerial development, although concessions had to be made for the requirements of mass-production on occasion. However, as was to be proven by the Second World War, the marrying of science, industry and the military in the correct manner allowed a high degree of technical development from all sides in the productive process. The failure of less advanced or organized industrial systems resulted in part from the fear of standardization of production which, it was believed, would hinder advancement and development. The Allies in the Great War, however, confounded such thinking and were able to mix mass-production with an increasing front-line technological superiority. The reality proved to be that once effective mass-production and procurement techniques were in place the process became highly responsive to demands and moreover was able to offer technical leaps which became apparent in the production process. Naturally, a degree of this success was because of the greater availability of resources, but it is also the case that the more responsive economies of the West fared better than the military-command economy of Imperial Germany. Such a system as the latter could only really work when the entire economy was rigidly structured and organized as was to be the case in the Soviet Union in the Second World War.

Undeniably, the most significant features of air power in the Great War were the role of the aircraft in reconnaissance and observation and also the role in convoy protection, yet it is for the birth of serious strategic bombing and massed air fighting that the war is remembered. Paradoxically, ground-attack operations which had proven relatively effective in 1918 were quickly relegated in the post-1918 era, while strategic bombing, which had proven little, came to prominence. For what was to come later, the First World War was certainly a crucial formative period, but in terms of direct impact on the conflict itself it is a fair summation that the Great War did a good deal more for air power than air power contributed to the eventual outcome.

Chapter Four

The development of air power doctrine and theory, 1918–39

In terms of world history, the Great War was undoubtedly a watershed. The major European powers had effectively exhausted themselves over the four years of conflict to such a degree that long-term geopolitical trends, already evident to some prior to the war, were now becoming all too apparent. Germany had, to all intents and purposes, been eliminated as a world power and the face of eastern Europe was irrevocably altered. Even the supposed victors, Britain and France, were in reality no longer capable of pursuing active foreign policies such as they had before 1914. If the Second World War was to bring about the end of the age of European supremacy, then the Great War was to lay the foundations for such far reaching change. In grand strategic and political terms, the world after 1918 was radically different to that of four years earlier and it was to the politicians, leaders and strategists of the immediate post-war years that the task of managing this transition fell. The post-1918 sentiment that the Great War had been the "war to end all wars" was in truth nothing more than sanguine speculation, for the war had done little to solve the underlying problems of the western world. More-over, the perception that future wars could and would be eliminated was held largely by those for whom a widespread restructuring of the world's power systems was unnecessary. This effectively equated to those who had won, or had at least maintained what they held or desired from, the First World War.

What was universally accepted by the world's major powers in the post-war era was the belief that a future re-fight of World War I was unthinkable and untenable. For the victors, another such conflict would not only be politically undesirable, but it could also actually be catastrophic and would probably result in the loss of everything that had been secured by the fighting of 1914–18. For the defeated or disgruntled of the Great War, a total economic war of the kind just fought not only offered the prospect of great hardship and misery but it also offered little prospect of success. Germany had lost in 1918 and in a weakened state why should the outcome in a future war be any different?

For all concerned, the post-war years posed significant strategic conundrums that required new solutions and methods of thinking. In essence, few believed that war had been eliminated, despite rhetoric to the contrary, and therefore what followed was an attempt to pursue political ends with military means without falling into the ruinous slaughter of the First World War. For the development of air power, the desire to synthesize a new type of war was crucial in propelling the development of air forces in particular directions in the interwar era. National strategies were to play an important role in shaping air policies in the 1920s and 1930s (see Chapter Five) but these strategies were in part the result of what air power theorists were claiming was and was not possible. While the logical progression was for strategy to fit to what air power had to offer, in some cases aerial theory adapted itself to what was desired, even when this was unrealistic, thus leading to distortions of air power development in the interwar period.

The development of air power thinking followed three distinctive lines in the 1918–39 era. The first, and for most advocates the most significant line of thought, was strategic bombing which appeared to offer the most comprehensive and revolutionary progression of warfare; perhaps even to the extent that ground and naval war would no longer be necessary. The second line of thought centred on the belief that air power provided the means with which to break completely the deadlock that had emerged in ground warfare for the best part of four years. It was argued that the spearheading of ground offensives by aerial artillery was the key to ending campaigns and wars quickly. Thirdly, the development of maritime air power was seen by some as being the key to maintaining or seizing the initiative in naval warfare. The use of aircraft to command the world's seaways was considered fundamental to the future of the maritime powers such as Japan, Britain and the USA.

In all of these areas, progression of thinking and doctrine continued apace throughout the interwar years and often caused inter- and intra-service friction. Part of this resulted from the characters and personalities involved in the disputes and from the degree of the public interest in aerial matters. Popular support was forthcoming because the airmen seemed to be offering a way out of the type of war that the Great War had degenerated into, and importantly, they were not tarred with the same brush as those who had led so many to their deaths at Verdun and the Somme. Of course, the truth was quite different: casualty rates in air forces in the Great War were usually higher than in ground units and airmen were sent to their deaths with as much disregard for human life as the infantry. However, popular perception was then, as now, much more powerful than reality. The proponents of air power were, in the eyes of the masses, railing against excessive military conservatism and this lent them considerable popular support, much to the chagrin of their leaders.

Additionally, friction was caused by the nature and character of those leading the fight for air power. Those who ended the war in positions of responsibility in the world's air forces were often younger than their similarly ranked colleagues, and arguably sought to assert their authority by belligerent advocacy of their position. Moreover, they were quite often inexperienced as high commanding officers which may also have been a potential source of trouble.[1] Clearly then, the desire for change and the nature of those advocating it was to shape the development of doctrine and theory to a significant degree and must be acknowledged when examining the progress, or at times the lack of it, in the interwar years.

The emergence of strategic bombing

The roots of strategic bombing theory lay back in the period before the First World War when conjecture grew as to how air power should be best employed. Whereas the more obvious examples of linking air power with armies and navies were more readily accepted, the notion that aircraft could be used in an entirely separate, or strategic, manner began to be debated. However, the grander notions of massed air fleets smashing cities and civilizations into rubble owed more to science-fiction and fantasy than to the realities of contemporary air power, although this did little to deter its advocates.

Nevertheless, many of the principles of later strategic bombing theory were evident and established long before the emergence of the more famous prophets of the 1920s and 1930s. The notion of the "knockout blow", in which a vast fleet of bombers would deliver a major punch to an enemy which would cause such chaos that surrender would rapidly follow, had been postulated before 1914. Notably, comparisons with naval strategy and doctrine were evident, leading to perceptions of air forces as "fleets".

The first aim of an air campaign would be the decisive aerial engagement, in the tradition of the "Trafalgar" theory of naval battles.[2] This would allow "command of the air" to be established, which meant that the enemy's air fleet would have been neutralized and thus would give the victorious air force free rein to do what they would.[3] The subsequent objectives would be the enemy's urban centres, and notably the capital city.[4] Bombing attacks, it

72

was argued by some, should attempt to defeat the enemy's morale by directly attacking civilian populations. It was considered that only military personnel could withstand such bombardment and not the general public. Others shied away from proposing these brutal strategies and pressed for bombing campaigns to target industrial and political centres to cause as much disruption to the enemy state as possible.[5]

The French writer Clement Ader was one of the most notable of the early air power advocates, speculating that Britain had most to lose from the rise of air fleets due to her particular geographical vulnerability to air attack. He also claimed that air forces should constitute an entirely new third service, rather than an auxiliary weapon to aid the infantry, artillery and cavalry.[6] In Britain, Sir Frederick Lanchester was probably the most significant air power theorist, publishing his ideas in *Aircraft in warfare: the dawn of the fourth arm* (London, 1916), although the ideas themselves dated back to a series of articles from 1914 and 1915. Some of Lanchester's mathematical calculations were similar to those used by the US RAND corporation in the Cold War era indicating the perspicacity of his thinking. In many other ways Lanchester was also remarkably prescient, for example stating long before it was proven that airships were too vulnerable for front-line use (Higham suggests that Lanchester's writing may have decided Churchill against naval airships in 1914). He also notably claimed that bombers would require escort fighters to protect them during bombing missions over hostile territory, a tactic that was too readily dismissed until 1943. If one were to seek a true theorist for British strategic bombing, more than anyone else it would be Lanchester, even if the RAF ignored some of his predictions. It is more than likely that Lanchester was read by Sir Frederick Sykes, Chief of the Air Staff, RAF (1918–19) and Sir Hugh Trenchard, the dominant chief of the RAF throughout its formative years (1918 and 1919–29).

The First World War had indicated the potential of massed bombing, but many problems had emerged once defenders had organized themselves. The French abandoned long-range bombing in 1915, the Germans tried first with airships, then with heavy bombers such as the Gotha and the Staaken, only effectively to give up by 1917. Despite claims that the cover of darkness offered a way out of the problem, many of the underlying drawbacks remained: navigation, excessive resource investment, targeting, true strategic value, and so forth. However, such difficulties were considered surmountable and by the end of the war the Allies were on the point of launching a sustained bombing campaign against German cities. Perversely, some air power advocates such as the American Billy Mitchell were disappointed that the war ended when it did as it denied them their chance to prove what their ever expanding fleets were capable of. However, if the war had continued into 1919 and the bombing campaigns had gone badly, the supporters of air power would almost certainly have glossed over the problems and explained away the failings as they had in 1915 and 1917 and were to continue to do so throughout the Second World War.

Post-war thinking nevertheless began to build on pre-war theorizing and on some of the lessons of the Great War, though of course only those lessons which supported strategic bombing. The US Army Air Corps set up a tactical school at Maxwell Air Force base in Alabama to consider the applications of air power, in a strategic and tactical sense, while in Britain the RAF also began thinking about the best use of massed bombing. As early as 1918, Sir Frederick Sykes, the then Chief of Air Staff of the RAF, had officially proposed a major plan for the creation of a massed bombing force capable of delivering severe blows to an enemy.[7] The plan was rejected by the British government on the grounds of cost and strategic necessity. However, it was in aeronautical journals such as the French *Revue de L'Aeronautique Militaire* set up in 1921, and the Italian *Rivista Aeronautica* (1925) that air power discussions really developed and it was from this latter journal that the much debated Douhet legend may well have begun.

The Douhet myth

Guilio Douhet remains the doyen of the air power "theorists", especially in the USA where he is considered the father of air power even more so than the native Billy Mitchell. It was notable that in the aftermath of the Gulf War of 1991 many air power advocates were claiming that the air campaign which had preceded Desert Storm had proved Douhet (and Mitchell) correct – air power, if used poperly, was the final arbiter of military success. Of course this was a very selective and partial reading of events, but the willingness to extol the virtues and righteousness of Douhet's philosophy without careful consideration of reality demonstrates how various myths and legends have grown and been fostered by generations of air power thinkers, writers and practitioners. Nevertheless, no matter how mythical their influence now appears to be, there is no denying that Douhet, and to a lesser extent Mitchell, have been, and continue to be, cited as the father figures of modern air power. Douhet had a stormy career as an officer in the Italian army where, surprisingly, he had little contact with air forces, only lasting in his post as director of the Aviation Section from 1913 to 1914. He was transferred after disciplinary hearings, only returning briefly in 1918, and again in 1922 when he was appointed Sub-secretary of Aeronautics by Mussolini. He soon left this position and concentrated on his writing from 1923. Lee Kennett even suggests that Douhet may never have learned to fly.[8]

However, it was for his writing that Douhet was to claim his place in air power history. He was certainly writing up his opinions before the Great War but controversy persists as to the extent and nature of his thinking at that time for there is no evidence that it was any more theoretically advanced than the work of other contemporary writers.[9] After 1918, Douhet became more involved in the debates concerning the future of war, though his writing was largely based on the strategic requirements of Italy in the post-war era, a point that is often overlooked.[10] The key text in Douhet's career was *The command of the air* published in 1921, and in an expanded and more strident form in 1927. It was here that the key points of Douhet's philosophy can be gleaned.[11]

In essence, his theory on the use of air power can be encapsulated quite briefly. He believed that in times of war there was no longer the distinction between combatants and civilians. As war was now a matter of whole nation states confronting each other, their civilian populations were now legitimate targets. It was also the case, Douhet argued, that ground forces could not bring about a rapid conclusion to a major war. Success had come to the Allies only after four years of attritional slaughter. The key to future war was the aeroplane, or more precisely, the heavy-bomber. Large formations of heavy-bombers, like the Italian Caproni designs, offered the means with which to deliver massive attacks on enemy centres of population and industry, which would bring about the collapse of the enemy's will to resist and thus would bring victory.[12] The only role Douhet foresaw for ground forces (especially in his later writings) was as a policing force to mop up resistance in the wake of the aerial assault. Indeed, Douhet believed that the maximum possible resources should be given over to building the bomber fleet. He felt that all other forms of military activity were now at best peripheral, and at worst a dangerous distraction from the decisive activity of strategic bombing. Of particular importance to Douhet was the attack on the enemy's morale, which of course was a euphemism for bombing civilians, for which he was quite willing to advocate the use of poison gas. Such measures, considered extreme by some air power advocates, were acceptable to Douhet because they would bring about a rapid end to the war and for Douhet that was the key. To his thinking there was little point in agonizing over the rights and wrongs of bombing: it had to be dealt with as a reality relevant to the 1920s.[13] His particularly apocalyptic vision of a future air war, with thousands of deaths caused by poison gas, was seen at the time as extreme and repulsive. However, it can easily be viewed alongside the threat of nuclear holocaust, a strategy accepted as a necessity in the post-World War II era.

A crucial part of Douhet's strategy and a point often overlooked, was Douhet's claim that the enemy's air power capability had to be neutralized before the massed bombers could be unleashed on the cities. The enemy air force had to destroyed, preferably on the ground, in order to seize command of the air. Moreover, it was crucial that the enemy be denied the ability to rebuild their air forces or resources would have to be repeatedly applied to defeating new enemy air fleets. The key in Douhet's thinking was to gain mastery of the air as an essential precursor to aerial bombardment, a point the RAF was particularly unwilling to accept in World War II.

However, Douhet's pivotal role in the formation of strategic bombing theory in the interwar era is highly questionable. His writing almost certainly had marginal influence and was read and acknowledged retrospectively. By the time Douhet's work became widely known in Britain and the USA, the future practitioners of strategic bombing in World War II had already established the precepts of their doctrine and planning, albeit in a flawed and incomplete fashion. Indeed, neither RAF commanders Arthur Harris or John Slessor claimed to have heard of Douhet before World War II.[14] Douhet's work was little read outside Italy until the 1930s and an English translation was not published until 1942. Moreover, there is no direct evidence of his work being used in the formulation of British strategic bombing theory in the interwar era. Whatever Douhet was writing was in any case similar in content to the thinking of other air power advocates and indeed to the doctrine being formulated or rejected within the world's air forces.[15]

Nevertheless, evidence of the wider impact of Douhet can be noted. The air power writer L.E.O. Charlton indicated the importance of Douhet's work in 1935,[16] and Arthur Harris' future right-hand man, Sir Robert Saundby, also later wrote of the Italian's important influence.[17] During the 1939–45 war the air power propagandist Alexander de Seversky used Douhet to support his drive for an independent air force capable of defeating America's enemies directly, without long and costly ground wars, resulting in the famous Disney cartoon *Victory through air power*.[18]

Criticisms of Douhet abound. For example, his bombers always got through and the impact of his raids were always calculated at their most destructive. There is no doubt that Douhet's vision was at times simplistic, but a key factor in his planning was the use of poison gas, never used in World War II. Consequently, the impact of the bombing raids he envisaged was never tested. Additionally, the key goal of destroying the enemy's air forces was never the first priority of the strategic bombing offensive until *Operation Pointblank* in 1943. Still further, a key element in Douhet's strategy was the surprise bombing attack and the inability of defences to respond quickly enough to prevent such raids. In the 1920s this was, to an extent, legitimate thinking but, with the advent of radar and high-performance interceptor fighters in the mid-1930s, Douhet's whole strategy was undermined. Douhet can perhaps be criticized for not expecting defences to develop at all whilst bombing technology would, but in the environment of the 1920s there did not really appear to be an answer to the surprise bombing raid.

However, Douhet's most important contribution to the development of air power lies in the perception of his influence rather than the reality. It is clear that Douhet was not a pioneering theorist. Others were or had already outlined the potential of air power in much the same way. Nor was he a clear strategist. Although the essence of his thinking can be found in *The command of the air*, a complete view can only be obtained by piecing together a picture from many sources. As Claudio Segre has argued, the most fitting epithet for Douhet, like Mitchell, may well be prophet.[19] His impact on defining and crystallizing bombing theory was at best peripheral but in encapsulating the essence of strategic bombing for those pressing for a greater role for air power in the period leading up to and during the Second World War, Douhet's prophesying was well suited.[20]

The development of strategic bombing theory and doctrine

Strategic bombing theory in the interwar era took root in a number of air forces, but only in Britain and the USA was it to have a major influence in shaping air power policy, although its influence in Germany and the USSR is often too readily overlooked. However, as was to be demonstrated in the Second World War, it was predominantly the RAF and the USAAF which sought to fulfil the notions of strategic bombing. Interwar theory was to be shaped by a number of considerations, often little related to the prevailing realities of air power. Clearly, air forces were acting against a backdrop of political pressure to ensure that the attritional slaughter of the trenches was avoided in future wars, and in an environment of burgeoning fear and interest in air warfare, the so-called growth in "air mindedness". Moreover, air forces had to wrestle with more mundane matters, such as inter-service squabbles with the RAF defending its hard won independence, while US airmen attempted to carve out their own separate identity. All of this, as much as technology and practical application, was to shape the development of strategic bombing theory after World War I.

In the RAF such theories were considerably influenced by Sir Hugh Trenchard even before he became Chief of the Air Staff (CAS) in 1918, for during the later stages of the war Trenchard had been commander of the long-range or strategic bombing forces in Europe. It was here that, with insufficient numbers of suitable aircraft to have much impact on German industry, he adopted a policy of dispersed bombing in the hope of undermining civilian morale. He even deployed his aircraft on interdiction duties to support the ground forces directly. Both of these policies earned him criticism from Britain, in particular from Sir Frederick Sykes. After the war, Trenchard became CAS largely because he was considered level-headed and unlikely to press for wild expansion schemes. However, he was a shrewd political operator and did much to ensure the survival of the RAF through the "locust years" of the 1920s by selling the idea of using the RAF as a cost-effective imperial police force. He also brought with him particular and developing ideas on strategic bombing, most notably notions on the "moral effect" of bombing on civilian populations. Trenchard even argued that the ratio of psychological to physical effects in the impact of bombing on a nation was as high as twenty to one. His ideas were fuelled still further by the reports of the British bombing survey teams, which had struggled to find much physical evidence of bomb damage in World War I and had thus emphasized what they perceived or hoped were the effects on German morale. In addition, the panic and chaos caused by Germany's modest bombing of London indicated what might be achieved by a concerted and sustained offensive. By the end of the 1920s, the emphasis on targeting morale was well established, and Trenchard's influence lingered throughout the 1930s and into the Second World War, long after his retirement in 1929.[21]

Paradoxically, despite the acceptance of strategic bombing in principle the practicalities were never properly investigated. Although RAF theory rested on delivering a "knockout blow", little time and effort was devoted to how this strategy was to be carried out. Fighters, either as escorts or as interceptors were dismissed as either sops to public concerns at their own defencelessness or as a dangerous dissipation of scant resources. Problems of navigation and bombing were largely glossed over and, indeed, it was not until the late 1930s that the RAF really began to investigate the problems of locating and then hitting a target – even one as large as a city. It wasn't until 1937 that the RAF set up a "Committee for the Scientific Survey of Air Offence" under the direction of Sir Henry Tizard, in the hope that this would do for Bomber Command what similar initiatives had yielded for Fighter Command. However, even this new approach was partly instigated by Bomber Command's grudging acceptance that fighter technology had improved, and that if they did not react to this, and indeed to Sir Thomas Inskip's review of defence (1937), they could be at risk.

However, it must be stated that the inability of the RAF to develop the doctrine necessary to prosecute their strategic bombing theories was in part a result of the poor funding of the service in the 1920s and early 1930s. Nevertheless, it is clear that near blind faith in RAF bombing strategy was required in the interwar era and the consequences of this myopia, which persisted during the first two years of the war, became all too apparent with the appalling casualties endured by Bomber Command until the closing stages of World War II.[22]

In contrast to the tentative British experience of bombing in World War I, the US Army Air Forces (USAAF) had nothing similar on which to base their interwar theorizing, although the results were studied. Vicarious learning is rarely absorbed and the history of war and conflict is no different. However, like the British they were able to formulate their thinking without having to consider the needs of the ground forces too much. In addition, the US Navy had its own air forces so maritime air power was also beyond the US Army's remit. Nevertheless, the US air forces contained within the army were determined in the long term to establish themselves as an independent force and it was the theory of strategic bombing or bombardment which appeared to offer the best chance of achieving this.

Although strategic bombing was to take root in the US Army Air Service (or Air Corps [USAAC] from 1926) it was to follow a different line to that pursued by the RAF. Initially, the Americans were influenced by the thinking of Colonel Edgar Gorrell, who had been appointed as head of Strategical Aviation and since 1917 had been studying strategic bombing. Gorrell was influenced by British ideas, and like the RAF he made the distinction between the "moral" and "material" effects of heavy bombing.[23] Whereas the aggressive "morale targeting" notions of the RAF partially reflected the offensive and combative British aerial experience of the Great War, and also reflected Trenchard's personality, the US Air Corps Tactical School (ACTS) based at Langley, Virginia, adopted a more measured approach. Initially, air power interest divided between pursuit, attack and bombardment aircraft but by the late 1920s the emphasis was shifting.[24] During the 1930s when the Norden bomb sight and new faster bomber aircraft designs became available, the belief of theorists based at the ACTS (by then at Maxwell Airbase, Alabama), such as Kenneth Walker, Donald Wilson, Laurence Kutter and Haywood Hansell, began to take shape and was to influence many World War II commanders, such as Curtis LeMay, Carl Spaatz and Ira Eaker. The new thinking was also prompted by the MacArthur–Pratt agreement between the US Navy and the US Army which delineated spheres of air power influence within the armed forces, and the USAAC was now to be responsible for defending American shores with land based bombers. This of course required the army aircraft to be able to hit a moving target at sea and thus a premium was to be placed on bombing accuracy.[25]

Essentially, unlike the British, the Americans took a particularly industrial-economic view of bombing. To their thinking, the key to bringing about success was to identify "key nodes" in the enemy economy and to target these for destruction by precision bombing. What these so called "key nodes" were and exactly how they would be destroyed remained to be developed, but the essence of US doctrine was already different to that of the RAF. This was reflected in intent, if not always in practice, in World War II. However, like the British, the US Air Corps believed slavishly in the ability of the bomber to by-pass defences, despite the protestations and arguments of Captain Claire Chennault, who taught pursuit aviation at Maxwell in the early 1930s.[26] Moreover, and again reflecting the British experience, the USAAC chose to disregard any empirical evidence from the Spanish Civil War and from the war in Europe prior to US entry. The ACTS preferred to rely on their statistical and scientific approach to strategic bombing and the bombing campaigns in Europe were dismissed as being partial, poorly organized and lacking in the correct doctrine and equipment.[27] Although the American air forces endured a steeper learning curve than the British in World War II, they too suffered from an unwillingness to deal with the practicalities of prosecuting a strategic bombing campaign and it was to take until 1943 for the US air forces to come to terms with the implications.

The development of strategic bombing theory in other major powers foundered not because of lack of prescience or stultifying military conservatism, as is often argued by the arch-advocates of bombing, but simply because it did not fit with national strategic aims or it was considered technically unattainable in the foreseeable future without an unwarranted investment of scarce resources. In addition, the legacy of the failed strategic bombing campaigns against Britain between 1916 and 1918 continued to shape thinking throughout the interwar era.[28] The Germans, though always adopting a more sceptical and pragmatic view, did seriously consider and study strategic bombing, especially when the Nazis came to power, but it never became properly established largely on the grounds that the limited available air power resources would be required to support ground operations more directly.[29] Unlike Britain and the USA who were protected from land based assault by geography, Germany would have to confront many hostile armies immediately on the outbreak of war. In addition, the German military were unconvinced by the claims of the air power advocates, including a number from within the *Luftwaffe*, and this view was supported by German airmen's experiences in the Spanish Civil War 1936–9.[30] Nevertheless, in the early stages of German rearmament from 1933 onwards, the political and deterrent effects of bombers were recognized in the creation of the "risk fleet", a force intended to deter enemies from interfering in German affairs until the

Wehrmacht was ready for war.[31] However, the technical practicalities of creating a strategic bombing force continually undermined efforts, and plans for a four-engined heavy-bomber were abandoned in the mid-1930s in favour of the ill-fated Heinkel He 177 long-range bomber. Nevertheless, on the outbreak of war, the Germans, thanks to their pragmatic approach to war, had in the *Luftwaffe* the most effective short-to-medium range bombing fleet in the world and, unlike the RAF, German air forces had solved many navigational and bomb aiming problems. Paradoxically, although the *Luftwaffe* was less inclined to strategic bombing, it was a more effective force for carrying it out than the RAF, certainly until 1941.[32] What the *Luftwaffe* lacked throughout were the resources to create a heavy-bomber fleet and, after 1940, they had no pressing need to do so.[33] Nevertheless, planning for a strategic bombing offensive against the USSR was in place in the summer of 1941, only to be abandoned when the demands of army support took over.[34]

French attitudes to strategic bombing were at best ambivalent and, in places, downright hostile. According to Pascal Vennesson, the French air force, only formed in 1933, rejected Douhet and his theories and remained very much at the beck and call of the army. However, it has also been argued that once nominally independent, the nascent French air force attempted to wriggle out of the army's clutches and build a more progressive doctrine which included dabblings with strategic bombing. This fused with the army's misplaced faith in the strategic defence (hence the Maginot Line), to which the air force was in reality closely tied, and served to cripple French air power in the interwar period.[35]

In Italy the prospects for strategic bombing looked better. Italy had carried out a bombing campaign during the First World War with some success and Douhet's writings were naturally more widely read in Italy than anywhere else. Moreover, Italy had an independent air force by 1923 with a manufacturer, Caproni, who already had experience of designing heavy-bombers. Still further, Italy's geographical position was such that aerial bombing on a sizeable scale was a viable option. Yet strategic bombing doctrine never became part of Italy's national strategy. Principally this can be attributed to a series of institutional and procurement failures. Not only was there no real consideration of doctrine in the *Regia Aeronautica*, but there was also no serious central planning or strategic overview. The failure of Mussolini's ill-disciplined fascist state bears testimony once again to the fact that, in order to develop air power effectively, a strong industrial, scientific and military structure needs to have been established with clearly defined national strategic goals. This was not achieved in Italy and consequently strategic bombing was never fully investigated because it was not a viable option.[36]

Strategic bombing in the USSR also looked to have distinct theoretical possibilities, once the chaos of the civil and Polish wars had subsided. Both Germany and Japan, the Soviet Union's two most likely opponents in future wars, were potentially vulnerable to strategic bombing, with their major cities being within reach of Soviet heavy-bombers. Kenneth Whiting argues that Soviet thinking on strategic bombing may have been influenced by Douhet's writing but the ideas proposed by A.N. Lapchinsky in the mid-1920s and Khirpin in the 1930s only held with the more general aims of Douhet's ideas and rejected the more extreme notions. In particular, and understandably considering the USSR's requirement for a large standing army, Douhet's claim that air power alone would be the central and decisive factor in future wars was discarded. Ultimately, and like the German experience, the VVS (the Red Air Force) abandoned its strategic bombing ideas in the wake of disappointing experiences in the Spanish Civil War and as a result of the Red Army purges.[37]

As can be seen therefore, strategic bombing as a means of winning wars was largely rejected by the armed forces of the world during the interwar period. Those who examined the possibilities came to the conclusion either that massed bombing did not fit with national strategy, or that it was not viable in the technological climate of the interwar era. Only in Britain and the USA, as a result of certain geographical, armed service and political circumstances, did strategic bombing really take root. Moreover, the nature of the doctrinal ideas codified in the RAF and the USAAF varied a good deal between each other and developed mostly in isolation, certainly without the influence of Douhet. However, in shaping the development of air forces and political attitudes to air power, especially in the 1930s, the idea of strategic bombing was a potent force, particularly in Britain and Germany and such issues will be dealt with in the next chapter. Generally, it can be seen that few believed air power had the ability to alter completely the nature of wars. At best it would be able to shape and influence ground and maritime war. Consideration in most armed forces turned to how best to use air power to support conventional war.

Land based warfare

While the advocates of strategic bombing spent the interwar era arguing that bombing of cities was the way in which a repetition of the Great War could be avoided, others sought to explain how the stalemate of 1914–18 had been broken and how mobility and fluidity could be restored to land warfare.

It was soon to be argued that air power was a constituent part of the formula required to bring speedy conclusions to land campaigns. Land warfare theorists such as J.F.C. Fuller and Basil Liddell-Hart, and the Soviet general Mikhail Tukhachevski, claimed that mobility and decisiveness could be brought back to ground warfare by the use of armoured vehicles, tanks, mobile artillery and, importantly, aircraft.

The role of aircraft in supporting ground offensives was to be developed throughout the interwar period in a much more restrained and less hysterical manner than strategic bombing, and it was also to be supported by experience to a far greater level. It was clearly much easier to develop doctrine and codify practice for ground support operations than for city bombing and there were a number of small scale conflicts in which combined ground–air tactics could be developed. In part, this led to a much more balanced assessment of air power in land warfare than was possible with strategic bombing. However, like its more prestigious and public counterpart strategic bombing, air power in ground operations was to be influenced and shaped by national strategic requirements, inter-service bickering and political forces, thus leading to a patchy and uneven integration into the doctrine of armed forces.

The crucial and pivotal problem confronting armies in the wake of the Great War was how to introduce mobility and decisiveness back to the battlefield. The armies of Europe had gone to war in 1914 expecting a rapid conclusion to the various campaigns and each endeavoured to emerge victorious from the expected decisive battle. Such a battle did not come and, especially on the Western Front, the next four years witnessed a series of arguably wasteful campaigns aimed at creating a breakthrough. Many factors combined to bring about the stalemate, one of which was the stultifying influence of air observation which frustrated attempts at generating surprise attacks. However, the key factor had been the dominance of artillery in dictating the nature of the battlefield. In this, air power again had been a key factor in its direction and support of artillery bombardment. By 1918, some of the armies of the great powers had come to terms with the requirements of the World War I battlefield. All arms co-ordination was the key with new technology, communications, tanks, aircraft and highly effective and well-directed artillery bombardments providing the means of winning battles with acceptable losses. The success of the British army, especially in the closing stages of the war, did seem to have provided the answer. Unlike the Germans in their initially successful offensive of 1918 which was spearheaded by stormtrooper infiltration tactics, the Allies realized the necessity of not outpacing their artillery cover, for without it they would be helpless cannon-fodder. The Germans were to discover this when they did indeed outdistance their supporting artillery in the 1918 offensive and consequently suffered fearful casualties. The slow remorseless advance adopted by the Allies in the later stages of the war appeared to have restored a degree of mobility to the battlefield.

However, questions remained. Some argued that the effects of the naval blockade and the attritional battles of 1915–17 had so undermined the Imperial German state that the army was collapsing anyway. It was just as reasonable to argue that the Allies had bludgeoned Germany to defeat, and the apparent success on the front line in 1918 had come about thanks to the disintegration of the German army and state, not because of a great leap forward in Allied military planning and organization.

The respective perceptions of how victory was achieved were to shape battlefield thinking in the interwar era. The French and British concluded that a combination of factors had brought Germany to defeat and that their armies had to a degree been successful in 1918. In a future war, the French in particular expected a period of defensive, attritional warfare, backed by economic blockade and preparatory to another remorseless advance akin to 1918. The key was the ability to survive the attritional phase of the war without suffering the heavy losses of 1914–17: hence, ultimately, the Maginot Line.

For Germany, however, the strategic requirements were very different. It was clear that, with the economic situation which confronted them in the interwar era, another long drawn out war would be fatal. What was required was a means of winning decisive battles and campaigns quickly. Mobility and momentum had to be restored to the battlefield in the early stages of a war and the slow remorseless approach of the Allies in 1918 was not the answer. It is clear that, to a significant extent, the requirements of national strategy were forcing the pace of theoretical consideration and doctrinal experiment in the interwar period. However, as will be explored later (in Chapter Five) this does not mean that national strategy was driven by battlefield capability, although it has been claimed that the doctrinal developments in ground and air warfare in Germany in the 1920s and 1930s, in part, resulted in a whole national strategy – the so-called *blitzkrieg*.[38]

The development of thinking on the use of air power in ground warfare progressed fitfully and unevenly during the interwar years, but it is with Germany that the formulation of the most effective doctrine for ground support operations is usually associated. Following the First World War the German general staff, now renamed *Truppenamt* and under the direction of General Hans von Seeckt, initiated a major survey of the military lessons of the conflict and the role of air power was an area of major interest. A series of studies involving over 130 officers and experts was instigated to examine the impact and role of aircraft in future war. Even though Germany was not allowed any military air power by the terms of the Treaty of Versailles, surreptitious analysis continued, conducted by Major Helmuth Wilberg, who was to become the most significant contributor to German air doctrine in the interwar period. These discussions concluded that Germany's defensive air strategy in World War I had been ill-founded and that, in future conflicts, fighters should be used to gain air superiority as an essential precursor to the effective deployment of Germany's own bomber and ground attack arm. Von Seeckt himself was an ardent supporter of air power, although he took a more pragmatic line than contemporary overseas advocates. This reflected general German policy towards the employment of air power, as indeed did von Seeckt's favouring of the use of air forces on deep interdiction duties rather than close air support operations.[39]

By 1926, air power doctrine had been codified by Wilberg into a single document entitled *Guidelines for the conduct of the operational air war*. The employment of air power in future wars was outlined in some detail. The use of the term "operational" was significant because it emphasized a flexible and non-doctrinaire approach. Although only a small number of aircraft and air support units were to be placed directly under the control of the army, the bulk of the air forces would still support the ground forces in a wide variety of interdiction duties once air superiority had been achieved.[40] Thus, German air doctrine did not tie the future *Luftwaffe* to a simple role of army support, but offered a doctrine based on widespread and general support for German armed forces at an operational and campaign level. Notably, however, strategic bombing was not emphasized.

German rearmament was transparent by 1935, and the considered doctrine of the newly created *Luftwaffe* was set down in another document, *Air force regulation on the conduct of the air war*. This was effectively to determine the employment of air power throughout the Second World War. Again, General Wilberg was involved as editor and joint author, although General Walther Wever, a late convert to the benefits of air power, was arguably the major contributor. In a very similar vein to the 1926 appraisal, the 1935 document argued that gaining air supremacy was a crucial first stage in the prosecution of a campaign. This, in effect, meant attacking the enemy air force with a series of knockout blows. Once the enemy air force had been eliminated, German airspace would be safe and the *Luftwaffe* would be able to concentrate on attacking the enemy's ground forces and on causing disruption and chaos in the enemy state. However, it was once again argued that the *Luftwaffe* could not win the war independently, in marked contrast to the doctrine of the RAF.[41]

It is also important to note that the subjugation of air power to the immediate needs of the army in a series of close support operations was also rejected. As Michel Forget argues, German air doctrine fell between the two concepts of close air support and strategic bombardment. Close support of the army was to take place, but the *Luftwaffe* would make a more operational or even campaign level contribution to a conflict. This would allow a flexible approach to the use of air power, although clearly the ultimate aim was to provide the right conditions for the ground forces to win the campaign.[42]

Luftwaffe doctrine crystallized during the Spanish Civil War, as much valuable experience and practical learning was added to the theory developed since 1918. The Germans maintained a force of 100 aircraft and 5,000 personnel in the Condor Legion which contributed significantly to Franco's victory. Close air support operations, previously eschewed by the *Luftwaffe*, grew in importance following the Condor Legion's experiences in Spain and a special unit was established to develop the means of supporting Germany's armoured forces in a concerted manner.[43] However, problems persisted and the delay between the call for air support and the actual raid remained at some hours. Generally, *Luftwaffe* aircraft were ill-suited to close air support operations.[44] Moreover, it is worth noting that on the outbreak of the Second World War only some 15 per cent of the *Luftwaffe* had been designated to offer close support to the army, thus undermining the frequently quoted myth that the German air forces were specifically designed and constructed to support armoured warfare.[45]

It can be seen that the operational requirements of the German state were to be met and supported by the *Luftwaffe* in any future war in an attempt to win decisive and rapid campaigns. The rejection of massed bombing was in part driven by the geostrategic position of Germany and the place of the army at the head of the armed forces. It would seem logical therefore that France would follow a similar pattern in placing the need to succeed at an operational level first and foremost, even if the desire to change the nature of modern battle was not a priority following the victory of World War I. However, French army/air force planning failed to meet this challenge and, by the Second World War, the French air forces had not developed an effective doctrine for the employment of aircraft to support the land war or, more importantly, the forces to prosecute such a strategy.

Doctrinal wrangling was the major cause of the failure of the air forces in World War II. Throughout the interwar period, especially after the creation of the independent *Armee de l'Air* (the French Air Force) in 1933, the army and the air force leaders squabbled over the use of air power in support of the land war. The army emphasized the use of aircraft to cover reconnaissance and observation and the screening of French ground forces from air attack. It was in essence a World War I formula, although it must be stated that by the mid–1930s the importance of bombing operations was also being considered. The air force attempted to emphasize the importance of the air battle to gain air superiority, and in this the bomber would be the key, they claimed. The strategy was to eliminate the enemy air force by bombing raids and offensive action, and the potential was there for strategic bombing raids, even though it seems unlikely that this was ever seriously considered. However, the spirit of consensus was lacking and views rapidly polarized.[46]

French air power doctrine was confused throughout much of the 1930s, a by-product being the disastrous BCR (*Bombardement Combat Reconnaissance*) aircraft, which was supposed to meet a wide variety of air power requirements but instead resulted in French air power planning and design being led down a blind alley.[47] The adage that a horse designed by committee would turn out as a camel is particularly apposite, and the BCR has been described as a "two-engine, eight-ton, underarmed and underpowered dinosaur".[48] In wider terms, without a clear goal and with an aero-industry still steeped in the practices and thinking of the past, the French were left with far too much to do by the late 1930s.

The air minister, Pierre Cot, intervened in 1937 to bring French air doctrine under some form of control. The army's view effectively prevailed, with the need to deny enemy air forces the ability to roam over French air space considered a priority. Consequently, *Plan V* was initiated to build many more fighters. However, this scheme was incomplete by the outbreak of war in 1939. Although the basis of *Plan V* was not in itself misguided, it did reflect again the defensive nature of French strategy. The French air force's belief that the battle for air superiority required offensive and aggressive action akin to German thinking was also not without merit, although quite possibly the *Armee de l'Air* had a hidden agenda by wanting to demonstrate that an independent strategy and thus an air force free from being shackled to the army was necessary. However, the generally defensive posture adopted by the French armed forces surrendered the initiative and allowed the dispersed fighter defences, as existed in 1940, to be swamped by the *Luftwaffe*.

The British experience reflected the nature of general strategy and the prevailing doctrine of the RAF, which was based principally around strategic bombing. Army co-operation was considered to be of limited importance and consisted at one stage of just one squadron, although four was the more usual figure.[49] In light of the political aim not to deploy another large army on the continent and to rely on economic, political and strategic bombing threats, this was logical.[50] However, the British army's perception of the role of air power was particularly outdated and conservative. Moreover, whereas the *Luftwaffe* and even the *Armee de l'Air* investigated close operational level co-operation between the army and the air force, in Britain this was not the case to any significant degree, especially after the dabblings with offensive armoured warfare had faded in the early 1930s.[51]

Nevertheless, some rudimentary doctrine was formed though not in a coherent and co-ordinated fashion. The RAF was anxious not to get drawn into expensive and wasteful ground-support operations of the type carried out in World War I, where loss rates had been excessive to say the least. Where artillery and machine-guns could do the job then aircraft should not be employed, it was argued by official manuals. The role of the fighter was to gain and maintain air superiority.[52] Only when the enemy army was in retreat, or was close to a breakthrough, should air forces be deployed on hazardous close air support operations. The problems of co-ordinating aircraft and ground forces were remarked upon by some, such as John Slessor, following imperial air policing operations, but empirical learning of this type was never really formulated into a true doctrine.[53]

The US Army's Air Corps (USAAC) followed a similar pattern of doctrinal development to the RAF in its attitudes to land warfare. In much the same manner that strategic bombing theory dominated thinking in the RAF to the detriment of all other forms of air power (until the British government enforced a shift towards air defence in 1937), so too was thinking and doctrinal development at the Air Corps Tactical School at Maxwell, certainly from the late 1920s. Some even argued, as they did in Britain, that the use of air power to support the army, and indeed the navy, was a dangerous diversion of limited resources. The lessons of World War I, limited as they were for the US Air Service, had little impact and the Third Attack Group (formed in 1921 to examine close air support) drifted away from the role during the interwar period. Airmen posted to ground support units worked in virtual isolation, spread out across the USA as they were, and there was no cohesive policy towards the employment of air forces to support the army nor indeed which aircraft would be best suited to such duties. The development of doctrine and theory did not really get underway until the lessons of the German *blitzkrieg* began to filter back to the USA from Europe in 1939.[54] However, in spite of this, the technological advances in the USAAC were significant and, although the doctrine did not exist for their effective use, new types of aircraft such as the A-20 were being procured in the late 1930s. In addition, the US Marine Corps, free from the desire to establish independence, developed more considered and pragmatic theories on the use of close air support, and were able to hone them in Haiti and Nicaragua. Importantly, dive-bombing was established as an accurate and effective technique.[55] (See Chapter Five.)

The Soviet Union was again a state which could have been expected to develop a system of army co-operation air forces of some note in the interwar era, especially under the general influence of the armoured warfare theorist Mikhail Tukhachevski, prior to his apparently pointless execution in the Red Army purges of the late 1930s. In fact, by that time, doctrine in the *Voyenno-vozdushnyye sily* (VVS – the USSR's air force) did emphasize army co-operation and support but was undermined by a lack applied thinking and technological development, failings which were largely a consequence of Stalin's decapitation of the Red Army.

The strategic requirements of the Soviet state were quickly identified by Trotsky, when he stated in 1923 that the first call on air power was to co-operate closely with the Red Army. Mikhail Frunze, a successful commander from the civil war, took the significance of air power still further, viewing it as part of the new revolutionary nature of warfare and as such being particularly suited to the revolutionary Soviet state. Frunze believed air power to be a crucial, though not decisive, factor in warfare and when he succeeded Trotsky as war commissar he moved to forge a firm link between air power and the army. Unlike the German operational view of air power, air forces in the USSR were largely attached directly to Red Army units for close tactical support, as laid out in the Provisional Field Regulations of 1923.[56]

However, the development of doctrine in the VVS was hindered by a number of factors. Initially, the plans of Frunze and Marshal Tukhachevski for a modern, technological and well equipped army, backed by a sophisticated air force, foundered on the failure of the nascent Soviet industrial state to provide anything more than a poorly equipped mass infantry based army. By 1929, aviation, armoured and technical personnel made up only ten per cent of the Red Army. Moreover, at a doctrinal level, Frunze's ideas were rather too closely based on traditional military thinking. Frunze saw aircraft as the replacement for cavalry, disrupting the enemy rear zone, but notions of air superiority battles and of attacking the enemy air force were not uppermost in his thinking. In addition, Frunze was saddled with revolutionary ideology, which led to contradictions in his philosophy of air power. While he claimed that too much reliance on the technological aspects of war was overly bourgeois, he also stated that an army without air support could not function.[57]

Doctrinal thinking was clearly muddled, though the basic tenet that the air forces should more or less directly support the army was accepted. The approach to how this was to be achieved was less than sophisticated or properly thought out, and was moreover undermined by the purges of the late 1930s. Unlike the French, who could not make their minds up, the Soviets failed to develop an effective doctrine and an air force to support it because they were unable to manage their resources effectively. The USSR failed the organizational test of air power prior to the Second World War, although the purges were also a major factor, and the VVS was to take until 1943 to create an effective ground support air force, much the same length of doctrinal learning time as the RAF and the USAAF.

In contrast to strategic bombing, air support for armies was determined by levels of developed doctrine and training rather than prevailing levels of technology. The *Luftwaffe* had few if any high quality close air support aircraft, yet by 1939 it was a potent ground attack force owing to its carefully honed doctrine. In contrast the US air forces had many new and technologically advanced aircraft, but lacked the doctrine to apply them successfully. In addition, the debate concerning procuring dedicated ground attack aircraft, or using swing-role aircraft such as fighter-bombers, as in World War I, had yet to be resolved..

On the outbreak of war only the pragmatic, and thanks to the Spanish Civil War, experienced Germans were in a fit state to conduct ground support operations with any degree of effectiveness. In the summer of 1940 the failings of British and French planning and doctrine were to be contrasted ruthlessly with the relative efficiency and flexibility of the *Luftwaffe*.

Maritime air power

Maritime air power had progressed considerably in the First World War, mirroring the advances made in other areas of air power development. Aircraft on maritime duties had greatly extended reconnaissance ranges, provided essential air cover to convoys and offered the means of direct attack on naval vessels. The British were the leaders in the field with 12 aircraft handling ships in the Royal Navy and some 3,000 aircraft available in 1918.[58] The future of maritime air power, certainly in Britain, most probably in the USA and, latterly, in Japan, looked secure.

As always, many commentators recognized the potential of air power to influence maritime operations but in the post-1918 era the world's major naval powers struggled to come to terms with the prospect of air power at sea. It was to take many years for navies to accept that aircraft could play a potentially decisive role in maritime warfare. However, the large navies of the world did investigate what air power had to offer and the much repeated myth that naval staffs and thinkers alike dismissed aircraft as mere fancies in the interwar era is simply not true. The rate of change in naval thinking did vary greatly but was shaped by geostrategic requirement and constraints of finance as much as by institutional conservatism.

Maritime air power divided into two sectors. First, there were land based air forces which sought to intercept and attack enemy naval units, and which also carried out the important role of defending seaborne trade. Secondly, and of greater interest to naval thinkers in the interwar period, there was carrier-borne aviation which developed rapidly in some navies up to 1939. During the interwar period the development of doctrine in these two respective fields was, however, uneven and in some cases, despite pressing strategic need, almost non-existent.

The experience of World War I had clearly illustrated to armies the crucial nature of air power in the conduct of land campaigns, while strategic operations had also been undertaken to a certain extent between 1915 and 1918 and in any case had a host of vociferous advocates. In contrast, maritime air power laboured partly because it had neither the weight of evidence, nor the popular support enjoyed by its other air power cousins. Consequently, it suffered markedly in Britain, developed in a distorted manner in Japan, and in the US Navy was still struggling to assert itself in 1941 when the Pearl Harbor raid decided matters in a peremptory manner. Elsewhere, maritime air power, often for quite legitimate strategic reasons, was considered to be at best peripheral and even occasionally a dangerous distraction.

The role of the American air power advocate Billy Mitchell in the development of maritime air forces, as well as air strength in general, has usually been overstated. Certainly, like Douhet, his influence was less as a strategist or theorist and more as an advocate and even as a vociferous publicist.[59] Mitchell, the then Assistant Chief of the US Army Air Corps, was instrumental in setting up a series of trials in the early 1920s aimed at proving that aircraft could influence naval operations decisively. In 1921, the ex-German battleship *Ostfriesland* was sunk by bomber aircraft and, even though the conditions were ideal for air operations and the target was stationary, the event was of considerable symbolic importance.[60] Prior to this, US naval officers had argued that no battleship could be destroyed by air attack alone. After the sinking of the *Ostfriesland* they were constantly forced into evaluating how to defeat the air menace. Unlike Douhet, Mitchell's views on air power emphasized the wide ranging capabilities of the aircraft, rather than just the strategic. This view was in part dictated by the more isolated strategic position of the USA in relation to any potential enemy who might instigate a strategic bombing campaign. Therefore, Mitchell's primary concern was to unify air power into a coherent force in the USA and thus, in his opinion, ensure continental defence. His overstated views and harsh criticisms of the US Navy and Army eventually led to his downfall and court-martial but his exuberant "crusading" for air power has brought him his place in air power folklore, particularly in the USA.

Unsurprisingly, the most significant developments in maritime air power in the interwar era emerged in the major naval powers of the world: initially Britain and the USA, and then from the late 1920s onwards, Japan. The geographical positions and national strategies of these powers were crucial factors in the scale and impact of development and doctrinal advancement must be viewed in the context of the international situation in the interwar period. Japan and the USA were already on a long term collision course and any future confrontation would of course take place over the vast expanse of the Pacific Ocean. As such, air power had the potential to be highly effective, initially as a reconnaissance and scouting force and ultimately as an aggressive arm. Speed, mobility and the offensive aspects of air power eventually came to predominate, leading ultimately to fast carrier groups, where the aircraft carriers had little armour in order to increase aircraft handling capacity, speed and endurance. It was expected that such forces would operate beyond the range of land based bombers and would be able to evade surface vessels.

The Royal Navy, however, had other priorities. It was expected that their emerging carrier forces would have to operate in and around Europe and the Mediterranean, as well as in the Far East, and consequently would have to operate with the very real threat of surface attack and land based air assault. This duality was in part to result in the Royal Navy developing armoured carriers with smaller complements of aircraft. These were of limited value in long-range oceanic operations, in which they were to become embroiled in 1942.

However, the development of air power doctrine in the British forces was hindered in other ways. While the USA and Japan had dedicated naval air arms, the Royal Navy had to rely on the RAF to provide its aircraft and aircrew, even on board carriers. The RAF, however, was little interested in any form of maritime air power, save using its larger flying boats for imperial duties. Consequently, and despite protestations from the Royal Navy, the maritime air force suffered from a distinct lack of interest on the part of its parent body, and the so-called "dual control" problem emerged. It was not until 1937 that this curious situation changed and the fleet air arm was put under the direct control and ownership of the navy. This was much too late to have a marked effect on British carrier based aviation by the Second World War.[61]

The Royal Navy (RN) itself had grand schemes for carrier air power during the 1918–39 period. A bold plan for the construction of seven fleet aircraft carriers, to be supported by an assortment of trade protection and light carriers was developed, only to founder for a variety of financial and organizational reasons. The RN suffered from being the leading naval power in 1918 and a conservative "wait and see" policy emerged, resulting in a reactive posture that allowed the Japanese and the Americans to seize the initiative. This combined with the dual control problem and financial constraints to hinder and indeed retard air power development in the RN. However, it should be noted that even though British carrier procurement and production was repeatedly cut back, the battleship arm suffered even more, thus deflecting the anti-air power myth that has been directed at the Admiralty in the inter-war period.[62]

Doctrinal debate also centred on land based maritime air power which had played a significant role in protecting Britain's trade routes during the First World War. This duty was effectively jettisoned in the interwar period as the Royal Navy claimed that the U-boat had been defeated by asdic (sonar) and the practice of convoying. The RAF was more than happy to accept this as it allowed them to withdraw resources from this activity. Moreover, and in spite of a series of tests and trials in the 1920s and 1930s, the development of a land based maritime air force capable of attacking enemy naval vessels also came to very little. The RAF argued that their massed bombing force would be able to deal with such naval threats, even without specialized training. The Royal Navy was only willing to admit that aircraft could observe and at best annoy major naval vessels and so, consequently, never pressed too hard for an increase in maritime bombers. World War II, and indeed the bombing trials of the interwar years, proved that this policy was hopelessly flawed and inadequate.[63]

By World War II, Britain had no properly considered aerial anti-submarine doctrine or aircraft capable of fulfilling such a role; no effective maritime striking force other than a small number of antiquated torpedo bombers (the most effective aircraft in trials in the 1920s/30s had been the dive-bomber, but unlike in Japan and the USA, this was rejected by the RAF as being too specialized); and no capable carrier air arm. The RN still had a narrow view of the use of aircraft in naval warfare and aircraft were to be deployed as reconnaissance and hindering forces rather than as decisive attacking units. In view of this position in 1939, it is all the more remarkable that the RN was willing and able to launch the Taranto raid against the Italian fleet in 1940. This perhaps demonstrated that the RN was constrained by circumstances more than desire in the interwar era.

The US Navy had certain advantages over its British counterpart and this, in part, enabled a more forward thinking approach to maritime air power. Principally, the lack of a central air force which also included naval aircraft, as in the RAF's case, allowed the US Navy to focus on maritime air power in its own way, free from interference. The influence of Mitchell in the early years was quite important as his unremitting pressure prompted the

Chief of Naval Operations, William Benson, to create a Bureau of Aeronautics (BuAer), dedicated to naval aviation, in 1921.[64] However, the most influential figure in the development of maritime air power in this period was Admiral William Moffett, the Chief of the BuAer until his death in 1933. Moffett forced the pace of maritime air power development and ensured that the air faction in the navy made its voice heard.

Japan was already regarded by the USA as the most likely future enemy and it was expected that US forces would have to carry out an offensive strategy to take the war to Japan.[65] The role of air power in such planning grew throughout the interwar period. It was expected that the US fleet would have to operate against land-based Japanese air forces and thus would require carrier based aircraft to counter this threat. Even the battleship minded "Gun Club" in the US Navy was infiltrated by admirals who recognized the value of air power, even if only in a supportive role. In 1927, an investigative board was set up to examine the place carriers should hold within the fleet, made all the more urgent with the arrival by the end of that year of two fast carriers, the *Saratoga* and the *Lexington*.

As the interwar period went on, tactics were developed for the combined use of carrier-borne dive and torpedo bombers. In particular, a series of Fleet Problems (naval manoeuvres) identified that, in order to make the most of their advantages of speed and mobility, the carriers should operate almost independently of the battleship line. This caused considerable debate throughout the navy with the traditional battleship officers arguing that the carriers should act as the scouts and reconnaissance units of the navy, and that ultimately it would be the big guns of the battleships which would decide the outcome of a battle. However, the weight of evidence began to accrue against this more conservative view of carrier warfare. Increasingly, an offensive and independent carrier doctrine was developed. In 1932, Admiral Yarnell led the fast carriers on a successful sneak air raid of Pearl Harbor, upstaging the Japanese by nine years. Subsequently he argued for the use of six to eight fast carriers in a war against the Japanese.[66]

Despite this, on the eve of war, US naval air doctrine, advanced as it was, was still to a large extent tied to supporting the battleship line. Although independent carrier doctrine had been developed, the struggle for supremacy within the US Navy had not been decisively won – it was to take the Pearl Harbor raid to achieve that. Nevertheless, the overall importance of air power to the defence of US possessions and interests in the Pacific and Asia had been accepted and was latterly considered the key to the defence of the Philippines.

Maritime air power in Japan developed along similar lines to the US Navy, although initially for different strategic requirements. Japan had identified the

USA by the early 1920s as being the most likely opponent in a future war over Japanese expansionist ambitions in Asia. This was to become even clearer as the 1930s went on when the European imperial powers confronted each other once again. While the Japanese army struggled to assert itself against China, and worried over the potential actions of the Soviet Union, the Imperial Japanese Navy (IJN) concentrated on how best to deal with a US threat to further Japanese activity in southeast Asia.

The Japanese had had their own carrier fleet founded on the *Akagi* and *Kaga* of later World War II fame since the late 1920s, but when more expansionist ideas began to take root in the Japanese military from the early 1930s, then the problem of confronting the USA's offensive carrier aviation became a real issue. The IJN feared the potential of the US carrier fleet: it was on offensive operations that carrier aviation came into its own. However, it was perceived that Japan would have to fight an essentially defensive war against the USA, once initial gains had been made, and it was in this early phase that the Japanese aircraft carriers could prove their worth. Moreover, as the future commander of naval operations, Admiral Isoroku Yamamoto, concluded in 1933 Japanese carriers would offer the best means of blunting US fleet operations.

However, the doctrine that had been developed by the mid-1930s placed the Japanese carrier arm firmly in a subsidiary role to the main battleship line which still dominated the IJN's thinking. Initially, Japanese planning had centred on a defensive attritional strategy which aimed to weaken a US fleet advancing across the Pacific with submarines and land- and carrier-launched air strikes. When sufficiently damaged, the US fleet would be attacked and destroyed by the Japanese surface fleet. This was considered to be the only way to even the odds in light of the US fleet's 30–40 per cent superiority in tonnage in the mid-1930s. By the late 1930s, under the direction of Admiral Yamamoto, the IJN altered its strategy to include a knockout air strike against the US fleet to buy time for Japan to seize the initiative in the resource rich southeast Asia. However, even in this scenario, carriers would only prepare the ground for the Japanese surface fleet and once again the war would end with a Jutland style showdown.[67]

The doctrine, so effective in the early stages of World War II, really began to crystallize under the tutelage of the prescient Commander Minoru Genda, who can be identified as the true doctrinal father of Japanese naval aviation. Genda had been arguing since the mid-to-late 1930s for a major expansion of Japanese land and sea based air power, even at the expense of surface fleet construction. However, the Naval Staff's Third Replenishment Plan for the period of 1937 to 1942 effectively rejected his calls, placing first priority on matching the US Navy's battleship strength.[68] Genda persisted and in 1940 he formulated the plan that a large group of carriers operating together would offer more effective fighter protection (though in fact each carrier would only be operating fewer fighters) and a greater volume of anti-aircraft fire. Moreover, the offensive punch of such a carrier group would be considerable indeed, increased by the need for fewer fighters. Genda's ideas caused a rethink in the IJN and in April 1941 the First Air Fleet was formed comprising all the fleet carriers then available. Under the leadership of Admiral Chuichi Nagumo, with Genda in a prominent role, manoeuvres were carried out to test the capability of the fast carrier fleet. The principles of Genda's doctrine formed the basis of the Pearl Harbor operation, a raid intended to destroy the American carrier fleet, rather than the battleships, symbolizing the importance attributed to the US Navy's carrier force.[69]

However, although Japan's carrier fleet was the most effective force of its kind by 1941, equipped with superior aircraft and better trained aircrew than even the US Naval air forces, the place of aviation in Japanese strategy, even naval strategy, was not central. Despite what they were to achieve at Pearl Harbor and in the first few months of 1942, the Japanese navy at an institutional level never truly accepted the predominant nature of aviation in maritime warfare. Battleship mentality still ruled in the IJN, precipitating the wasteful construction of the super battleships *Yamato* and *Musashi*, and more importantly leading to the fruitless and vain search for the decisive battleship confrontation with the US fleet, which the Japanese navy expected right up until 1945 to decide the war either way. The IJN was still clinging to the idea that a Jutland style battle would be the culmination of a Pacific campaign. What the majority in the Japanese fleet failed to realize was that the fast carrier strike force they had pioneered had relegated the battleship to a subservient position of supporting and protecting the carrier.[70]

The emphasis on the decisive battle also hindered the other crucial role of maritime air power for Japan – trade defence. The British experience of World War I, which had reinforced the IJN's desire for a Jutland style showdown, did not also lead to the Japanese seriously considering how to defeat a commerce raiding threat to their sea communications. For a nation as equally dependent on seaborne trade as Britain, the lesson of the U-boat offensive in 1917 and 1918 should have been a chastening one. Yet the important role of aircraft in defeating this menace was not acknowledged by the battle-oriented IJN. Such duties were considered unfitting for the airmen of the navy and, consequently, by World War II no doctrine of aerial trade defence had been formulated. The real disaster occurred when the IJN continued to do little about this problem as the Second World War went on.[71] (See Chapter Seven.)

On the outbreak of war, maritime aviation doctrine in the major naval powers was not fully formed. The US Navy understood most about the nature and potential of maritime air power, especially carrier aviation, but was still developing the means with which to carry out its thinking. In addition, the place of the fast carriers was still partly linked to the battleship line, a duty only finally abandoned courtesy of the Japanese Pearl Harbor attack. It is also worth noting that the US Army, like Bomber Command in the RAF, believed that large formations of heavy-bombers could destroy naval forces. This notion was to be swept away by repeated failures in Europe and the Pacific, where throughout the war not a single active major naval vessel was sunk by high altitude bombing. The Japanese had developed the most effective carrier strike force and the air doctrine to use it, but the rule of battleship based strategy persisted. In essence, the maritime air force and its supporting doctrine had been developed but the direction and long-term strategy for its use had not. The Royal Navy was in the most parlous state by the end of the 1930s in terms of equipment, but its doctrine was also underdeveloped. Though the RN was to carry out the famous carrier strike on the Italian fleet at Taranto in 1940 (which greatly impressed both the Japanese and the Americans) the geographical and strategic constraints of fighting a continental based power such as Germany, and a second rate naval power such as Italy, resulted in a conservative outlook. It should be stated that the British did not require a fast carrier force to fight Germany and the resources were not available until very late into the 1930s to construct such a force to operate against the Japanese, or possibly the Italians. However, the bomber dominated doctrine of the RAF and the Royal Navy's conservative views on the capacity of air power to dominate maritime operations, either against naval or submarine threats, did seriously hinder the development of maritime air power.

Conclusions

For the most part, air power doctrine in the interwar period developed according to national strategic requirements, for obvious and logical reasons. In general, the maritime powers created carrier and land based air power suited to their perceived needs, and the doctrine for the effective use of such resources was likewise formulated. Those powers who were able or wanted to avoid major continental commitments such as Britain and the USA saw in strategic bombing a way of doing just that. Conversely, the continental powers turned their attention, with varying degrees of success, to establishing how best to use air power to support their armies. What is clear is that, for the most part, doctrine was formulated in isolation from the famous "theorists". Neither Douhet nor Mitchell for example could be said to have directly precipitated national air strategies.

Significant advances were made in the field of doctrine, most notably by the Germans and their pragmatic approach to the employment of air forces in support of land war, and by the Japanese and Americans in the field of carrier-borne aviation. In other areas, technology drove doctrine with varying degrees of success. The emergent technology of radar in the mid-1930s precipitated Britain's advanced air defence system, which served them well in 1940, and the doctrine for its use came in its wake. In contrast, US aircraft designs were highly advanced in a number of areas, yet the doctrine did not exist or was flawed.

More often than not, however, doctrine lagged some way behind contemporary technology. In many ways, air power advocates recognized the potential of air forces and were prescient in their claims. Where they went astray was in arguing that their theories were immediately attainable. Air forces and their supporters continually miscalculated what was realistically achievable, especially in the field of strategic bombing, and this more than anything has fuelled the notion that air power failed in the Second World War. This is because it has usually been measured against the hopes of the interwar theorists.

Nevertheless, the formulation of theory by the world's air forces , if not always coupled with the doctrine to support it, opened up political and strategic opportunities in the 1930s as the world lurched back towards war. Effective air support for ground forces appeared to make war look more decisive and acceptable again, clouding the memories of World War I, while both Britain and Germany went on to use the fear of strategic bombing for political and diplomatic ends in the 1930s. Such policies were brought about by the perception of what air power could achieve in modern war, a legacy of theoretical thinking from the end of World War I, and even before, rather than an acknowledgement of what was technically possible.

Chapter Five

Global air power, 1918–39

The Great War had laid the foundations for the growth of global air power. In the years 1914–18, sizeable aero-industries had emerged, air power had become an integral part of military operations and, perhaps most importantly, the aeroplane had become commonplace to many, especially in Europe and North America. Although the immediate post-war years were to witness the considerable contraction of military air forces, perceptions of the role and nature of air power had become firmly established in the minds of governments and societies alike. Over the next 20 years or so, the influence of air power and air forces spread across the world with the emergence of air transport, policing and imperial operations. Meanwhile, in the industrial nations the potential of the aerial weapon they had created, most pointedly the bomber, came to dominate foreign policy and strategic thinking for a period in a manner quite out of proportion with actual capability.

By the eve of World War II the "shadow of the bomber" was cast across the belligerents, although governments and military planners, while still concerned about the possible impact of bombing and the use of poison gas, now believed they could manage the situation. Of greater concern was the respective ability of indigenous aero-industries and economies to meet the future requirements of air forces. From the mid-1930s onwards, aerial technology had undergone a considerable revolution and the premium on membership of the first-rate air power club had increased dramatically. Few realized how important the close integration of technology and industry had become to maintaining top level air power status and effectiveness and for many the interwar period was to prove poor preparation for the coming exigencies of World War II.

Post-war demobilization and new air power policies

The end of the Great War brought major change to the face of Europe and, as states collapsed and emerged, so the effects were felt by their armed forces. Austria–Hungary had disintegrated and so too did its already struggling aero-industry. By 1919 neither Austria nor Hungary, by now separate states, had managed to keep any significant aircraft manufacturers in operation. The German air industry was still in reasonable shape by November 1918 but the Treaty of Versailles saw the effective dismantling of military air power in Germany by 1920. Civil aviation continued but limits were placed on the performance of such aircraft by worried Allied observers and the Germans persisted in finding ways around the restrictive limitations placed on them by the Allies. Paradoxically, the constraints and duress under which the *Reichswehr* had to develop air power, in close collaboration with civil aviation, forged close links between the military and the aero-industry itself, links which were to aid open rearmament in the 1930s.[1]

German air power also survived thanks to close ties with the Soviet Union, a secret product of the Treaty of Rapallo signed in 1922. The USSR required an input of modern technology to boost its flagging home aero-industry and wanted to glean as much as possible from the German military about their World War I experience and their ideas for the future of air power. The Germans, determined to keep some form of link with modern military air power, needed somewhere beyond the prying eyes of the Western Allies to carry out tests and to gain practical military flying experience. A pilot school and air testing centre were set up at Lipetsk, some 220 miles from Moscow, and the *Reichswehr* invested heavily in the formation of the airbase. To avoid flouting the Treaty of Versailles, officers sent to the Soviet Union for air training were temporarily retired from the German army, only to be reactivated on their return.[2] Therefore, under the shrewd stewardship of General Hans von Seeckt, the *Reichswehr* cleverly maintained a vestige of air power throughout the period prior to the advent of Hitler, thanks to the combination of links with the USSR and the civil air sector in Germany.[3]

Although the Germans benefited greatly from the USSR deal, the Soviets were not so happy. In the aftermath of their civil war and the struggle against Poland, in both of which air power played only a limited role, the USSR was determined to expand its air forces. The Western Allies had sent limited air support to the White Russian rebels and volunteer pilots and aircrew, from the USA and Britain in particular, had aided the Poles with some success against the Soviets.[4] From the links formed with the German military in 1922 the Soviet air force wanted modern training for its aircrew as well as technical and industrial help. The former was a fair success, but the attempt to aid new Soviet air production floundered following the economic downturn in Europe and the hyperinflation suffered by Germany. However, aircraft production did get underway under the direction of Mikhail Frunze who was an ardent supporter of the growth of a Soviet military industry to compete with the West. In spite of this, the Soviets still had to buy aero-engines from German companies. Indeed, by 1925, although the USSR no longer needed to go abroad for its aircraft, home based engine production had reached only 10 per cent of requirements.[5] The inability of the Soviet economy to provide enough aero-engines was one of many factors which prompted the much greater emphasis on rapid industrialization in the USSR from the mid-1920s onwards.

The victorious powers of World War I were also confronted with many problems in the years after 1918. Demobilization was far reaching and swift. In the USA the air service contracted from 190,000 in November 1918, to just over 10,000 by 1920 and, by 1919, 90 per cent of the aero-industrial plant had been discarded resulting in huge war surpluses. Moreover, aircraft production fell by almost 98 per cent inside two years of the armistice.[6] France also saw a marked decline in its air forces, although with prevailing international uncertainty, it was not as excessive as in the USA. In 1918 the French air arm had 90,000 officers and men which shrank to 39,055 by October 1920; 11,023 aircraft in November 1918 to 3,940 in March 1920, although 3,050 were in storage; and the aero-industry contracted from 183,000 workers to 3,700 by 1921.[7] The RAF also rapidly diminished from 293,532 officers and men in November 1918 to 37,981 by October of the following year.[8]

However, while the powers of Central and Eastern Europe and the USA virtually disappeared from the international air power scene for the 1920s, the French and British, with greatly increased imperial responsibilities and a climate of financial stringency, were forced to adapt to a wholly new strategical and political situation. In fact it was Anglo-French hostility which caused the first "air scare" of the interwar period, when concern grew in London at the threat posed to British security by the larger French air and submarine forces. Although France did have a larger air force than Britain in the 1920s, the reality was that no threat was ever posed to British security. The French were far more concerned about Germany, still in their eyes the major factor in determining long-term European stability.

In Britain, however, the perceived French air threat was skilfully used by Sir Hugh Trenchard, the RAF's Chief of Air Staff (CAS), to help maintain air force independence at a time when the threat of reabsorption into the army and the navy was still on the political agenda. Although it is usually argued that strategic bombing was kept in reserve by the RAF during the

1920s until a more politically opportune moment arrived, John Ferris has argued that Trenchard displayed the RAF's true attitudes towards massed bombing during this French air crisis. The CAS argued that the French air threat was very real, of considerable potential, and that the only way to deter it was to build a bomber fleet of roughly equal capability. These were very similar to the arguments used in the 1930s against Germany and had considerable impact on thinking in the RAF.[9]

The link between the new air weapon and political strategy was also already forming. The British government was concerned not to allow any foreign power a potential hold over Britain. In much the same way that Germany could not be allowed to threaten Britain with naval power in the years leading up to World War I, so France could not be allowed to hold an air power advantage that might in the future force Britain into a diplomatically compromising position. The belief that the bomber could not be defended against, and that the destructive potential of massed bombing was huge, became embedded in government thinking during the early 1920s, even though Trenchard had exaggerated considerably merely to gain political and financial advantages for the RAF. Moreover, although the expansion of the RAF's home defence force was undertaken with sporadic success, many of the industrial and technical problems encountered in the expansion of the 1930s were uncovered during the 1920s but were conveniently forgotten.[10]

Air power and the wider world

Although strategic bombing was a cornerstone of RAF philosophy by the early 1920s, it alone was not enough to ensure the survival of the world's first independent air force. The second and arguably the most important policy adopted by the RAF to this end was that of "substitution", which involved using aircraft as replacements for the navy and the army in imperial policing and control duties across the globe. In an era of financial stringency, the RAF was able to make itself immensely popular with the British government by carrying out such operations at considerably less cost than the other services. Trenchard coupled the imperial card with the potential threat of French aerial aggression and hence ensured the survival of the RAF.[11]

Air power proved to be an effective arm in imperial operations and duties and was introduced into many overseas territories and campaigns by western powers, thus emphasizing the effect that air power, the most technologically based of weapons, could have on populations totally unused to it. Once again it was clear that the gap between the respective military capacities of modern western industrial states and the rest of the world had widened significantly, a trend noticeable in imperial expansion dating back to the mid-to-late nineteenth century.[12]

The British were faced with a number of imperial problems in the immediate post-war era and the RAF was soon being utilized in control and policing duties, at much lower cost than the army, which hitherto would have been expected to carry out such operations. The first such campaign was carried out in Afghanistan in 1919 in the so-called "Third Afghan War" and, in spite of difficult operating conditions, air raids were carried out on Kabul, Jalalabad and Dakka along with leafleting designed to demoralize the Afghan troops. Despite initial panic, however, the Afghan troops and tribesmen learned to fight back, and three aircraft were brought down. But the psychological effect of the raids, especially when the Afghan capital was targeted, was considered by the RAF to be a clear indication of the potential of air power to operate effectively in defence of the empire, although naturally the army disagreed.[13] The case for air policing was boosted by the Somaliland campaign in 1920 against the Dervish uprising, led by Mohammed bin Abdulla Hassan. Aircraft were used to some effect with reconnaissance and bombing raids being undertaken, and the governor of Somaliland even went so far as to claim that the RAF alone had, in effect, won the campaign.

However, the most famous example of imperial policing undertaken by the RAF occurred in Iraq between 1922 and 1925. The British had become embroiled in the convoluted politics of the region following the Great War and a rebellion had broken out in 1920. Forced to commit men and equipment, by the end of the year there were 17,000 British and 85,000 Indian troops stationed in Iraq to combat the rebels.[14] With concern mounting at this growing and excessive commitment and expenditure, Winston Churchill, the Secretary of State for Air and of the War Office, in conjunction with Sir Hugh Trenchard, formulated a plan for controlling Iraq through air power, supported by a small ground force. The plan was sold to the cabinet largely on the grounds of greatly reduced cost, and was a key factor in ensuring the survival of the independent RAF. The impact was considerable and in conjunction with political and diplomatic initiatives, control of Iraq was eventually re-established. Annual British expenditure in Iraq fell from £23.36 million in 1921/22 to £7.81 million in 1922/23, the first year of air control. By 1927 the figure had shrunk still further to just £3.9 million.[15] The High Commissioner, Henry Dobbs, even commented in 1925 that "air control has been . . . brilliantly successful" and that policing of Iraq with ground troops alone would not have been feasible.[16]

The RAF was also used in imperial policing and control roles in India, Aden, Africa, Transjordan and Palestine. In areas of open country and against widespread populations aircraft were of considerably greater value, but in regions such as Palestine from 1920 onwards, air power proved less successful. Against urban rebellions, unless the British forces were willing to indulge in repeated bombings of civilians in towns and cities, the aeroplane was of little direct military value.

Air power was also used in an imperial prestige role in the interwar era, with long-range cruises down the Nile and across Africa being undertaken, in addition to flying boat visits to Australia, Singapore and Hong Kong. Again these duties were largely political, aimed at demonstrating the strength and determination of the British to police and support the empire. Moreover, the cost of such operations was again much lower than using naval cruisers, and arguably the impact on populations unused to flying machines was more impressive.[17]

The impact of these imperial policing and control duties on British air power was probably mixed. While the substitution policy ensured the survival of the RAF during a difficult period, it contributed little to the growth of the RAF as a modern air force. Indeed, although it can be argued quite effectively that the methods developed for imperial control and policing had no real effect on RAF doctrine. There were lessons to be learned, notably that bombing of populations did not have the psychological impact envisaged and certainly not once counter-measures were developed, however rudimentary these may have been. Moreover, for the maritime air forces, used to conduct long-range flying boat cruises during the interwar era, the effects of the imperial role were quite damaging. Trade defence duties were jettisoned to concentrate on long-range flying boat operations and thus the lessons of the Great War concerning the value of air power in anti-U-boat operations were lost, with serious repercussions in World War II.[18]

The French and Spanish were also involved in imperial air power operations during the interwar era. In 1921, Abd al-Karim led a rebellion in Morocco against Spanish rule, the so-called Rif War 1921–6, with considerable early success. The Spanish force used aircraft sporadically and ineffectively until the air forces were concentrated and directed to pursue a plan of systematic bombing of crops, villages and livestock, even resorting to the use of poison gas. However, the tactics did not bring about the decisive victory expected and, after 1924, the Spanish returned to orthodox tactical support operations. Like the British, they realized that attacks on the civilian populations were ineffective and possibly even counter-productive. Direct tactical support, however, was viable and often very effective as there was no realistic way for the rebels to hit back.[19]

The French were to show greater aptitude for organizing their air effort when they too confronted al-Karim in 1925 when he led his forces from Spanish to French Morocco. The French air forces developed *Groups Mobile* consisting of armoured cars, motorized infantry, light tanks and air support. These anti-rebel units proved remarkably effective, surpassing even the RAF's achievements in their imperial activities. It was readily accepted by the French, and by al-Karim himself, that the rebels' inability to defend themselves against air attack was a significant factor in the success of the air forces deployed against them. The tactics used emphasized tactical level support duties: reconnaissance, observation, bombing and strafing. Long-range bombing did take place on occasion when fighting lulled, but even then it was concentrated on encampments and fortifications, there being no evident recourse to the "terror" style tactics of the Spanish.[20]

The USA also deployed air power in imperial style operations between 1927 and 1933 when US forces were deployed in support of the Nicaraguan regime during the Sandino War. Marine Corps aircraft were used for re-connaissance, observation, close tactical support, communication, supply and medical evacuation duties against the *Sandanista* rebels. During these operations the marines pioneered the first systematic use of dive-bombers, eschewed by the US Army Air Service and by the RAF. Partly as a con-sequence of the work of the marines in the Sandino War, the dive-bomber was adopted by the US Navy during the 1930s. The air operations in Nicaragua were considered largely successful, most notably in two battles, at Ocotal and on El Saraguazca mountain. Again, it was demonstrated that enemy forces incapable of properly defending themselves were especially vulnerable to air attack, even in difficult operating conditions such as those in Central America.[21]

Perhaps the most extreme example of air power being deployed by a western power against non-Europeans in the interwar period was, however, the Italian–Abyssinian War of 1935–6. The common perception of the conflict is one of a modern, well-equipped, technological army demolishing a rag-tag band of tribesmen. But although the Ethiopians were poorly equipped and at times badly led, they fought with great tenacity and resourcefulness against fearful odds and ultimately with little hope of success. The Italians used air power extensively throughout the campaign with considerable im-pact, whereas, paradoxically, tanks proved to be somewhat disappointing. Some 872 bombing missions were undertaken, including many which dropped poison gas bombs, although in direct attacks on the civilian population only limited effectiveness was noted. Once again it was tactical ground support that brought greatest success. Predating the *blitzkrieg* tactics of World War II, it was noted that air support was particularly effective in leading ground assaults, though because of the poor bomb load capacities of Italian aircraft attacks still relied heavily on artillery.

The Ethiopians, although severely disadvantaged by their inability to combat air attack effectively, did start to begin to deal with the problem by concentrated use of rifles, machine-guns and even *Oerlikon* cannon. The Italians lost 16 aircraft to ground fire, usually while on close-support tactical duties, emphasizing the lesson of World War I that such duties were decidedly dangerous.[22] Generally, the campaign yet again indicated the vulnerability of ground forces to air attack if friendly air forces either did not exist or were unable to contest air superiority. However, it was concluded by American observers and analysts that, although air power had been of tremendous help and had probably brought about a speedy end to the conflict, it was not decisive. Clearly, the aerial bombing attacks had not brought about the collapse of Ethiopian resistance.

In general, the air power campaigns conducted by the western powers around the globe had proved a number of important points. The most significant was the distinction between modern, industrial military strength and traditional, man-power based forces − a distinction now clearer and more divisive than ever before. Indigenous, non-industrial societies had no real answer to the aeroplane. They could on occasion deal with modern infantry, limited artillery and even tanks, but aircraft were on a different level, not necessarily in terms of the actual physical damage they could inflict, but in their psychological impact. It was clear that an army backed by air power had a distinct and considerable advantage over an army lacking such support. The colonial campaigns indicated that armies with no defence against properly organized air forces could not operate effectively, and thus air power, while not capable of winning campaigns single-handedly, was a pivotal factor.

The effects of the imperial campaigns on home based air power were strictly limited. Although it was more ammunition for the air power advocates, the air forces themselves learnt very little and operations against poorly armed rebel forces were no measure of effectiveness against modern armed forces. However, the strategy of deploying air forces in imperial roles did lead to a few minor distortions. The RAF's maritime air force concentrated on long-range flying boat cruises at the expense of anti-submarine warfare, but the development of British air power in general continued unaffected by its imperial duties. Indeed, although it was retrospectively perceived that the bombing of native rebels had fallaciously proven the value of aerial bombing, there is little evidence of any direct link. Doctrinally, the imperial experience merely reiterated lessons already learnt in World War I, and it was on a wider political scale that these campaigns had their impact.

Air technology and civil aviation

The technological development of aviation in the interwar era saw a number of important advances that were to influence air power in the Second World War. However, many of these innovations came about, not as a result of military efforts, but of civil aviation. In a period when government expenditure on the military was severely curtailed – certainly until the mid-1930s – many of the most significant advances were the result of private funding and the development of airlines and air-mail routes. Germany in particular, despite restrictions imposed by Versailles, worked hard to build a civil aviation industry to maintain some form of military aero-industry in the post-war years.

With the aero-industries suffering from post-war contraction and the likelihood of military investment almost non-existent, the survival of aviation rested with other fields of development. The end of the Great War yielded a considerable surplus of material, and many of the first airlines relied heavily on ex-military aircraft, such as Breguet 14s and De Havilland DH4s, but as safety measures and controls were introduced and as the ex-military aircraft began to reach the end of their serviceable lives, so new and more specialized aircraft began to be introduced.

The first airlines were set up in the immediate aftermath of the Great War linking many of Europe's major cities. The ex-military connection was illustrated by the French Farman Company beginning operations between Paris and London with converted Goliath bombers, and many other early airlines were similarly built on the backs of military designs, that at times were less than ideal for their purpose. The Dutch airline company KLM was set up in 1919 as was Britain's Imperial Airways and a whole host of other more ephemeral companies came and went during the first few years.[23] International rivalry, especially between imperial powers, grew fierce and notions of national prestige often led to significant government involvement.[24] Routes were developed across the globe and as competition grew fiercer and operating laws and practices became more stringent, the strongest airlines with the best services survived, while those unable to raise new capital or meet the requirements fell by the wayside. In Europe, the German civil aviation industry, backed by the Weimar government in an attempt to compensate for the lack of a military air arm, prospered greatly and by 1927 German airlines covered greater distances with more passengers than their British, French and Italian competitors combined.[25]

By 1930, many of today's current airlines had become established: KLM was flying to the East Indies; Air France to Indochina and Africa; Lufthansa across Europe and the USSR; Pan-American across the Pacific, the Atlantic and South America; and Imperial Airways throughout the British Empire. The airlines made few large orders, but they were crucial to the survival of the aero-industries. During the 1920s, European firms were predominant but by the 1930s the US firms such as Boeing, Lockheed and Douglas were beginning to dominate the world market. In part this was due to the growing need of the aero-industry for advanced construction techniques and modern engine tools to build the increasingly sophisticated civil aircraft. These were the products of a highly advanced industrial economy and here the USA had a significant lead.[26] Once again the trend of air power making increasingly heavy demands on home economies was evident. Crucially, the geopolitical structure of the USA more readily supported aircraft as a viable means of transport, whereas in Europe circumstances – shorter distances, which made air transport too costly compared to other forms, as well as political rivalry – dictated that large scale air transport never became established to the same degree prior to 1939. It was a trend that was to bring predominance to the US based aviation industry with significant results on the ability of the economy to produce what was needed for success in World War II, especially in air transport a field in which the USA led by some way. Importantly, when the age of mass military air power arrived it was the USA more than any other nation which had the infrastructure in place to facilitate rapid expansion.[27]

The importance of civil aviation began to emerge when a new generation of airliners was introduced from the mid-to-late 1920s. While military aircraft continued to be wood and fabric bi-planes, the demands of efficiency, speed and performance dictated that airlines had to offer more to stay profitable. Many features later to be crucial to the development of military air power in the late-1930s were developed by civil aviation: cantilever wings (i.e. without rigging and struts); metal based construction; retractable undercarriages; navigation equipment; pressurized cabins – to name but a few. The design philosophy of the aircraft that emerged, such as the Junkers G-23 and the Fokker F.VIIa, was to have a direct influence on military aircraft design and development in the build up to war.[28]

In addition to the advances made in aviation technology, thanks to the civil sector, innovation came as a result of the variety of air races and contests much in evidence in the 1920s and early 1930s. The most famous of these were the Gordon Bennett Trophy and the Schneider Trophy, the latter being a competition for aerial speed racing which was eventually awarded to Supermarines of Britain after being won for the third successive time in 1931. The winning design was the direct forerunner of the Spitfire fighter of World War II. Many other competitions were held, testing aircraft distance and altitude endurance, with much of the development experience

Table 5.1 – Average fighter performance, 1915–55

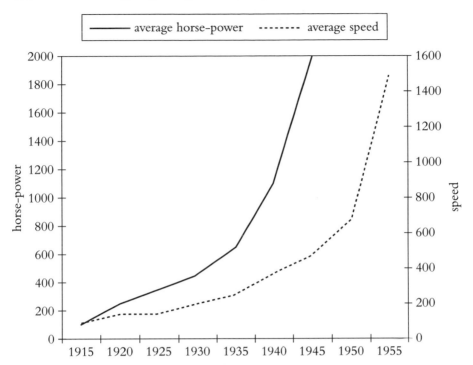

feeding into civil and military designs at a later date. The record-breaking tests and competitions of the interwar era pushed the limits of aviation still further. In 1920 the USA held the altitude endurance record at 33,000 feet, increased it to 43,000 by 1930 and surrendered it to Italy in 1938 at 56,000. To coincide with these advances came cold-weather technology, pressure suits, oxygen systems, pressurized cabins and so forth. All of these contributed to fighter, photographic reconnaissance, and high-altitude bombing technology in World War II.[29]

The period of the mid–to–late 1930s saw a remarkable acceleration in aviation technology as the results of the design work of the 1920s began to come to fruition. The wooden based bi-plane models which had become established in air forces around the world as a result of the Great War began to disappear to be replaced by all-metal cantilever-wing monoplanes with high-performance engines and dramatically improved navigation and flight control systems. The basic fighter of early 1930s vintage was little removed from its World War I predecessor in terms of basic design and armament. Between 1918 and 1935 engines had improved from around 225 hp giving

Table 5.2 – Average bomber performance, 1915–55

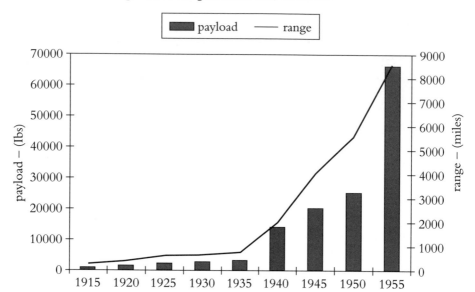

speeds of 125 mph, to 500 hp producing speeds in excess of 200 mph. Yet within three years the Messerschmitt Bf109 and the Supermarine Spitfire had horsepower of over 1,000, speeds measured at around 350 mph, significantly increased operating ranges and, perhaps most importantly, between three and four times the armament of the older bi-plane fighters.[30]

The dramatic improvements in aviation design and technology from the mid-1930s onwards helped to create, in the era of the Second World War (from 1935 to 1950), a period in which air forces were technologically advanced enough to make a telling contribution to the war effort, but not so advanced that the aero-industries could not mass-produce in vast quantities. As Richard Overy has stated,

> a war fought five years sooner would have resembled the limited air combat of the First World War; a war fought ten years later would have produced aircraft that were so technically complex and expensive that "mass-production" air power would have been almost impossible.[31]

Nevertheless, the air power demands being made of economies after the technological advances of the mid-1930s were still sufficient to drain between 40 and 50 per cent of war production during World War II.[32]

110

Rearmament – air power and strategy

By the early 1930s, it was becoming clear that the world situation was deteriorating. Both in Europe with the advent of Hitler and in the Far East with the increasing belligerency of Imperial Japan, international security was again in jeopardy. The failure of a variety of arms elimination and reduction talks and the effective disintegration of the League of Nations combined to create a world order quite different to that of the 1920s. The threat of war, while not immediate, was increasing and in order to confront this new situation the major powers began rearmament programmes, abandoning the retrenchment of the 1920s.

Air power was to play a significant role not only in shaping and determining rearmament policy but also in developing national strategies. In Britain and Germany the dominance of strategic air power was considerable, although there were significant differences in the approaches of the two powers, approaches which were to become increasingly divergent as the decade progressed. Both states, but especially Britain, were to place great faith in the political and diplomatic power of the bomber – faith that was quite out of proportion to the weapon's real capability. However, this was the key to the place of the massed bombing force in strategic planning. It was not what it could achieve, but what it appeared to be capable of. It was the beginning of deterrent theory being a basis of national strategy, a trend that was to come to fruition in the nuclear era.

The influence of bombing on strategic planning was clear by the end of the 1920s and early 1930s as the shadow of the bomber loomed large. The fear of the bomber had become a major factor in strategic thinking, partly as a result of the experience of World War I, limited though this was, partly because of the claims of the air power prophets and the consequent impact that this had on the general public, and partly because of the arguments proffered by the air forces themselves. Books such as *Invasion from the air, Air reprisal, The gas war of 1940* (written in 1931), *Der luftkrieg* and *Die erde im flammen* all served to build the picture across Europe of a future war being dominated by highly destructive air raids.[33] In Britain the fear was even more deep rooted, fed by books such as P.R.C. Groves' *Behind the smoke screen* (London, 1934), J. Griffin's *Glass houses and modern war* (London, 1938) and L.E.O. Charlton's series which included *War from the air* (London, 1935). The evidence that emerged from Spain during the civil war, in particular the bombing of Guernica, further emphasized the impact on civilians and the devastation which followed. In Britain especially, the fear of the bomber was a significant factor in the determination of national strategy. The repeated attempts by governments, although ultimately fruitless, to ban the aerial threat through international agreement were clear reflections of the peculiar place of the bomber in western consciousness. More than any other weapon, the aeroplane, with its potential to attack the heart of the nation state directly, was seen as the ultimate weapon of modern war.[34] The threat of the knockout blow, although widely disputed by many military analysts and, quite naturally, by the navies and armies of the world, markedly influenced government policy in Britain. The Air Staff fed the government horrendous casualty figures – 20,000 in London on the first day of an aerial assault, 150,000 in the first week. Moreover, they emphasized, the morale of the civilian population was much more susceptible to collapse than that of the military.[35]

The British were also deeply conscious of the damage done to their geostrategic position by the bomber. Prior to World War I, thanks to the English Channel, the British had to fear only naval threats to their security and these had been negated by the superiority of the Royal Navy. However, with the advent of the aerial threat, the British were no longer secure from direct attack. They were as vulnerable as any other European power to aerial bombardment, if not more so. For a nation isolated from the physical devastation of war, unless self-inflicted, for the best part of 900 years it was a chastening experience, an experience also to be encountered by the USA in the 1950s.

Although not affected to the same degree by the fear of the bomber, many other states across Europe were also concerned with the threat of massed bombing and measures evolved in an attempt to deal with the problem. Two political responses to the shadow of the bomber emerged: restraint or deterrent. The former floundered in a sea of mistrust and antipathy. Although the preferred option of the USA and Britain, few in the West believed that the USSR, which on paper had the largest air force in the world, could be trusted to honour any air disarmament agreement. The feeling was mutual and, in any case, the rise of Nazi Germany, French insecurity and the generally deteriorating international situation swept away the likelihood of any air disarmament agreement succeeding. The second response, that of air deterrence, although in the short term damagingly expensive to economies recovering from the 1929 financial crash, and in the medium term inadequate as a means of containing German aggression, ultimately laid the foundations for Allied survival in World War II by creating a significant and sound air power base. Indeed, if the Allies had not adopted deterrence and rearmament as a means of dealing with Hitler in 1933, the consequences could well have been catastrophic once the Second World War had broken out.[36]

Germany also subscribed to the deterrent effect of air power, although for different reasons to Britain. In the early stages of rearmament, there was considerable fear of French or Polish invasion should it become obvious that Germany was intent on a programme of military rebuilding. Erhard Milch, the Secretary of State of the RLM (State Air Ministry), requested a new study of Germany's air power needs in the wake of Hitler's accession to power. Dr Robert Knauss, a future commander at the Air War Academy, offered a deterrent plan based very much on the theories of strategic bombing as a supposedly cost-effective means of providing Germany with a viable defence. Aerial defence was not practical, Knauss argued, and only a large fleet of bombers would provide a true deterrent effect as all states feared massed aerial bombing.[37] The plan was initially accepted by Hitler and Goering and a bold programme of expansion was initiated.

However, although support persisted for strategic bombing in Germany, economic practicality and strategic necessity precluded the creation of a strategic bombing force. The German aero-industry and the economic resources available did not allow for a major heavy-bomber construction programme, and more importantly, such a plan did not fit with developing national strategy. Air deterrence diminished the prospects of war, while the Nazi state was ultimately determined to change the face of Europe, through force if necessary. The two concepts clearly did not work together, and by 1936 the more broadly based Wever doctrine of air power, which emphasized the concentrated use of air forces on an operational and campaign level to support ground offensives, had been more or less adopted.[38]

Moreover, the experience of German air forces in Spain during the Civil War further underpinned the contentions of the *Wehrmacht*, and indeed many within the *Luftwaffe*, that massed bombing was not the decisive factor the air power advocates claimed it to be. Nevertheless, the diplomatic and political power of strategic bombing and its effect on Britain in particular was understood by the German government and used in the strategic and diplomatic decision making process.

Ultimately, however, deterrence relies on credibility, both in a technical and a political sense. First, a deterrent must be considered technically practical and viable by all sides and this was not the case in the interwar era. Many air power advocates believed air power could act in the apocalyptic manner envisaged, but many did not and certainly if doubt persisted to any degree in the minds of policy makers then the deterrent was undermined.

The deterrent also had to be backed up with a credible diplomatic policy that emphasized the willingness of the "deterrers" to use their air weapon if necessary. Although Germany clearly had an aggressive foreign policy and was apparently willing to use force, the Western Allies did not paint themselves in the same way. The policy of appeasement totally undermined the deterrent effect that the RAF's bomber fleet might have had. The repeated willingness of the British to compromise in the face of German aggression proved two things: first, that they were unwilling to use their bomber force because they were fearful of going to war, or secondly, that they did not believe that their bomber fleet was effective as a weapon of war and therefore could not risk calling Hitler's bluff.[39] In either case, the deterrent effect of strategic bombing was compromised. The theory of deterrence had run ahead of technological capability, and the latter was not able to catch up until the nuclear age.[40] Nevertheless, the deterrent effect of air power was to play a significant role in shaping air and national strategic policies in the age of rearmament.

Munich stands out as the most obvious example of air power, or more pointedly the fear of air power, influencing foreign policy. Allied rearmament was barely underway by 1938, while the perception of German air power was one of fear and intimidation. Whatever the realities of German air strength, or indeed the true capabilities of aerial bombing in the late 1930s, the apparent helplessness of the British and French in the face of a *Luftwaffe* "knockout blow", undermined the resolve of Chamberlain and Daladier to stand firm. Both the British Chiefs of Staff and the French Chief of Air Force General Staff argued that an air war in 1938 would be disastrous. They needed more time to deal with the larger numbers of aircraft required and with the technological revolution which had rendered large parts of the world's air fleets obsolete.[41] The French air force considered that 80 per cent of its 1,350 aircraft was inadequate for a modern war in 1938, while the RAF had only 100 Hawker Hurricanes and 3 Supermarine Spitfires to meet the German air threat, a force considered totally inadequate. It would be wrong to argue that perceived air power inferiority was the deciding factor in the adoption of appeasement at Munich, but it was certainly a contributing factor. As President Roosevelt's ambassador in Paris reported after Munich, "If you have enough airplanes you don't have to go to Berchtesgaden".[42]

Air rearmament – building for war

With the slow but inexorable breakdown of the international scene, and with the failure of attempts to eliminate bombers, so the pressure grew for military rearmament on a scale unknown for 20 years. The expansion of air forces, be it for deterrent purposes or otherwise was shaped and defined by a number of influences which brought about the types and nature of air forces which fought the early stages of the Second World War.

The place of air power in national strategy was quite naturally crucial to the level of development and expenditure on air power in respective nations. Establishing likely threats and the required counter-measures necessary, or indeed in identifying long-term goals and building air power resources to meet such aims, were all part of the difficult process of aerial rearmament.

Germany sought a broadly based and comprehensive military programme into which air power fitted at both diplomatic and military levels – the former to provide a threat to intimidate opponents, the latter to support the possible land based conflict. Britain, with limited financial resources, was desperate to avoid another continental commitment on the scale of World War I and the massed bomber fleet was viewed as a means of doing just that by preventing a war from breaking out in Europe – the deterrent effect. Much more could be spent on the RAF at the expense of the army thanks to protection afforded by the English Channel. The French were not so lucky. Even with the Maginot Line, the French considered the land battle the most crucial part of their national strategy and in spite of the *Armee de l'Air*'s efforts to broaden air power thinking, the limited air rearmament which took place was still largely shaped and influenced by notions of supporting the army. The USSR, technically the largest air force in the world throughout the 1930s, also placed most resources in army support, although dabblings with long-range bombing also took place. The USA, even more isolated than Britain, was able to concentrate its air power resources on long-range bombardment and on naval air power, while Japanese air power was directly subordinated to the demands of the army and the navy. In essence, it is clear that air rearmament choices had to be made, and while airmen around the world saw potential in many aspects of air power, degrees of value on respective forms of air strength had to be established. Combining an understanding of doctrine and air power capability and fitting it to national requirements was the first step on the road to rearmament, although, of course, it did not always produce effective air forces. Inter-service rivalry was a cause of skewed investment, as was slavish adherence to dogma, and such distorting influences often interfered with what might have been considered the correct path of aerial development.

However, a crucially important influence on air power rearmament was the ability of states to build what was eventually decided upon. The aero-industries of the early-to-mid-1930s were in no fit state to meet the ever increasing demands of military expansion. Only the USSR had been embarked upon a programme of aerial expansion since the 1920s. All the other states had seen drastic reductions throughout the period, and Germany, despite the efforts of the *Reichswehr* to hide its air power base in the USSR and amongst the civil aviation industry, had to build its military aero-industry virtually from scratch. Aircraft, especially modern military aircraft, were expensive and complex pieces of kit and the resources needed to produce them *en masse* were for the most part lacking. Quite simply, the aero-industries were unable to deliver what their governments wanted in anything like the quantities desired. Both the British and German air expansion programmes hit snags and production always lagged behind orders and, with the pressure of the growing air arms race that developed from 1935 onwards, the failings of industry were received in states of near panic.[43]

The effects of the arms race were at times quite marked and, in the long-term, of considerable significance. The increasing pressure to build vast numbers of bombers to maintain huge air fleets for essentially political and diplomatic reasons, especially when Britain and to a lesser degree Germany were subscribing to notions of deterrence, created "shop window" air forces with little in the way of substantial reserves. By the late 1930s concern was growing in British circles that the RAF was merely a facade with little depth and in Germany, likewise, there was concern that the *Luftwaffe* had been swollen for purposes of deterrence by the continued construction of aircraft totally unsuited to front-line operations.[44]

The problem of estimating the opposition's true air strength remained a considerable problem throughout the air arms race. Curiously, German intelligence persistently underestimated the strength of the British aero-industry and its output, while the Allies overestimated the capacity of the German aviation industry. In Britain this was in a part because of the excessive concern over bombing and the public statements of politicians such as Churchill, who were attempting to turn British attention towards the threat of German expansion. In reality, German air strength was based on large numbers of training and ex-civil transport aircraft and overall aircraft production in Germany was never as high as the British believed. Conversely, German military intelligence gathering proved inadequate, at times believing British aircraft production to have reached only a third of its actual output.[45]

Arguably, the most significant impact on the air arms race occurred with the rapid advances made in aviation technology from the mid-1930s onwards. The technical leap, especially in high-performance monoplane fighters, shifted the balance of air power considerably. The bomber began to be viewed as being vulnerable and in consequence the British Prime Minister Stanley Baldwin's claim that "the bomber will always get through" no longer seemed so certain.[46] While the advocates of strategic bombing in the RAF and in the US Army Air Corps still believed in the strength of the bomber fleet, others began to question the whole validity of the strategy. The Germans and the Soviets, with their experiences in the Spanish Civil War, and with other pressing demands on air power, came to the conclusion that city bombing was not as significant as had been believed. Moreover, with advances being made in early warning radio direction finding equipment, most notably in Britain from 1935 onwards, the probability emerged that a bombing offensive could be defeated.

The British government, never convinced by the bomber as a means of waging war in the first place, began a significant shift in policy in 1937. It was clear that the deterrent effect of their bomber fleet was negligible, as Hitler was still pursuing aggressive foreign policies. Yet it was still costing the British government a great deal of money, more than the National Government was willing to pay. In 1937, Sir Thomas Inskip was appointed Minister for the Co-ordination of Defence and he effectively abandoned the previous policy of threatening Germany with a large RAF bomber force. He argued that the role of the RAF was to defend British airspace, not to bomb Germany into submission, although that role may have value should a war develop.[47] Essentially, British foreign policy, in conjunction with the French, was defensively oriented. Both western European powers expected any future war with Germany to be a refight of the Great War and thus they should fight to their strengths. They recognized that their own initial military strength was weak compared with Germany, but they also believed that the Nazi state was economically vulnerable and thus could be undermined by a blockade as it had been in 1914–18. Anglo–French strategic planning called for a defensive war, to throw up a wall behind which the Allies could capitalize on their economic superiority and defeat Germany in a long haul war. The French army and the Maginot Line would occupy the *Wehrmacht*, while the RAF would keep the *Luftwaffe* away from the British Isles.

It can be seen that the emphasis in British air power policy had altered towards air defence, now considered feasible thanks to early warning radar, high-speed monoplane fighters and properly organized civil defence. Inskip and the British government rejected the claims of the RAF that there was no viable defence to aerial bombardment, but quite apart from the fact that Britain could no longer afford to continue the air arms race with Germany, the switch to air defence fitted more naturally into British foreign policy.

The high point of the bomber based expansion plans called for the creation of a 90 squadron fleet with 1,659 bombers, but in the wake of Inskip's report this was reduced to 77 and 1,360 respectively, while fighter strength was to be increased from 476 to 532.[48] The importance of air power and in particular air defence to British planning was emphasized during the Munich crisis when the Chiefs of Staff informed Chamberlain that the British air forces were simply not ready for war and nor would they be in a fit state until mid-1939 at the earliest.[49]

On the outbreak of war, British air power was still in a state of flux, with increasing and highly sophisticated air defence forces, principally based around the Hawker Hurricane and Supermarine Spitfire, at least equal if not superior to anything the *Luftwaffe* could deploy. However, most other elements of the RAF were equipped with obsolete or unsuitable aircraft. Indeed, RAF Bomber Command was to suffer badly in the early stages of the war, having to fight with aircraft unfit for the grand designs of its senior officers. Britain's most notable achievement in the years leading up to World War II was the transformation of its aero-industry from a small and inefficient sector in the early 1930s to a sophisticated mass-production line by the end of the decade. British aircraft production outpaced the much larger German economy by 1939 and continued to do so until 1943.[50]

Although the French followed similar strategic principles, of defence and preparing for a long-haul economic war, their attempts to fit air policy to meet such needs failed. From a position of superiority in the early 1920s, French air power fell away dramatically and by the outbreak of war was largely equipped with inadequate numbers of obsolete designs. In essence the French aero-industry, without strong direction from the military and political establishment, and hampered by poorly considered planning and procurements processes, not rectified by attempts at restructuring and re-organization in 1936 and 1937, was quite unable to cope with the demands made of it in the late 1930s (see Chapter Four). Like the British, the French shifted the emphasis of their air rearmament programme towards fighter defence in the late 1930s with the advent of the so-called *Plan V*. In discussions with the British in 1938, it was considered that the revamped *Armee de l'Air* should confront the *Luftwaffe* while the RAF should deal with the threat from the Italian *Regia Aeronautica*, illustrating the faith the French put in their aero-industry's capacity and ability. However, unlike the British, they were unable to develop new designs in any quantity rapidly enough to meet the *Luftwaffe* in 1940. The *Armee de l'Air* and the French aero-industry needed more time than Hitler was to allow them.[51]

German front-line air power on the outbreak of war was considerable, but its base was weak and its long-term planning flawed. Economic constraints were always a problem, with small scale fuel production, lack of foreign currency and an aero-industry of limited size being the most significant. The inability of German industry to provide efficient engines for the proposed heavy-bombers, the Dornier Do 19 and Junkers Ju 89, led to their cancellation and consequent diminishing interest in strategic bombing.[52]

Nevertheless, between 1933 and 1936 the aircraft industry expanded by 800 per cent and military air power consumed 40 per cent of the defence budget. Once the initial burst of energy and enthusiasm had spent itself, however, problems in long-term planning emerged, problems which the existing structure was unable to cope with.[53]

The poor overall and central direction of air rearmament was a major factor in the long-term failure of the *Luftwaffe*, with the leadership of Herman Goering of particular significance. His position as Hitler's right-hand man was initially of value to German air power, ensuring adequate resourcing but, in the long-term, Goering's failings became apparent and ultimately ruinous. He was largely concerned with numbers and, like the British, became embroiled in creating a large front-line force of aircraft to add to Germany's and his own personal prestige. He ignored pleas for greater investment in supplies, spare parts and logistical support, leaving the *Luftwaffe* in a parlous state once the war had developed.[54]

The failings of Goering were partly alleviated in the mid-1930s by the shrewd stewardship of Erhard Milch, State Secretary at the Air Ministry. Milch, an able and well-connected, if abrasive organizer, was able to keep German aircraft production roughly on target until the major expansion schemes of the late 1930s emerged. By this time, however, he had been sidelined by Goering's appointment of Ernst Udet as Technical Director of the *Luftwaffe*. Udet was a colourful and energetic character, but his disruptive input merely served to fragment control and direction in aircraft procurement. His fascination with dive-bombing led to the redesign of the Junkers Ju 88 which increased its weight from seven to twelve tons, resulted in a decrease in speed from 500 kmh to 300 kmh, and delayed production for a year.[55]

Hitler's scheme to expand the *Luftwaffe* five-fold after 1938 was completely unrealistic and would have taken the equivalent of the entire German defence budget from 1933–9, 85 per cent of the world's aviation fuel production and bankrupted the nation.[56] Nevertheless, in spite of the reality, the future *Luftwaffe* Chief of Staff, Hans Jeschonnek, argued that Hitler should be supported in his plan as its intention was sound, if not entirely practical.[57] Whereas production targets had been met until 1936, after that date expansion stagnated and central direction evaporated, thanks to the interference of Udet, Wever's death (*Luftwaffe* Chief of Staff), Goering's empire building and sloth and the simple economic constraints of the German aero-industry. Much of this was hidden both from the outside world and from Hitler who was constantly fed what he wanted to know by Goering. Under the pressures of war, the inherent flaws and failings in the German aircraft procurement and production process were eventually to lead to the collapse of

German air power in the face of concerted Allied attack. However, in the short-term the large front-line force created by Goering, coupled with a more prescient and appropriate *Luftwaffe* doctrine was to prove remarkably adaptable and effective.

In stark contrast, Soviet rearmament policies prior to the German invasion in June 1941 laid the foundations for rapid growth in the VVS (Soviet Air Force) after the invasion (*Operation Barbarossa*), but left it open to the initial German onslaught. The five-year plans and the emphasis on heavy industrial expansion in the 1930s served to put the VVS in a strong position by the end of the decade. Modern aircraft had been introduced, such as the I-15 and I-16 fighters and the SB-2 and TB-3 bombers, and the total frontline strength of the VVS (some 2,500 aircraft in 1937) dwarfed that of other powers.[58] Soviet fighters were a match for anything other than the latest German designs as indicated by the experiences of the Spanish Civil War. It was clear that as a result of the five-year plans, deficiencies in aircraft and aero-engine design as well as production techniques had for the most part been eliminated.

The crisis in the VVS, as with the rest of the Soviet military, occurred as a result of the purges of the late 1930s, a process in which the officers and leaders of the VVS suffered disproportionately. Alksnis, commander of the VVS since 1931, along with Khripin, his deputy, were eliminated in 1937 and many other leading airmen went with them. Around 75 per cent of the VVS's senior officers were victims of the purges. In addition, the aero-industry also suffered, with research organizations and design bureaux also coming under scrutiny.[59]

The impact of the purges fused with a major reorganization of the VVS as a result of the poor showing in the Winter War against Finland in 1939–40. This was still underway when Germany invaded. Nevertheless, with a strength of some 10,000 aircraft in June 1941, the VVS was able to absorb horrendous casualties, with over half its force destroyed on the ground in the early stages of the campaign, and still recover, demonstrating the depth of the industrial base and central organization forged during the 1930s.

Italian air power flattered to deceive throughout the 1930s, and while the *Regia Aeronautica* (RA) pontificated on strategy and won plaudits for its technical capability, it eventually came to near disaster in the campaigns of 1940–43. Problems had begun to emerge in the RA in the 1930s for a number of reasons. First, like other right-wing dictatorships, the leader, in this case Mussolini, took an active and unhelpful interest in military affairs. Il Duce attempted to keep control of all three services but was of course unable to maintain an effective direction in Italian defence policy making. Moreover, his contradictory ideas of a traditional rural based community sat in stark contrast to his ambitious overseas plans of conquest, which of course required a thriving modern industrial economy. Secondly, the Italian aero-industry suffered badly in the economic recession of the early 1930s and the fascist economy's response was to become introspective and isolated. This merely led to it falling behind the rest of the major world air powers as the decade progressed and, by the outbreak of war, Italian engines in particular lagged behind their major adversaries. Thirdly, the lessons of the Spanish Civil War passed unnoticed by the RA. While the Germans and the Soviets learned a great deal, the Italians were protected from their own inadequacies by German efficiency and know-how and by the failings of the aircrew they faced. Thus, the fact that they were confronted by technically superior air-craft did not filter through to the upper echelons of the Italian armed forces.

Finally, and perhaps most importantly, in the 1920s the Italians split their aircraft procurement procedures into two distinct political and technical camps. The former, the *Direzione Generale del Genio e delle Costruzioni Aero-nautiche* (DGCA), held the final say on aircraft procurement but repeatedly ignored the advice of the *Direzione Superiore Studi Esperienze* (DSSE), where the scientific and technical know-how was lodged. Consequently, when the DSSE wanted to purchase Caproni RE2000, F5 and Ca165 aircraft in 1938, the DGCA ignored them and ordered Macchi Castoldi MC 200 and Fiat G50 and CR42 models. All of the latter types were to be considered in-adequate and obsolete during the Second World War. When war came to Italy in 1940, the RA was totally unprepared, equipped as it was with outdated arms and with no overall central doctrine of operations. Notably, even the newer monoplane fighters being introduced were outclassed by their opponents.[60]

Japanese air power, in effect protected from the concerns of overseas bombing, and with considerable learning experience gained from the many conflicts undertaken by the Imperial Japanese forces in the 1930s, was able to develop a fairly high combat effectiveness and proficiency – as the Western Allies were to discover in 1941/2. Designs of aircraft and training were well established, and in the latter case considerably superior to their western counterparts. Of the major air powers of World War II, Japan developed last and it was not until after the First World War, with French and British help, that the Imperial Japanese air forces began to emerge. Steady increases in aircraft production and development continued throughout the turbulent 1930s (445 in 1930 to 5,000 in 1941) and the experiences of actions against Chinese and Soviet forces in particular proved invaluable.

The aero-industry in Japan, however, followed a similar pattern to that found in the other Axis powers. Co-operation between the navy and the army was already slight and fierce competition continued to foul relations throughout the war. This spilled over into aircraft procurement and production and there was no attempt to co-ordinate aircraft development between either services, or indeed between the major manufacturers (Mitsubishi, Nakajima and Kawasaki). With an economic base already weak and under-developed in comparison with the US, this lack of homogeneity and single-mindedness in pulling the aero-industry together compounded with no overall direction and control in the aircraft development and production process to fragment the sector and to dissipate effort, with serious consequences in World War II.[61] Moreover, the harsh and brutal training programme used by the Japanese for pilot and aircrew training, the navy especially, sowed the seeds for rapid decline once the war with the West had broken out. No strength in depth was created and once the admittedly superb front-line aircrew had been lost in the battles of 1942 the Japanese were completely unable to rebuild and expand their air forces.

Although the USA was the last of the major belligerents of World War II to become embroiled in war, the foundations of the rapid growth in aircraft production which dwarfed the output of all other nations after 1940, had already been layed. The mass-industrial base, and more importantly its use of technological innovation to create a sophisticated and responsive economy gave the US aero-industry a major advantage over its contemporaries and was the cornerstone of Allied air power superiority during World War II. As the world situation deteriorated from the mid-1930s onwards, the administration began a series of rearmament programmes to bolster US defence. Research establishments set up to guide and administer aviation science switched the emphasis of their work to applied military research and development.[62]

In the aftermath of the Munich crisis and the importance of air power in the strategic bargaining that had gone on, the Roosevelt government began the process which would see a whole new generation of aircraft emerge just as the USA went to war in 1941. The US Army Air Corps saw a 90 per cent officer and 140 per cent enlisted men personnel expansion, while a target of 5,500 aircraft was set to be achieved as soon as was practicable.[63] Already being equipped with the famous Boeing B-17 heavy-bomber, the procurement of new modern aircraft types such as the Lockheed P-38 Lightning, Curtiss P-40, Republic P-47 Thunderbolt, Consolidated B-24 Liberator and the Douglas A-20 Havoc demonstrated the depth of the US aero-industry and its ability to meet the demands and needs of the armed forces on an unrivalled scale. The US Navy also saw the expansion of its naval air arm in the mid-to-late 1930s, with a range of new aircraft carriers being constructed, such as the *Yorktown, Enterprise, Wasp* and *Hornet,* to add to the veteran *Lexington* and *Saratoga* and, prior to the attack on Pearl Harbor, a major programme based around the *Essex* class of carrier had already been initiated. A congressional bill of 1935 called for a naval air reserve of 6,000 pilots to support the regular naval aircrew, and priority was being given to naval aircraft development to close the gap on Japanese models.[64] Nevertheless, on the outbreak of war, of the US Navy's front-line carrier aircraft, only the Douglas Dauntless dive-bomber could be considered acceptable.

The massive plans for the expansion of US air power were still to a large extent beyond the capability of the US aero-industry, certainly in peacetime, but after Pearl Harbor the capacity of the US economy, and its modern, sophisticated approach to mass-production was to pay dividends.

Conclusions

Between 1918 and 1939 the role of air power in world affairs expanded considerably, influencing national strategies and foreign policies alike, especially in the 1930s. The 1920s had witnessed the permanent foundations of air strength, in spite of the massive demobilization following the Great War. The roots of air power were laid by carefully considered service policies and equally by the emergence of civil aviation. This non-military market was the force behind technological advancement during the 1920s and early 1930s as military forces, in the West at least, endured the so-called "locust years". Much of what was to shape aircraft development in the mid-1930s dated back to the development of civil aviation in the preceding years. By the 1930s, as war loomed again, the importance of air power to strategic thinking was marked, and on occasion, perceived technical capability drove policy in certain directions. The "shadow of the bomber" was a major influence in the formulation of state policy, particularly in Britain and to a lesser degree in Germany, but also across much of the industrial world. At Munich, deficiencies in air power strength played an important part in shaping British and French policy.

Yet, despite perceptions, air strength remained weak or flawed in all nations and was palpably unable to meet the demands and expectations made of it. Although Germany embarked on a major *Luftwaffe* expansion scheme in the 1930s, the foundations of such growth were undermined by the inadequate development and direction of the aero-industry. Ultimately, this was to be a contributory factor in Germany's defeat in World War II. Conversely, the British underpinned their long-term air strength by a co-ordinated industrial effort. The USSR, the USA and Britain took a long sighted and industrial view of air power, and short-term capability was compromised in order to secure long-term strength. The short-term was not aided by certain events (such as Stalin's purges) or by financial stringency, or indeed by pursuing the more grandiose claims of the extreme air power advocates. Nevertheless, when conflict came in 1939 the benefits of aero-industry organization and expansion in a "total war" environment were to become self-evident, even if it did not appear so in 1940 and 1941.

Chapter Six

The war in Europe, 1939–45

Undoubtedly, the apogee of total war and, indeed, mass air war emerged in the 1939–45 conflict. In 1939, air power was considered a key component of military and naval activity, and some even saw the value of strategic bombing as a means of defeating enemy powers. By 1945, the value of air supremacy had been demonstrated by the Allies' crushing air strength and its pivotal role in the defeat of Germany. The apocalyptic visions of Douhet and his contemporaries finally, on the face of it, came to fruition with the mass destruction of Dresden, Tokyo and latterly Hiroshima and Nagasaki. By the end of the World War, air power not only played a crucial role in deciding the outcome of ground offensives and naval operations, it also promised to elevate (or degenerate) war onto an entirely new plain. Ultimately, war had become so "total" that the conflict threatened to subsume the political element which had always been the very impetus for war itself.

Air power and strategy

Despite all this, to be fully effective, air power had to be integrated into an overall strategy for the prosecution of the war which involved other services and a combination of routes to victory. The belligerent powers linked strategy and air power with varying degrees of success at different points in the war. For example, the *Luftwaffe* led the way in the early years of the war being a vital, indeed possibly defining, component of *blitzkrieg*. As Germany enjoyed staggering success between 1939 and 1941, so the high profile of air power in precipitating such victories in part led the Allies to develop air forces of such overwhelming superiority that, from the spring of 1944, they enjoyed air supremacy on a previously unprecedented scale. Paradoxically, the *Luftwaffe*, despite its apparent trailblazing, disintegrated as the war progressed, being the first casualty of the attritional war into which Hitler had led his state. The roots of German failure and Allied and Soviet success in the air war can in part be traced back to the pre-war years when the foundations of the later massive expansion of the aero-industries began. Aircraft production and development was a microcosm of the war as a whole. The Germans, at a higher state of front-line military readiness in 1939, made their advantages tell, sweeping away inferior powers with bold and risky offensives against which the rearming and ill-prepared British and French could not react quickly enough. However, those that survived such as Britain and the USSR, and those beyond the range of direct German aggression, such as the USA, were able to muster their superior economic strengths and go over to the offensive. While Germany initially proved unwilling and latterly unable to expand its air forces sufficiently, if at all, their opponents, with long-term air expansion and re-equipment programmes already underway, surged ahead of the Nazi state and its diminishing and haemorrhaging air power strength. Confronted with a series of punishing air offensives, over Germany itself, over the Atlantic, and finally in support of the massive land forces which from late 1942 onwards began the inexorable advance on the Nazi state, German strength and power was crushed.

Land warfare – *blitzkrieg*

It is all too often assumed that German air power in World War II was largely deployed in close support of the army, contributing considerably to the success of the armoured offensives which epitomized *blitzkrieg*.[1] However, as has already been indicated, the *Luftwaffe* was a broadly based force with no constricting central doctrine, other than that its resources should be used generally to support national strategy. Dabblings with strategic bombing, which many in the *Luftwaffe* itself continued to support, persisted, although limited resources, the lessons of the Spanish Civil War and the demands of war reduced such efforts to the periphery. Nevertheless, in the 1939–41 period, the technical and doctrinal efficiency of the *Luftwaffe* was such that it was far more capable of carrying out a strategic bombing campaign than the British.[2]

The flexibility of German air power was, in the early stages of the war, its very strength and, paradoxically from 1941 onwards, a fundamental weakness.

While the *Armee de l'Air*, and to a lesser extent the Soviet VVS, were tied to close support of the army, the *Luftwaffe* was able to deploy its air resources in more general "operational" level support of the *Wehrmacht*, shifting from air superiority efforts to medium-range interdiction of enemy rear zones, then to psychological city bombing raids, and finally to close air-support duties. The disparate and multi-purpose *Luftwaffe* was well suited to such activities, and the technological advantage it held in operational aircraft and training, as well as superior numbers, were the cornerstones of early success.

Far from being the dedicated spearhead of the panzers, less than 15 per cent of the *Luftwaffe* was designed as a close support force for the army in 1939,[3] and the level of importance given to aerial bombing of cities, even in an operational sense, was illustrated by plans for the heavy bombing of Warsaw during the Polish campaign of September 1939, plans only abandoned due to the inclement weather.[4] However, the *Luftwaffe* carried out a general campaign of mostly indirect, but also close and direct air support of the army with considerable success, even though much still had to be learnt. Such was the level of improvization in the *Luftwaffe*'s support of the *Wehrmacht* that a whole host of co-ordination, liaison and communication problems emerged that had to be solved as the Polish campaign progressed and it was testament to the efficiency of the German military that such glitches were relatively easily negotiated. In part, this success was down to the work of Generalmajor Wolfram Freiherr von Richthofen, a veteran of the Spanish Civil War, in establishing lines of communication between ground units and air forces. For much of the war, Richthofen's Fliegerkorps VIII acted as the primary close air support force and found itself moved from sector to sector as required.[5] Nevertheless, response times between calls for close air support and air attack still stood at some hours.[6]

The early stages of the air campaign were marked by the *Luftwaffe*'s efforts to gain air superiority over the Poles, considered essential in pre-war planning. The Polish air force could only muster some 800 aircraft, of which just 463 were frontline types, to meet the *Luftwaffe*'s near 2,000 aeroplanes.[7] Moreover, the German aircraft were predominantly modern whilst the Polish types were obsolete, best illustrated by the disparity between the PZL P-IIc and the Messerschmitt Bf109 air superiority fighters (over 100 mph difference in top speeds). However, contrary to popular belief (fuelled by the claims of the Germans themselves[8]) the Polish air force was not destroyed on the ground during early German bombing raids and kept on fighting until shot out of the sky by superior German fighters and highly effective ground based anti-aircraft firepower.[9] By September 17, over two weeks into the war, having lost over 75 per cent of its frontline force, the Polish air force withdrew to Romania giving total air supremacy to the *Luftwaffe*.[10] Thus, the Polish air force was never able to intervene in any serious manner with the efforts of the German ground forces, while the *Luftwaffe* was able to conduct highly effective army support operations throughout the campaign, virtually at will. The importance of maintaining the ability to contest air superiority was already being proven. Once the enemy had free rein in the air it proved to be a crippling disadvantage for friendly ground forces.

The *Luftwaffe* was well satisfied with its efforts in the Polish campaign. It had coped with certain air-to-ground communication problems (which were to persist into 1940 and beyond), had demonstrated considerable operational flexibility and had proved itself adept at seizing control of the air. Indeed, a plan of aerial operations was established over Poland that was to form the basis of *Luftwaffe* success over the subsequent two years. The plan was predicated on general and operational air support of ground operations, eschewing both dedicated close air support and strategic bombing. The formula was repeated in the rapid German descent on Scandinavia in April 1940 when air superiority was again a critical advantage, even forcing the much vaunted Royal Navy, still predominantly a surface force, back to the British Isles.[11]

However, it was in the campaigns in the Low Countries and France in May and June 1940, which saw the rout of larger Allied ground forces by the German military, that the real value of the *Luftwaffe* in supporting ground offensives came to be understood by the Allies. In 1940 the *Luftwaffe* was the one major arm the Germans possessed which was numerically larger than the forces opposing them. In ground forces the *Wehrmacht* was considerably outnumbered, and it was to be operational effectiveness, Allied failings and luck that was to bring about the collapse of the West in six weeks, a feat that had eluded the Imperial German army for four years. The *Luftwaffe* had 1,300 bombers, 380 dive-bombers and 1,210 fighters deployed in support of *Operation Fall Gelb* (Case Yellow, the code name for the invasion of the West) while the Allies mustered some 1,151 fighters and 1,045 bombers and ground-attack aircraft.

However, the deficiencies ran much deeper than the figures indicate. First, the Allied air forces were heterogeneous and lacked centralized control and direction, in marked contrast to the *Luftwaffe*. Aside from the few British Hurricanes and Spitfires and a very small number of Dutch Fokker types, the *Luftwaffe*'s aircraft were technically superior to anything in the Allied inventory, and it was particularly in bomber attacks on German forces that the RAF and the French *Armee de l'Air* were to suffer. However, the most important factor in the Allied defeat lay in the doctrine of employment of the available resources. The *Luftwaffe* was used to support the direction of the campaign in a generally co-ordinated manner, massing aircraft to create air superiority where required and sweeping the skies of the more widely dispersed Allied air forces.

The offensive opened, as was becoming the norm, with an attempt by the *Luftwaffe* to cripple the enemy air forces on the ground. The Dutch, Belgian and French air arms were badly mauled on the first day but, as in Poland, the *Luftwaffe*'s attacks were indecisive. However, again following the Polish pattern, the real defeat of the RAF and the French *Armee de l'Air* came when they attempted to intervene in the ground war by attacking German land forces. The losses from both German fighters and flak defences were prohibitive. Within two days, half of the Allied aircraft in the combat zone had been destroyed and, by 20 May, with the situation for the British Expeditionary Forces deteriorating the RAF had abandoned the continent.[12]

Perhaps the act which best illustrated the role air power played in *blitzkrieg* came with the audacious breakthrough across the Meuse which decided the outcome of the campaign.[13] Here, a screen of fighters covered the crossing from Allied reconnaissance aircraft, and German close-air support bombers, notably the Junkers Ju 87 "Stuka", kept the French defenders under constant bombardment. Allied attempts to strike at the unexpected breach in their defences came to nothing and incurred heavy losses, despite the simultaneous diversion of the *Luftwaffe*'s main efforts to the elimination of Dutch resistance. In this brief northern air campaign the ending of Dutch resistance, largely as a result of the bombing of Rotterdam, indicated the psychological effect aerial bombardment could have.[14] The Allied armies were thrown back in chaos and disarray, a state maintained by the dominance of German air power which constantly disrupted and harried the retreating British and French units. By June the campaign was over, the French eliminated and the British driven back across the English Channel.

The success of the Germans had been staggering and the *Luftwaffe* had played a significant part in the victory. Its fluid, flexible and concerted use of air power had proved far more effective than the rigid dispersed doctrine of the French, but this mirrored the overall approach of the two powers. The Germans had achieved surprise and, importantly, had been able to maintain the speed of their breakthrough, in part, by relying on the *Luftwaffe* to provide support. The Allies were unable to respond quickly enough, because of unco-ordinated decision making, poorly considered planning and due to the intervention of the *Luftwaffe*'s interdiction operations which prevented rapid movement and response by defending forces. In marked contrast to the Ludendorff breakthrough in 1918, which outdistanced its supports and was eventually pummelled by redeployed Allied artillery, the 1940 offensive never allowed the Allies enough time to reorganize and this was partly as a result of the suppressing effect of German air attack and the inability of the French and British air forces to prevent it.

However, the shortcomings of the *Luftwaffe* were soon to be exposed by the RAF. The first indications had come during the Dunkirk evacuation of 25 May to 2 June 1940. Goering had argued that the *Luftwaffe* would be able to smash the fleeing British on the Dunkirk beaches and in the English Channel but it was prevented from doing so by the intervention of modern and well-equipped RAF fighters. The limited range of the Bf109, which was operating from bases some distance from Dunkirk, and the vulnerability of the *Luftwaffe*'s bombers to British fighters became all too clear. The *Luftwaffe* lost 240 aircraft to the RAF's 177. For a numerically much superior force this was hardly a catastrophe, but it was a rude shock to the *Luftwaffe* as well as a foretaste of things to come. Moreover, due to the limited powers of recovery of the German aero-industry, these were losses which could not be sustained indefinitely, especially in light of the high attritional rates even a victorious air campaign such as that in France incurred. (Losses had been around 30 per cent.[15])

The attempt to spearhead the invasion of the British Isles with the *Luftwaffe* was a plan that had already been discussed and rejected by the German Air Ministry in 1939.[16] Nevertheless, in view of the overwhelming naval superiority of the British, control of the air was considered essential. In the same way that the *Luftwaffe* conducted any other campaign, the suppression of the enemy air force was the first step to victory. Unfortunately, the *Luftwaffe* was confronted by a number of significant problems on a scale it had not yet encountered and arguably the lack of a dedicated purpose was in part to be its undoing.

The *Luftwaffe* failed for a number of reasons, many indicative of the German air force's inherent shortcomings. A series of tactical failings only partly exposed by the Polish, Scandinavian and French campaigns were ruthlessly exposed during the Battle of Britain, emphasizing that the *Luftwaffe*, although broadly capable, was not actually particularly proficient at anything. Its mainstay air superiority fighter, the Bf109, had too limited a radius of operations to act effectively over the British Isles, thus exposing the German bomber fleet to the RAF's high performance fighters, against which they were hopelessly vulnerable. Notably, the campaign over Britain was the first time the *Luftwaffe* had encountered a properly organized air defence system specifically designed to meet the challenge of an air war. Crucially, the *Luftwaffe* had, in no particular way, been developed to conduct such a focused offensive.

In the intelligence gathering war the Germans continued to follow their pre-war predilection for underestimating their enemies' resources and capabilities.

Already unaware of the British aero-industry's true production capacity, the *Luftwaffe* failed to appreciate the performance of the Hurricane and Spitfire fighters, overlooked the significance of the RAF's early warning radar and markedly overestimated the effectiveness of the *Luftwaffe* itself. It was considered that RAF Fighter Command could be eliminated in just four days; the rest of the RAF and the British aero-industry in four weeks.[17] Conversely, the British, despite overestimating the strength of the air forces facing them, were already beginning to gain intelligence gathering advantages from the breaking of the German encoding device, *Enigma*.

The *Luftwaffe*, partly as a result of poor intelligence and partly thanks to ill-considered strategic decision making, was to change its direction a number of times throughout the campaign. Worse still, even when night-time bombing of London had been adopted there was no considered policy of targeting and effort was dissipated between morale, transportation and the aero-industries, with the consequence that none was particularly affected. In addition, the *Luftwaffe* was forced to fight with a number of other strategic shortcomings and failings. Primarily, the strategic position was such that the *Luftwaffe* was forced to fight over enemy territory, a significant multiplying effect in rates of attrition. Whereas the RAF could recover many of its pilots and nurse home damaged aircraft, the *Luftwaffe* lost downed pilots and aircrew for good and crippled aircraft were often unable to make the hazardous return flight to France.

Arguably, the most fundamental strategic problem facing the *Luftwaffe* was that of making the RAF fighters come and fight. Even if the campaign had gone more in favour of the *Luftwaffe*, there was nothing stopping the RAF from withdrawing its fighters north, out of range of the *Luftwaffe*, and conserving its resources for countering the attempted German invasion. With German naval and invasion forces at a premium, to risk landings with the threat of RAF fighters screening the Royal Navy from the *Luftwaffe* as it attacked the German fleet was probably too much of a gamble, even for Hitler. The problem of forcing an enemy air force to come out and fight and thus expose itself to attrition was one faced by the Allies in 1942 and 1943. Until US bombers forced the *Luftwaffe*'s hand and made it fight for control of the airspace over Germany, there was no real way of crippling German air power in a drawn out "imposed" attritional struggle.[18] In 1943 the Allies had the capacity and wherewithal to deal with the situation; in 1940 the *Luftwaffe* did not. Ultimately, the *Luftwaffe* was simply not up to dealing with the problem of Britain in 1940 and the losses inflicted by the RAF at the crucial times of the battle were enough to break the nerve of Goering and Kesselring, who were all too aware of their air force's true incapacity to withstand much pain.

German forces switched to the blockade and demoralization of Britain over the winter of 1940–41, but they were again unsuccessful, and Hitler's attention was lured east to the potentially rich pickings of the USSR, for many years his ultimate goal. The *Luftwaffe* was afforded just enough time before the launching of *Operation Barbarossa* in June 1941 to make good the losses suffered over the British Isles and in France. However, the quality of its pilots and aircrew was already declining as the experienced personnel of Spain, Poland, Scandinavia and France had been whittled away by the very high rates of attrition endured even by victorious air forces. Clearly, the *Luftwaffe* which prepared for the invasion of the USSR was not the force it had once been.[19] In spite of the potentially much larger scale of operations across the USSR, the size of the German air force remained much the same in 1941 as it had been for the campaigns of 1940. Indeed, Goering and his staff were horrified at the prospect of launching their under-prepared and ill-supported air forces on the Soviet masses. The perspicacious Air Ministry secretary, Erhard Milch, on hearing that Hitler and his staff believed that the campaign would be over before winter 1941 predicted a four year long war and began ordering winter clothing for the *Luftwaffe*.[20] To compound the problem, resources were being stretched still further as Germany's commitments grew across the continent. Already committed to maintaining the air war over northwest Europe, albeit on a reduced scale, the *Luftwaffe* was also being called upon to conduct operations over the Balkans. This included the massed bombing of Belgrade, which resulted in the deaths of some 17,000 people and culminated in the airborne invasion of Crete. In addition, at the height of *Operation Typhoon*, the attempt to capture Moscow in the autumn and winter of 1941, Field-Marshal Kesselring's Second Air Fleet was sent to the Mediterranean theatre to aid the ailing the *Regia Aeronautica*, particularly in North Africa where German troops and armour had recently been despatched under the aegis of Erwin Rommel.

Nevertheless, to support *Operation Barbarossa* the *Luftwaffe* was able to deploy 2,775 aircraft, 65 per cent of its total strength. For the first time however, the *Luftwaffe* was confronted by an enemy air strength much larger than its own, for the VVS (the Red Air Force) had some 8,000–10,000 aircraft in all in June 1941 with around 6,000 initially deployed in Europe. Once again the German plan adopted the tried and tested methods, beginning with a major attack on the VVS on 22 June. Despite warnings, the Soviet armed forces were surprised and some 1,200 VVS aircraft were eliminated by the *Luftwaffe* in the first eight-and-a-half hours of operations, 1,800 by the end of the first day, 4,000 after a week's fighting, and by September a staggering 7,500 VVS aircraft had been accounted for.[21] The rout of the VVS mirrored the near collapse of the Red Army as a whole, but despite the spectacular success of the German armed forces they were unable to secure the total victory they required. The VVS was able to survive and, in contrast, serious shortcomings in the *Luftwaffe*'s capabilities were starting to become all too apparent.

The most basic problem, and one largely glossed over in the planning of *Operation Barbarossa*, was the sheer scale and size of operations that the *Luftwaffe* was being called upon to perform. Although only a crude indicator, the aircraft per square mile ratio on the Eastern Front in 1941 was around 2, whereas in the West it had been between 10 and 15.[22] Quite simply, there was physically only so much the *Luftwaffe* could achieve as the campaign wore on into the autumn and winter, constrained as it was by the vicissitudes of the Russian climate and, importantly, by the burgeoning demands of the *Wehrmacht*'s ground offensives. Moreover, the logistical crisis was already a cause for serious concern. Supply lines stretched back for hundreds of miles, and the active units were having to operate from dirt tracks and muddy fields.

Operational ready rates in front-line units slipped to just 40 per cent by the time of the Moscow offensive, and the sortie rate fell by almost 50 per cent.[23] In previous campaigns direct close support operations for the army had taken up some 25 per cent of the *Luftwaffe*'s sortie effort. In the Russian offensive this figure hovered around 60 per cent, a trend not welcomed by Goering's staff in view of the excessively high attritional rates suffered on such duties.[24] The significance of this shift in combat effort was that less offensive action could be taken against the VVS directly, or against operational, rather than tactical, level targets. Indeed, sophisticated plans for a strategic bombing campaign against Soviet industry had to be abandoned because resources were being diverted to more pressing duties.[25]

The *Luftwaffe* was clearly successful in carrying out this expanded role, but its equipment was no better suited or designed for such operations. The Ju 87 Stukas and Henschel Hs 123 bi-planes were the only dedicated close support aircraft and, although they were later bolstered by the modification of Bf 109s and FW 190s into swing-role fighter-bombers, the only purposely designed ground-attack aircraft introduced by the *Luftwaffe* throughout the war was the Henschel Hs 129 and this proved to be a profound disappointment. The logical outcome of having to deploy more resources to army support was the allocation of twin-engined medium bombers, such as Heinkel He 111s, Junkers Ju 88s and the rapidly obsolescing Dornier Do 17s to such duties, duties for which they were clearly ill-suited.

By the end of 1941 the true extent of the task facing the German armed forces was clear. The *blitzkrieg* had proven to have limitations, and now once embroiled in an exhausting attritional war the failure of German industrial and economic planning and management prior to 1941 became all too apparent. Although the *Luftwaffe* continued to play a part on the Eastern Front, by the time of Kursk in 1943 the VVS had made good the technological, training and doctrinal shortcomings that had contributed greatly to its near collapse in 1941. Additionally, the Soviet aero-industries were swamping the *Luftwaffe* with vast numbers of new aircraft. At Kursk, the *Luftwaffe* mustered some 1,500 aircraft, while the VVS could deploy close on double that number.[26]

A clear indication of the crisis the *Luftwaffe* was facing had already emerged in 1942 when training programmes were cut short to allow new aircrew to get to the front line faster. The idea was for them to finish their training at the front line. However, ill-prepared as they were, active *Luftwaffe* units shielded raw airmen from dangerous operations to allow them to settle in. Unfortunately, this had the effect of increasing attritional rates on experienced pilots and crew, exacerbating the underlying problem. Additionally, new aircrew suffered greater accident rates as a result of their inadequate training. Clearly, the technical ability of the *Luftwaffe*, which their enemies sought to copy, slowly declined as the war went on, although perversely doctrine reached peak effectiveness in 1943.[27]

In assessing the impact of the *Luftwaffe* on conduct of the *blitzkrieg* campaigns it is clear that the German air forces were technically and doctrinally superior to the enemy air forces confronted, arguably with the exception of the RAF's air defence system. The rearmament of the *Luftwaffe* in the wake of the technological advances of the late 1930s had handed Goering's force a considerable advantage over the opposing air forces. Moreover, the *Luftwaffe*'s flexible approach to war, almost an anti-doctrine, allowed great adaptability in the face of a variety of problems. With more considered training and technical development, partly as a result of the Spanish experience, and because of the large amount of campaigning the *Luftwaffe* was involved in during the 1939–41 era, tactical German air superiority followed, and it was incumbent on the Allies to catch up.

However, it must also be remembered that the air forces arrayed against the *Luftwaffe* rarely offered serious opposition. Generally, they were technologically inferior, or in the process of absorbing a new generation of aircraft. The French and Soviet air forces were caught in the middle of major re-equipment programmes. Within the RAF only fighters were at the cutting edge of aerial technology while their bombers were obsolete, rendering close air support operations untenable. Additionally, the doctrines of the air forces confronted was also in a state of flux. The French *Armee de l'Air* was deployed in concert with national strategy, based on static linear defence, akin to the First World War. This allowed the *Luftwaffe* to mass its resources where required and saw the local French air units swamped and destroyed.

The VVS had switched its thinking to a dedicated policy of army support, but the purges and the resulting chaos of the late 1930s and early 1940s left the Red Air Force almost impotent by the time of *Operation Barbarossa*. Still further, aside from the VVS, all the air forces attacked by the *Luftwaffe* were numerically weaker as well as largely technically inferior.

The aerial *blitzkrieg*, more than anything, demonstrated that widening gulf between first rate air powers and other less well-equipped and advanced states. Countries such as Germany, France, Britain and the USSR were able, in theory at least, to produce top class air forces in large numbers but the other states upon which Germany cut its military teeth were not in the same league. Poland, Denmark, Norway, Netherlands, Belgium, Yugoslavia and Greece simply did not have the technical ability or economic capacity, or both, to offer serious aerial resistance to a well-equipped and broadly pre-pared air force such as the *Luftwaffe*. The real test of the *Luftwaffe*'s early war effectiveness came during the French campaign, when technical, training and operational capability handed the German air force its greatest victory. How-ever, its limitations as a major air power were demonstrated over the British Isles, its first campaign against a similarly competent air force, and over the vastness of the USSR, when the physical limits of a broad based air force lacking deep-rooted support were met, reached and found to be wanting.

Maritime air power

The role of air power in the maritime war between 1939 and 1945 appears to be of little significance when compared with the war over Europe itself. Indeed, the nature of maritime air power was largely dictated by the Euro-pean war being a continental based conflict and direct confrontation be-tween Axis and Allied maritime forces, be they air or sea based was limited. Nevertheless, in one respect the deployment of air power by the British was crucial to their survival in the war and, in another, demonstrated clearly the inadequacies of their surface based fleets when confronted with land based air forces. In the Mediterranean, notable operations were carried out, par-ticularly the Royal Navy's raid on Taranto in 1940, but for the most part even this campaign was decided by land based confrontation.

However, the Battle of the Atlantic was one of the pivotal campaigns of the European theatre. On two occasions the German U-boat fleet threatened to close down the Allied shipping lanes into and out of the British Isles, first in 1940/41 and subsequently in 1942/43. The first crisis came in the second winter of the war when Commonwealth trade protection forces alone had to endeavour to keep the transatlantic supply routes open in the face of a determined submarine offensive that came very close to forcing Britain out of the war. Once the German U-boats had access to the French Atlantic ports from the summer of 1940 onwards they were able to operate much further out into the Atlantic and stretch the trade protection forces to near breaking point.

The British survived the crisis by organizing and increasing their trade protection forces and one of the most significant roles was played by the aircraft of RAF Coastal Command. Long-range aircraft patrolling ahead and around merchant ship convoys were able to force German U-boats to dive to avoid detection. Once underwater the submarines were unable to keep up with, let alone close, with Allied convoys. While the Allied aircraft lacked the ability to attack and sink U-boats, certainly until 1942/43, their deterrent effect was absolutely crucial to British survival. It did not matter how many U-boats were sunk, the Atlantic campaign was decided by how many merchant ships could be safely escorted across the Atlantic and back again. The role of air power in gaining victory in this first serious attempt by the German U-boats to blockade Britain into surrender was crucial and is often underestimated.[28] The value of sufficient air cover was often disputed by advocates of the bomber offensive who wanted all available long-range bomber aircraft used to attack Germany directly. This left Coastal Command short of the resources it needed to secure the shipping lanes. The fact that defeat in the Atlantic would in fact have meant defeat in the war as a whole curiously evaded the minds of those who saw no value in the redeployment of a small fraction of the Allied air forces to keep the U-boat menace at bay.[29]

The second U-boat crisis to face the Allies came in 1942 and 1943, first when German submarines had free rein over the eastern seaboard of the USA prior to the Americans properly organizing their anti-submarine defences, and then latterly during the mid-Atlantic air gap fiasco. This second issue arose due to a lack of "very-long-range" Liberator aircraft being allocated to mid-Atlantic air patrols. Other shorter range aircraft simply did not have the range to cover the passage of convoys right across the Atlantic, and consequently German U-boats took to attacking Allied convoys in this so-called mid-Atlantic air gap. That it took until April/May of 1943 for this gap to be closed when the resources were available over a year before again seems mystifying, but such aircraft as were available were earmarked for the Pacific by an unhelpful US Navy, and for the bombing offensive by the RAF and the USAAF. Undoubtedly the lack of central direction for the Atlantic air forces and the determined and single-minded approach of the "bomber barons" were the root causes, but the overall strategic direction of the Allied forces must be open to criticism.

Table 6.1 – U-boat losses to RAF Coastal Command, 1939–45, % of total losses

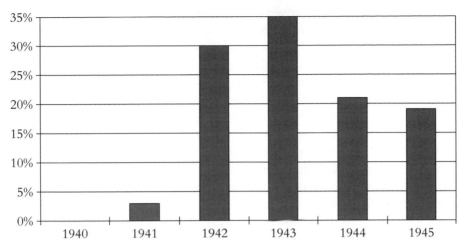

Source: Buckley, *The RAF and trade defence*, p. 186.

The importance of air power in defeating the U-boat threat principally rested with the simple deterrent effect of patrols, but from 1942 onwards the offensive capability of the RAF's Coastal Command dramatically increased. The use of operational research techniques and the incorporation of new technologies helped to tilt the balance decisively in favour of the Allies. The German submarine fleet countered with radar and radar detection advances of their own, but mirroring the war as a whole, as 1943 went on their ability to keep up with the Allies' leaps in air power technology declined. Coastal Command accounted for the destruction of more U-boats than any other service in the last three years of the war. The Germans pushed the limits of U-boat design still further and the new Type XXI model threatened to negate the aerial advantage of the Allies. However, the damage had been done and the war was drawing to a close with air power having contributed significantly to victory in the Battle of the Atlantic. It was clear once again that mobilizing the scientific and industrial communities for modern war was essential.

Air power's growing superiority over surface shipping was also demonstrated during the war in Europe, principally by the Germans. Whereas the British relied heavily on their surface navy to provide protection to seaborne operations, the Germans, lacking a sizeable naval arm of their own, were forced to use aircraft to combat the Royal Navy's (RN's) supremacy. The RN, lacking effective carrier based air power, proved to be extremely vulnerable to land based air attack as demonstrated during the Norway debacle of 1940, in the defence and evacuation of Crete in 1941 and off Malaya when the *Prince of Wales* and *Repulse* were sunk in December of the same year. The necessity of air cover for the RN in 1940 if it were called upon to break up a German invasion force seems therefore even more vital. The scant carrier based air forces of the RN did play a sporadic role in the European theatre, crippling the Italian navy at Taranto, bringing about the destruction of the German battleship, *Bismarck*, in 1941 and in offering air cover to convoys, although this became prohibitively expensive if deployed within range of enemy air forces.

Ultimately, the role of maritime air power in the European war was, aside from the Atlantic campaign, largely peripheral to the outcome of the war. Nor did such air power in Europe keep pace with the advancements of the US and Imperial Japanese navies. This however, is not necessarily a severe criticism. It should be remembered that strategic constraints and requirements shaped the progress of air power and the need for advanced carrier fleets in Europe was small. The British, with limited resources, viewed Europe as a higher priority than the Far East, where it was hoped that the USA would support British interests against the increasingly belligerent Japanese.

Arguably the one area where the European based nations failed to appreciate the value of air power was in the trade war. For the British this was a fundamental failure. As an island state highly dependent of sea communications and trade links, the strategic need for air cover of such routes was imperative, and it was a need that had been demonstrated by the First World War. However, such a failing was repeated more emphatically by the Japanese, and the Germans too, for the most part, did not truly recognize the potential of trade war, hence the small number of U-boats available on the outbreak of war.

Industry, science and technology

The demands of air power on aero-economies and their supporting industries during the Second World War were huge. While the direct impact of air power on the conduct of war had contributed greatly to the creation of what is now loosely termed "total war", the secondary impact of the air power revolution, on economies and aero-industries, also brought about the development of the new type of war. As has been stated, air power was much more expensive both to develop and maintain as an effective military force. Its unit cost in research, design and personnel training surpassed even the most expensive use of resources on the army or navy. Still further, the

cost of keeping an air force operational in wartime conditions grew enormously as wastage and attritional rates, as well as accelerating obsolescence,
threatened to swallow up available aero-industry resources. Already in the
late 1930s the rate of technological progress in aircraft design and technology
had stepped up dramatically, increasing demands on industry and still further
on a state's scientific base. Far more than in the Great War, the effectiveness
of air power was to be dictated by technological advances and invention and
indeed, the ability of a state's aero-industry to keep up with or even surpass
the technology of the enemy was essential to success.

The cornerstones of success were essentially twofold. First, a state had to
be able to maximize its productive capacity to maintain and expand its air
power potential. It was clear that effective air forces were crucial to modern
warfare and the ability of industry to provide the aircraft and equipment
required was essential. In this industrial war, the Allies were to be considerably more successful than their Axis opponents. The roots of the decline of
the *Luftwaffe* as an important fighting force from 1941 onwards can in part
be traced to the failings and inefficiencies of the German aero-industry in
maintaining its lead developed during the pre- and early-war years. In part
this decline was linked to the second pivot of air power success: the ability
to harness and integrate all that science, technology and mass-production had
to offer. Again, in this field the Allies were to leap ahead of the Axis powers
as the war progressed. Although the Germans were able to design new
aircraft and develop cutting edge technologies, they were palpably unable to
produce them *en masse*, resulting in the growing inferiority of *Luftwaffe*
aircraft not only in terms of numbers but also in levels of technical capability.

For example, the Messerschmitt Bf109 was the backbone of the German
fighter arm throughout the Second World War and, indeed, in 1939–40 it
was equal to the Spitfire, the leading Allied design. However, Allied fighter
aircraft designs developed markedly as the war went on, resulting in new
superior types such as the Tempest, Thunderbolt, Mustang and Lightning,
all of which were available in huge quantities. Of the *Luftwaffe* replacements
only the Focke-Wulf FW190 was introduced with widespread impact, although of course it was still massively outnumbered, and later jet designs
such as the Messerschmitt Me 262 were hampered by production problems,
ambitious specifications and political meddling.[30]

In addition, the production war was not just about aircraft design, but
rested equally on the development of supporting technology. Again the
Allies were able to outstrip the Axis powers in Europe by maintaining a high
level of technical input into the air war, an input which Germany could not
match indefinitely with such limited resources. With tremendous effort, near
parity was maintained until 1943 when the Allies surged ahead leaving the

Table 6.2 – Aircraft production, 1939–45

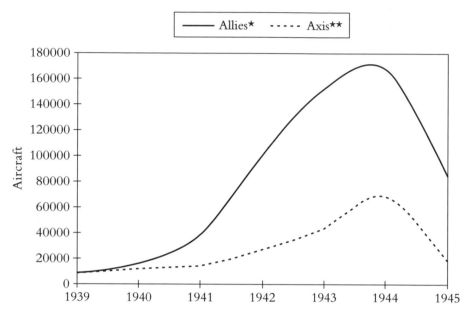

* = Britain and Commonwealth, plus USSR from 1941 and USA from 1942. Does not include France.
** = Germany, plus Italy between 1940–43 and Japan from 1942.
Source: Overy, *The air war*, p. 150.

Germans trailing in their wake. Once behind it was clearly beyond the Axis to catch up.

Allied success was based on a number of inherent and created advantages. The initial states of the British and US economies lent themselves to rapid expansion, for both had a pool of untapped labour, a legacy of the 1930s. Moreover, in the pre-war years, western economies had concentrated upon capital goods production – the end product – whereas their German counterparts had, in an effort to defeat unemployment, developed heavy industry. During the exigencies of war it proved highly problematical to solve difficulties in end production, and German output suffered as a result, while the Allies found it much easier to harness pools of labour and resources and forge them into the required industries.

The most important factor in the development of Allied superiority lay in the identification, at a high level, of major air power expansion as a strategic precursor to success. From 1936/37 for example, the British began preparing for a potential wartime expansion of its aero-industry. A framework was put in place such that if war broke out it could be quickly filled and used to facilitate rapid increases in aircraft production. The shadow scheme was one particular example whereby a company from another sector of industry would begin producing aircraft by copying the practices and production techniques of a successful aeroplane manufacturer. This allowed boosted production, without each new company having to endure a long and arduous procurement process, and concentrated technical development with experienced firms.

The identification of air power as a crucial component in long-term national strategy was a key factor in Allied success, and both the capitalist West and communist East aimed to make aircraft production a major priority. All intended to push their industries to the utmost in order to maximize output. The British revised their monthly output upwards to 3,000, while the USA, once embroiled in the war, intended to reach a target of 125,000 aircraft per year.[31] Soviet aircraft production was already the largest in the world in 1939, but plans were in hand for the transfer and development of production east of the Urals, in order to be able to survive a German assault.

German planning was much less ambitious, with the result that as higher targets were not even aimed at they were never going to be attained. Greater concentration was placed on the army's needs and this was linked with the belief that a war was unlikely to last very long anyway. Thus improvements in aircraft production beyond what had already delivered *Luftwaffe* superiority by 1939 were deemed unnecessary. In any case, Goering had the existing aero-industry working to capacity, or more precisely, what was considered "capacity" by a slack and inefficient planning administration.[32] The willingness to accept the *status quo* was in part caused by Goering's attempts to demonstrate to Hitler that he was doing his utmost and that everything possible was being squeezed out of the German aero-industry, and partly caused by the continuing underestimation of British aircraft production. There were no major plans for realistic expansion in the German aero-industry until the mid-war period, and by then it was much too late. Clearly, the Axis powers did not match strategic requirements with economic demands and by not even attempting to reach high production targets until 1942 they undoubtedly hindered their efforts.[33]

Planning and administration were yet more areas where the Allies held considerable advantages and the development of an integrated approach to aircraft procurement and production was something the Germans could not match, despite considerable effort. The British created the Ministry of Aircraft Production under the tutelage of Lord Beaverbrook, the Americans had the Aircraft Production Board and the Soviets the Commissariat for Aviation directed by Kaganovich and Yakovlev, all bodies which for the most part were effective and willing to wield power as necessary. Decision making was linked to an integrated process combining government, industry and science, all backed up with a flexible and responsive body of administrators.

In contrast, in Germany the central planning process was disparate, confused and severely hindered by Nazi ideology and the nature of the German state and its corresponding parts. Essentially, Germany was a fragmented society with many competing interests and struggling power groups. Debate will continue as to whether this was deliberately engineered by Hitler in order to retain power, or as seems more likely, that such confusion reigned because of the inefficiency and inadequacies of the Nazi regime. But it is sufficient to state that it was not conducive to effective production management, especially in the field of air power, more reliant than any other on the close co-ordination and integration of various parts of the economy and state. The problem was not aided by the power wielded by the military over the production process and the inability of Goering to restrain the competing parts of his personal empire. One facet of the German failure was Goering's placement of party lackeys in important positions, positions for which they were clearly not suited.[34] It has even been argued that poor organization and planning led to more production being squandered than was lost to Allied bombing.[35]

Inefficiencies in production were not aided by the German preoccupation with diversity and technical excellence. Both are ultimately requirements in modern warfare – a suitable variety of high quality equipment necessary to do the job – but balance must be maintained as to the level at which pursuit of the most effective designs starts to undermine front-line strength. Yet again, it was a lesson learned well by the Allies, but never clearly understood by the Axis powers. Whereas the Allies standardized around a small number of aircraft designs of sufficient military capability, the German procurement process resulted in the development of 86 models, fatally dissipating effort and technical ability.[36] In this, the role of Ernst Udet was particularly important, prone as he was to manipulation by eager aircraft manufacturers. The results of his inadequacies became clearer when Erhard Milch returned to prominence in 1941, following Udet's suicide. Milch was effectively forced to abandon the next generation of aircraft being developed by the *Luftwaffe* because they would not be in service for some time, and production of aircraft for the front line was desperately required immediately.[37] Hence his decision to make the *Luftwaffe* soldier on with modified but ageing designs in order to fill the gap in output in the short term. Ultimately Milch's gamble failed but there was little else that could be done at the end of 1941.

Later programmes, aimed at developing a generation of new aircraft one step ahead of the Allies, resulted in excellent designs with considerable potential. However, they were hampered by Germany's crumbling war effort, lack of resources and yet further political meddling, the most famous case being Hitler's insistence on the Me262 jet fighter being modified to act as a bomber. Moreover, in the case of the V1 and V2 weapons, they consumed vast amounts of resources with few tangible benefits. It is estimated that, in the closing stages of the war, the "V" programmes consumed the equivalent resources required to produce 24,000 fighter aircraft, and it is clear where these resources would have been better deployed.[38]

In contrast, the Soviets concentrated on quantity and adequate quality. By basing the development of the VVS in essence around two fighters, the Yakovlev 9 and the Lavochkin 5, and two bombers, the Ilyushin 2 Shturmovik and Petlyakov 2, all rugged and dependable designs, the VVS sacrificed a modicum of technical innovation as a price for simplifying the production process.[39] Moreover, the Western Allies were able to standardize around modern aircraft that were either in the early stages of procurement on the outbreak of war, or were able to improve and develop existing designs to a greater degree than the Germans and then mass-produce them quickly. In part this came as a result of the close integration of military and civilian personnel in the production process, a fusing which proved far smoother and easier than in Germany. Importantly, the sophisticated mass-production processes, eschewed by the Germans as capable of producing only cars and refrigerators, enabled a two way process by which new ideas and innovations could be introduced without fouling up production to a detrimental level. The procurement and introduction of the Rolls-Royce Merlin engine equipped Mustang in 1943 was a classic example of the responsive nature of the Allied production process.[40]

The second cornerstone of Allied success lay in the field of science and technology, an area in which the Axis were slowly but surely emasculated as the war went on. The integration of technology and science into the air war was critical because, more than any other arm, aircraft required protection from obsolescence to remain viable. The Allies again mobilized their scientific communities to considerable effect, indeed to a level the Germans could not match. Technology was crucial in areas such as radar, navigation and bombing in particular, but in most aspects of the air war the need to harness scientific developments was crucial. The British were effective in getting the most out of a weaker scientific base, aided by the enthusiastic support of Churchill (through Professor Lindemann) and indeed the RAF itself, which recognized the vital nature of scientific research and development. In particular, the RAF developed operational research units in each command and these shaped the strategic bombing offensive and the Battle of the Atlantic markedly.[41] The USA started from a much stronger base, but in many ways followed the British pattern. As in Britain, the vital nature of maintaining "cutting edge technology" and utilizing it in a military context was clearly understood. Operational analysis, already well established in the USA, was enthusiastically adopted by the US air forces, again to considerable effect.[42]

The British and Americans were also able to pool their resources to a significant degree, gaining considerable advantages from an expanded scientific community and base. Centimetric radar received a boost from international co-operation and of course the development of the atomic bomb was enhanced in the middle stages by the co-ordination of Allied efforts. Moreover, the Allies had access to the wider world's scientific resources, access which of course was denied to the Axis powers.

For Germany the mobilization of its strong scientific community and establishment proved inordinately difficult, though many problems were self-inflicted. In the same way that the *Luftwaffe* and the Nazi hierarchy failed to appreciate the role civilians and industry had to play in the air war, so they unwittingly contrived to undermine their own scientific efforts. The strength of the German scientific community had already been eroded by the loss of eminent personnel thanks to the nature of the Nazi state, in particular the manner in which it tried to direct research. Many scientists left to work abroad and eventually ended up working for the Allies, thus compounding the failure for Germany.[43] In the direction of its research, Germany was equally lax, not creating a central body until 1944, and in the organization of scientific development, effort was sporadic at best and riddled with party sycophancy. Actual design and research continued to be of a high standard but the poor co-ordination and imbalance in the relationship between state, military and science bodies resulted in dissipation and duplication of effort.[44]

In contrast to the Germans, the Allies took a particularly pragmatic approach to research, emphasizing applied rather than pure research. The harnessing of scientific innovation in a functional military context was the key in the West, whereas Germany's tradition of pure research and invention was more time consuming and restricted rapid application in the military. The contrast in these approaches resulted in short-to-medium term Allied superiority, but in long term developments in jet and rocket technologies, the advantages lay with the Germans, although they would probably have been made redundant by the inadequacies of their mass-production techniques.

Ultimately, the pattern of German failings in scientific development and research mirrored the shortcomings evident in most aspects of the Axis air war effort. Whereas the Western Allies with their pragmatic, flexible and more sophisticated capitalist economies could cope with most of the demands of the air war, the German model could not. Inadequate in central organization and long term planning, prone to political interference and wracked with petty squabbling, it was as much as could probably be expected that Speer and Milch got out of the German economy what they did. Nevertheless, during the Second World War the Allies' supremacy was overwhelming and, more than in any other area, the advantages of the Allies and failings of the Axis were no more ruthlessly demonstrated than in the field of air power.

Land warfare – the Allied recovery in the East

Whereas the *Luftwaffe* began to haemorrhage from 1941 onwards, their enemies began to learn from them and develop their own effective ground support air forces. The VVS and the Western Allies' tactical air forces developed along different paths, reflecting the contrasting nature of the air war on the Eastern and Western Fronts. From the low point of 1941, the VVS, backed by a massive air expansion programme, slowly synthesized its early war experiences into a highly effective tactical air arm doctrine.

The architect of the VVS's major reorganization was General A.A. Novikov, who pushed the Red Air Force even more along the path towards becoming a dedicated army support arm. The last vestiges of strategic air power thinking were effectively marginalized during this period and only some 4 per cent of VVS activity was devoted to long-range bombing throughout the war.[45] Novikov copied some of the tactics employed by the *Luftwaffe*, and tied air units to the army forces they were to support, in a similar fashion to the early development of air-ground co-operation in western armies. By 1943, tactical co-ordination had improved considerably and the introduction of new aircraft and weaponry began to place VVS air power ahead of the *Luftwaffe*, not only in numbers but also in effectiveness.

The aero-industry, forced to relocate by the advancing German army, quickly re-established itself east of the Urals. Much retooling and reorganization had been undertaken since the debacle of the winter war against Finland and the nature of the Soviet economy, which emphasized central planning, aided the expansion of the aircraft industry considerably. Standardization around certain rugged and dependable aircraft designs simplified production matters, although more advanced models were introduced from the mid-war onwards. Despite the chaos and privations caused by the German invasion, Soviet aircraft production increased dramatically from late 1941 onwards, from 1,630 per month in 1941 to 2,907 by 1943.[46] The arrival of lend–lease aircraft from the USA aided the Soviet recovery, but too much is often made of this, for the bulk of the 14,000 deliveries came much later in the war, and only amounted to some 12 per cent of Soviet combat aircraft used in the war.[47]

However, the increase in quantity was matched by simultaneous qualitative progression. The design bureaux expanded significantly during the months leading up to and after 22 June 1941, incorporating new designers such as Yakovlev, Lavochkin and Ilyushin to add to the long established Tupolev and Polikarpov. Obsolescent I-16 fighters were superseded by new Yakovlev and Lavochkin fighter variants. Early Yaks resembled French models, but by 1942/43 Yak-9 and Yak-3 models rivalled the Spitfire and Mustang in performance. The Lavochkin types did not have the same effect as the Yaks but nevertheless, the La-5 and La-7 were capable air superiority fighters. Notably, the VVS mirrored the RAF and the USAAF in using fighter designs as swing-role, fighter-bomber, ground-attack aircraft. However, dedicated heavy ground-attack aircraft such as the Ilyushin Il-2 Shturmovik and the Petlyakov Pe-2 bombers dominated on the Eastern Front where enemy fighters were never available in enough concentration to make their deployment too costly. Notably, the famous Shturmovik was quite vulnerable to high-performance fighters, but its heavy armour gave it excellent protection against anti-aircraft gunfire. As the land offensives swung backwards and forwards across Russia, new types of ordnance appeared in the VVS's inventory between 1942 and 1943, causing consternation in the *Wehrmacht*. Air-to-ground rockets and hollow-charge anti-armour bombs, coupled with the ever increasing numbers of Shturmoviks, and supported overhead by increasingly aggressive VVS fighters, handed localized air superiority to the Soviets wherever they required it.

However, their strategy was notably different from their western counterparts. It was never considered essential, or indeed feasible to attain complete air supremacy across the Eastern Front in the way the combined tactical western air forces sought to dominate western Europe. In part this was also due to the doctrine of tying the VVS to close air support operations only, and thus this prevented a more concerted air strategy from developing. The VVS was used to support the ground offensives by adding its weight to the massive and concentrated firepower the Red Army was able to bring to bear against the *Wehrmacht* by 1943. VVS fighters were deployed primarily to attain local air superiority over the battlefield and prevent the *Luftwaffe* from intervening with any effect. This was certainly successful, but was limited in objective and the *Luftwaffe* was arguably able to survive on the Eastern Front in a way that the RAF and the USAAF never allowed it to in the West. It is notable that diminishing German air resources were deployed on the Eastern Front from the late summer of 1944 because they could survive and have some effect there, while in the West they would be wiped out.

However, the VVS's strategy, or more accurately the Red Army's strategy, should not be criticized unduly. The scale of operations over the Eastern Front was vast, a factor identified by the *Luftwaffe* during and after *Operation Barbarossa*, and the size of force required to mount an air supremacy campaign akin to that in the West would have been beyond even the capacity of the Soviet economy. Moreover, unlike western armies, which used air power to make good the deficiencies in their ground forces, and to keep casualty rates as low as possible, the Red Army was quite effective as it was. Far from being a technically backward mass infantry army as is often perceived in the West, the Soviet forces were a highly effective mass-firepower force, which itself, like its western counterparts, became concerned with diminishing manpower resources by 1944.[48] Air power was a major factor in the increase in effectiveness of Soviet forces from 1943 onwards especially, but they were never as dependent on it as the armies of the Western Allies.

Land warfare – the Allied recovery in the West

For the RAF and the USAAF, the importance of the Mediterranean campaign in the formulation of an effective army support air doctrine was crucial. Whereas the VVS was thrown in at the deep end, the western air forces were able to develop their tactical air forces against much more limited opposition in North Africa and Italy, before applying the lessons *en masse* in the invasion of northwest Europe in 1944.

In the aftermath of their rout from the continent in 1940 the British Army and the RAF began a long debate as to the true role of air power. The RAF, with its more independent background, was able to maintain that air power should be used on a much broader scale than that adopted by the VVS, with the result that air–ground support operations were integrated into a broader air power strategy, which included strategic bombing and, from 1943 onwards, a general air supremacy campaign across Europe.

It was in the Western Desert from 1941 onwards that Air Vice Marshal Arthur "Mary" Coningham (the sobriquet being a corruption of his New Zealand Maori roots) began the formulation of British tactical air doctrine. Coningham's influence on this process was considerable, to such an extent that his model was adopted for the rest of the war, and copied by the USAAF once their own tactical air command structures had been found wanting. British failings in co-ordinating air power with ground offensives in operations up to *Crusader*, General Claude Auchinleck's major offensive of

1941, were largely resolved during the new operation thanks to a new system of air/ground co-ordination. While the ground offensive stalled, the Western Desert Air Force seized local air superiority and allowed effective air interdiction and close air support operations to be carried out.

However, Commonwealth air strength was not enough to gain control of the air, and the *Luftwaffe* was still capable of contesting air superiority to such an extent that air support was not enough to save *Operation Crusader* and, ultimately, Auchinleck's job. Nevertheless, the expanding desert air force continued to improve its tactical capability, reducing response time for air support (radioed request to air strike) from *Operation Crusader*'s two to three hours to Alamein's 35 minutes.[49] In these early days, the Allies utilized the Hurricane and the US Curtiss P-40, or Tomahawk as it was known in the RAF, as swing-role fighter-bombers.[50] The fighter-bomber in World War II had in fact been pioneered by the *Luftwaffe*, but RAF Fighter Command saw bomb equipped Hurricanes and Spitfires as a means of provoking the *Luftwaffe* to engage in aerial combat over France. This strategy produced only limited results, but the fighter-bomber, which was to dominate ground-support operations for the rest of the war, was nevertheless a logical progression from the air superiority campaign over Europe.[51]

The fighter-bomber was an effective air superiority aircraft, quite capable of looking after itself against enemy fighters, while being rugged and fast enough to absorb light flak damage and being too nimble to be hit by heavier anti-aircraft gunnery. The Hurricane and Tomahawk were eventually superseded in 1944 by Hawker Typhoons and Republic P-47 Thunderbolts, the latter being powered by an air-cooled engine which made it less susceptible to flak damage, probably making it the most effective swing-role fighter-bomber of the war. With a frantic air superiority battle raging for much of the 1942–3 period the advantages of the dual-purpose fighter-bomber were apparent. The dedicated ground-attack aircraft were less successful, being vulnerable to heavy flak and to enemy fighters which until 1944 remained a serious threat. In many ways, the success of the Shturmovik on the Eastern Front bucked the trend, but it survived because the density of fighter cover and flak defences was never high enough. It is difficult to imagine the VVS aeroplane surviving for long in the western theatre.

Rommel's final push towards Alexandria and Cairo ground to a halt for a variety of reasons but he was quick to note the value of Allied air power in Montgomery's eventual victory in North Africa. The RAF had gained effective air superiority, eventually attaining air supremacy, and Rommel's supply lines, rear zone and ground forces were attacked constantly. He stated,

The fact of British air superiority threw to the winds all the tactical rules which we had hitherto applied with such success. In every battle to come the strength of the Anglo-American air force was to be the deciding factor.[52]

While the RAF was finding its feet, the USAAF had to endure a similar learning curve. In April 1942 the USAAF had issued its Field Manual FM 31–35, *Aviation in Support of Ground Forces*. Unfortunately it proved to be a cumbersome and ineffective model. In essence it fell into the dispersed penny-packet approach to air support which had hamstrung the French in 1940. As Hallion has stated it was ". . . the kind of system that the British Army had wanted in 1939–41, until experience in the Western Desert taught otherwise".[53] The Battle of Kasserine Pass in Tunisia in 1943 was a dog's breakfast of an operation on the part of the US Army, and its attendant air forces. Each US "mini-air force" was distributed at corps level (too low) and thus was unable, and at times unwilling, to co-ordinate effort to gain air superiority, allowing the *Luftwaffe* to dominate.

The Kasserine fiasco resulted in FM 31–35 being abandoned in favour of FM 100–20, *Command and Employment of Air Power*, perhaps the most clearly laid out model of army air support operations of the war. Its basic three point plan consisted: first of gaining air superiority; secondly, conducting air interdiction operations against the enemy's rear zones to hinder reinforce-ment and resupply; and thirdly, attacking directly, in conjunction with ground forces, the enemy army itself.[54] The Allied tactical air forces largely stuck to these principles, which Coningham had already established in the RAF, and fine tuned them over Sicily and Italy. The most significant problems con-cerned communications, identification of friendly forces and ground–air liaison, and remedies were sought for them. Radio equipped jeeps aided rapid communication between air strikes and ground forces, and light spotter aircraft were adopted for artillery direction, a throwback to the Great War. Later these aircraft were used to control and direct close support and battle-field air-interdiction strikes.[55]

The essential precursor to such army support operations was, at the very least, air superiority and, in the best circumstances, air supremacy. By the time of the Italian campaign in 1943 the *Luftwaffe* had been greatly reduced in numbers and the Allied air forces for the most part enjoyed free rein over the theatre of operations. Additionally, new aircraft were appearing to open up a marked technological gap between Allied and *Luftwaffe* types for the first time. While Kesselring's forces soldiered on with the same models, perhaps slightly improved, such as Bf 109s, FW 190s and Ju 88s, the RAF and the USAAF enjoyed the arrival of P-47 Thunderbolts and P-51 Mustangs to attain air supremacy. As USAAF General Ira Eaker described it, the Mediterranean Campaign was the crucible for the development of Allied tactical air power.[56]

By the time of *Operation Overlord* in June 1944, Allied tactical air forces were able to do as they pleased as the air superiority war over Europe had been won thanks to the decimation of the *Luftwaffe* during *Operation Pointblank*, and especially by the US 8th Air Force following the introduction of the long-range escort, the P-51 Mustang. The fighter losses suffered by the *Luftwaffe* between January and June 1944 were immense: 2,262 pilots were killed, and in March alone 56 per cent of the available German fighters were lost.[57] The disparity in the air forces available for the invasion of France was immense: the Allies could call on 12,000 aircraft to the *Luftwaffe*'s 300.[58] True air supremacy was assured. The only concerted effort by the *Luftwaffe* to intervene in the western theatre from 1944 onwards came during the Ardennes offensive in December 1944. Self-inflicted failings such as shifting operational priorities, the lack of co-ordinated air and ground planning, no clear doctrine of air power employment and poor leadership combined with overwhelming Allied air power and *Ultra* decrypt warnings to cripple *Luftwaffe* efforts. Their intervention came to nothing.[59]

Allied air forces were crucial in preparing the ground for the invasion by crippling the French transportation network with heavy and medium bomber raids from the spring of 1944 onwards, the first major use of the strategic bomber force in an operational support role. From D-minus-46 a concerted bridge destruction campaign was initiated to break routes over the Loire and the Seine, and by D-minus-21 efforts were in hand for the reduction of *Luftwaffe* forces and airbases in Northern France. Airborne troops covered the flanks of the *Operation Overlord* landings themselves, fighters swept the skies of *Luftwaffe* resistance and bombers targeted strongpoints along the coast of Normandy.[60]

The RAF's Second Tactical Air Force and the USAAF's 9th Air Force played a crucial role in Normandy, perhaps more significant than any other army air support campaign of the war. The Allies' ground forces struggled in two particular ways. First, their operational effectiveness was markedly inferior to their German counterparts owing to a combination of: minimal or non-existent battle experience, compared to the Germans' five years or so; an inability to concentrate massed artillery firepower to support land offensives; and the inadequacies of Allied armour, which in sharp contrast to aircraft, was decidedly inferior to German equivalents.[61] The Allied advance from the beachheads acquired on D-Day itself was slow and painful and pre-invasion estimates proved to be highly optimistic. Montgomery, the field commander, suffered considerable criticism prior to the *Cobra* breakout from the American sector of the front at the end of July, but he was unwilling to expend his army's diminishing manpower resources in attritional frontal attacks if he could avoid it. This was the second major restraining influence on the Allied forces.[62]

Air power was the key to solving these basic military and political problems. The Allies' crushing superiority in the air was most certainly a key factor in the success of the Normandy campaign. German forces were hindered and attacked throughout the battle and the offensive against the logistical support of the *Wehrmacht* and SS troops was enormously successful. In general, the Allies won the campaign by a process of heavy attrition, which was often inflicted by Allied aircraft on German units as they advanced towards the battlefront and when they attempted to counterattack.[63]

The success story of ground support air power was again the fighter-bomber which proved the most potent aerial weapon, easily surpassing the effect of medium- and heavy-bomber raids, although latterly, and on occasion, these were usefully deployed.[64] Allied fighter-bombers, of which the RAF's Hawker Typhoon and the USAAF's Republic P-47 Thunderbolt were the main examples, were the bane of the German army's life from Normandy onwards. Such aircraft roamed freely overhead, attacked with little warning and were generally so swift that AA batteries had trouble downing them. The image of the fighter-bomber as a potent tank-killer is, however, something of a myth. The Typhoon especially gained a reputation for "brewing-up" German armour, a reputation that helped to allay some of the fears of the Allied ground forces, which were singularly outclassed by German tanks. In fact, although rocket-firing Typhoons were successful against mobile troops in general, they were largely ineffective at destroying tanks. The safest place on the battlefield during a Typhoon attack was inside a tank because they alone offered sufficient protection against anything other than a direct hit and rockets were notoriously inaccurate. However, German tank crews did not always perceive this to be the case and often baled out of their tanks at the first sign of air attack. Once again, ground troops exposed to air attack demonstrated limited powers of resistance, and in this respect armies of the Second World War followed their predecessors of the 1914–18 conflict. Nevertheless, fighter-bombers were highly successful, for they did cripple German armour: first by destroying its logistical support, and secondly by undermining morale. The number of undamaged but abandoned German tanks found by advancing Allied forces was testament to lack of fuel and lack of resolve in the face of unopposed air assault.[65]

In contrast, the medium and heavy bomber raids used to support Allied breakout attempts from Normandy illustrated decided shortcomings and problems, although they ultimately proved successful. There was already considerable resentment from the strategic air force commanders that their aircraft were being used in this tactical role, for which they were unsuited. There had been no intention of using the heavy-bomber fleets to aid the ground offensives directly but the situation in Normandy demanded it. Certainly, in the case of the crippling blow dealt to the Panzer Lehr division prior to the US *Cobra* breakout the use of four-engined heavy bombers as "super-heavy airborne artillery" could and did work. The carpet-bombing of German forces and defensive units caused stunning paralysis, albeit for a limited period, and rapidly advancing Allied ground troops quickly overran forces subjected to such attacks. Momentum was all too often lost, however. British armour was too slow to follow up the heavy bombing used to prepare *Operation Goodwood* and, as Ian Gooderson argues, fighter-bomber tactical air support would probably have continued to suppress German forces for longer had it been used properly during the battle.[66] During *Cobra* it was and the results were better.[67] Considering that the Allied forces had to learn how to use heavy-bomber support "in harness" during the campaigns across northwest Europe in 1944–5, the effectiveness was considerable. Mistakes and miscalculations were made but the ability of heavy-bombers to demolish and paralyse prepared defensive positions was clear.[68]

Tactical air support of ground operations in World War II developed into a fully fledged doctrine in the western Allied air forces by 1944. The RAF and the USAAF followed similar lines of operational level battlefield support to that pioneered by the *Luftwaffe*, the significant difference being in the resources employed and the application of technology and industry to meet the needs of the armed forces.

The *Luftwaffe*'s almost anti-doctrine approach to the air war, which emerged for a variety of reasons, allowed great operational flexibility, but ultimately undermined its efforts when confronted by a single-minded doctrine such as that of the Soviet VVS and the technical and numerically superior Allied air forces. The VVS, tied more closely to the direct needs of the army, took a narrower view of air operations than the western forces taking little interest in long-range air superiority operations. Consequently, while the *Luftwaffe* simply could not survive in the West by the middle of 1944, it still operated sporadically in the East. This, however, cannot detract from the effectiveness of the VVS in adding to and supporting the general superiority of Red Army operations from 1943 onwards. The attaining of air supremacy was both unnecessary and physically beyond them. Local air superiority was sufficient.

For the West, any measure capable of easing the pain of assaulting German occupied Europe was to be embraced and air power was just such a measure. The combined air offensive against the Axis powers gave the Allies massive superiority. By crushing the *Luftwaffe* the Allies were able to utilize air power as fully as possible. *Operation Overlord* and the rout of the German armies back to the Franco–German border, the destruction of the German Ardennes offensive in December/January 1944/5 and the eventual crossing of the Rhine in 1945 were all made possible by the overwhelming superiority of the Allied air forces. German accounts and reports of the war in the West from 1943 onwards repeatedly claim that air power was the key to Allied success. Even though casualty rates in the ground forces during the Normandy campaign were high (equalling and surpassing those of the Somme offensive of 1916), they would have been decidedly higher, and the forces deployed would have had to have been that much larger, to achieve victory without the level of air support that existed in 1944. [69]

The key to this success of air power was the destruction of the *Luftwaffe* from the middle of 1943 onwards, for without air supremacy the Allied tactical air forces would have had to engage in costly air superiority battles. This would have seriously undermined air support for ground operations and quite possibly compromised the *Operation Overlord* campaign. The ability of an air force merely to contest air superiority at critical moments was fundamental to the role that air power could play in ground operations. Denying prolonged periods of air superiority to the enemy and maintaining a presence over the battlefield greatly reduced the effectiveness of army air support. It was this inability of the *Luftwaffe* to pose any kind of threat to the Allied forces as they swept across France that undermined the considerable efforts of the German army.

The bombing offensive and Allied strategy

The strategic bombing offensives against Germany and Japan during the Second World War have provoked more comment and debate than any other air campaign in the short history of air power. Both on an ethical and a strategic level the rights and wrongs of the offensives have been the subject of a long succession of books, memoirs and articles and will almost certainly continue to elicit speculation and discussion. Clearly, the revolutionary nature of strategic bombing in widening and deepening modern war has been the factor which has set it apart from other uses of air power.

In terms of strategic bombing's impact on the outcome of the war the debate continues. However, despite the ethical and moral issues which surround the use of massed bombers to attack civilians, the value of the Allied bombing offensives to final victory should not be dismissed lightly, as many continue to do.[70] Moreover, when the more wide-ranging effects of the offensive are considered, such as the destruction of the *Luftwaffe* from 1943 onwards and the diversion of scarce resources to the defence of German airspace, then the impact of the offensive appears more pronounced. The Allied victory in Normandy would have been unthinkable without the vast and overwhelming support of the Allied air forces and if the attrition imposed upon the *Luftwaffe* had not been forced by the use of long-range fighter-escorts from late 1943 onwards then such air supremacy would in no way have been as complete. Debate over the strategic bombing offensive has too often been bogged down in retrospective quibbling over the amount of damage (or lack of it) done to the German economy and has glossed over the wider strategic requirements of the time. This is not to assert that mistakes were not made or that strategic bombing fitted neatly into an integrated Allied grand strategy at all times, or indeed that just because the Allies won, the systematic flattening of German cities, particularly from the autumn of 1944 onwards, was entirely justifiable on all counts. However, a wide perspective of the strategic bombing offensive's contribution to Allied victory needs to be appreciated.

The British, or more accurately the RAF, had been speculating optimistically about a future strategic bombing offensive since the end of the First World War. Nevertheless, government enthusiasm had never reached similar levels and indeed support for the creation of the bombing fleet in the 1930s had been based as much on its deterrent value as belief in its war winning capacity. However, as the Second World War developed, strategic bombing was to become a crucial aspect of British national strategy in the wake of the fall of France. While the war had been developing along traditional lines, support from the Chamberlain administration for the bombing of German cities was at best lukewarm and often openly hostile. The arrival of Churchill and the ejection of the British army from the continent changed everything. Britain's strategic position was such that any attempt to reinvade mainland Europe in the foreseeable future, in the face of the German army, had to be ruled out: direct confrontation was not an option. Britain simply did not have the resources or capability to defeat the *Wehrmacht* in open battle. However, Churchill considered prosecution of the war, in whatever form, to be essential. The alternative was tantamount to capitulation.

The British Chiefs of Staff formulated a new strategic plan in August and September 1940, which made the best of Britain's parlous state, offered a rationale for continuing the fight and made the bombing offensive a cornerstone of the war effort. The new strategy rested on three points.[71] First, Germany would be subjected to blockade to undermine the German economy, which the British considered susceptible to such indirect attack. The emphasis here was placed on weakness in raw materials, especially oil. Secondly, Britain was to adopt a policy of subversion, which included the raising of underground armies across Europe which would rise up at the appropriate moment to link up with a returning British army. The way would be prepared by the undermining of morale in Germany itself by a combination of covert activity and propaganda, and the third strand to British strategy, strategic bombing. Bombing would cripple the German economy, weaken the resolve of the people and bring the Nazi state to the point of collapse, at which point the underground army would rise up, and the British liberator army would return to Europe to mop up resistance.

In retrospect, the strategy was clearly constructed out of desperation and blind faith, for it relied on three routes to victory, two of which (bombing and subversion) had never really been tried before and the other (blockade) that had only ever worked in conjunction with traditional military offensives. The need for strategic bombing to work was clear: without it, and in a world where Britain and the Commonwealth were still acting alone, there was no hope of victory – merely survival. The importance was famously stated by Churchill in July 1940 when he claimed that the only way for Britain to defeat Germany in the circumstances of 1940 was to crush Hitler's state with ". . . an absolutely devastating exterminating attack by very heavy bombers".[72]

There were other pressing political forces at play. Churchill realized that Britain had to be seen to be acting aggressively in some way against Germany or morale at home would suffer. The belief among the population that the Germans were handing out crushing blows at will, against which the British could not respond at all, would eat away at the people's resolve and undermine all future efforts. The British people had to know and had to be shown that the armed forces were still fighting and that the German population was suffering too.

Still further, Churchill realized the vital necessity of eliciting US support and, importantly, material aid. Such help might well be compromised if the USA did not consider Britain reasonably secure and capable of furthering American political aims. The strategic bombing offensive was perhaps the only way of demonstrating to the Roosevelt administration that Britain was still fighting and was worth supporting. To this end it was arguably successful, considering the US government's attitude towards air power.[73]

In a similar manner, once the USSR had become embroiled in the war, the bombing offensive was the only realistic means the British had for supporting the Soviet struggle, however indirectly and limited it may have been. Stalin repeatedly called firstly for the British and then the USA to invade northwest Europe to relieve pressure on the Eastern Front. The

British understood that if the Soviets considered they were fighting Hitler single-handedly their resolve might crumble resulting in either surrender or some form of political deal. Strategic bombing of German cities was sold to Stalin, especially during his meeting with Churchill in 1942, as a realistic and important method of defeating Hitler. Indeed, Stalin was more impressed by the levelling of German cities by Allied bombers than by the arrival of Anglo-American forces in northwest Africa in November 1942 (*Operation Torch*).[74]

The USA did not need to rely on bombing to achieve victory. Although Roosevelt and his administration had become enthusiastic supporters of air power, and although the USAAF had been planning to conduct a strategic bombing campaign since the 1920s, there was no necessity for it to succeed. Nevertheless, Churchill, repeated scaremongering stories from Europe and US army intelligence reports, had effectively sold the idea of strategic bombing to Roosevelt, who along with Stimson, at the very least considered it a vital precursor to the invasion of northwest Europe.[75] Being particularly conscious of public opinion, the notion that bombing would prepare the way and make the job of the ground forces much easier and less costly in lives, also made the US administration firm supporters of the bombing offensive. Some in the USAAF, like the RAF, believed that bombing alone could win the war, but the combined resources of the USA, the USSR and Britain and the Commonwealth meant that it was no longer pivotal to Allied success. The war was to be won by a combined offensive of land, air and sea forces.

Thus, the place of strategic bombing in Allied strategy became less distinct after 1941 and it was not until the middle of 1943 that the combined bombing offensive became fully integrated into grand strategy, when, in addition to the more general aim of crippling the German economy, the destruction of the *Luftwaffe* and its attendant industries was cited as a main priority.

The early years of the bombing offensive seemed to indicate that the British strategy of 1940 was wholly unrealistic. Although the RAF had been pressing for the acceptance of strategic bombing as a viable method of prosecuting war since the 1920s, little of real value had been done to deal with the practicalities of conducting such a campaign. Navigation, aerial defence, bomb aiming and doctrinal development in general had been neglected, in part resulting in inflated expectations on the outbreak of war. Indeed, it is paradoxical that the nation which developed a highly sophisticated air defence system, and demonstrated its effectiveness against unescorted bombers in 1940 ignored the resulting implications and proceeded to mirror the mistakes of the *Luftwaffe*.

The fundamental philosophy of the RAF's bomber barons since the days of Trenchard's dubious influence on bombing policy was based on the breaking of enemy morale. (See Chapter Four.) This however, had been rejected in the years leading up to the outbreak of war in favour of bombing industrial and economic targets, thus bringing British thinking in line with the US Army Air Corps. From the autumn of 1937, Bomber Command started to consider what to target in Germany, but the degree of careful investigation into the most effective targets, and importantly how to hit them was still superficial.[76]

Once "unleashed" on the orders of Churchill in the summer of 1940, Bomber Command suffered a rude awakening over Germany. Daylight raids resulted in very heavy losses and were soon abandoned in favour of night raids, in the hope that this would evade the *Luftwaffe*'s preying fighters. To a degree this was successful, but it resulted in the increasing inaccuracy of bombing, which was already poor. The Butt Report of 1941, which was based on photo-reconnaissance information, was the first real test of Bomber Command's record. It was damning indeed and even Churchill's faith in the offensive was undermined. Its findings were that only some 20 per cent of bomber crews were getting within five miles of the target. Indeed, so inaccurate were the bombing raids, that the German authorities were often at a loss as to what the RAF was attempting to hit. Moreover, as losses at the hands of the increasingly sophisticated German night-fighters increased, with sinkings of merchant shipping in the Atlantic to U-boats for want of long-range bomber type aircraft mounting and with growing demands for more air resources to be used to support the Mediterranean campaign, the whole basis of the bombing offensive seemed to be about to collapse.

The campaign was saved by three factors. First, in February 1942 the Air Staff switched the premise of the offensive from destroying particular industrial targets to one based on a strategy of general area attacks on cities. This, it was hoped would hinder the German economy by dehousing, demoralizing and killing workers both at work and in their homes. Trenchard's philosophy was therefore, in part, resurrected by pressing circumstance. The RAF's new strategy was endorsed by Churchill's influential scientific advisor, Professor Lindemann (later Lord Cherwell).[77]

Secondly, Arthur Harris was appointed as the Commander-in-Chief of RAF Bomber Command in February 1942 and his influence was both marked and impressive. Whatever his detractors were to say later, he was a major factor in pulling Bomber Command together in 1942 and his single-minded determination, perhaps later a disadvantage, was ideal at this stage of the war. Paradoxically, he was not a true believer in the Air Staff's new morale-cracking stratagem, but did see significant possibilities in the straight-forward disintegration of Germany's industrial infrastructure using the policy of area bombing.

Finally, the Japanese attack on Pearl Harbor and the subsequent German declaration of war on the USA brought the Americans into the war. Agreed Allied strategy was predicated on the "Germany first" principle, and the USAAF was a firm and ardent supporter of strategic bombing and the potential of a joint offensive offered possibilities that it would have been foolish to ignore.

USAAF plan AWPD-1 (Air War Plans Division) called principally for the targeting of electrical power, transportation, oil and the German aero-industry, although in certain circumstances a final psychological morale-cracking knockout blow was to be considered.[78] The USAAF's plan was in essence to try just what the RAF had abandoned and was now telling its American cousins was unworkable: precision, daylight raids over Europe. Vicarious learning is difficult at the best of times and despite warnings from the RAF, the Americans were determined to test the capabilities of the B-17 Flying Fortress bomber and their own air battle doctrine.[79] Early efforts were often restricted to targets in northern France and within range of Allied fighter escorts, but when the US 8th Air Force (the strategic air force in Britain) began operating over Germany itself and started to encounter the *Luftwaffe* in strength, losses mounted and faith in the US techniques began to be questioned. The German fighters rapidly developed new tactics for dealing with the higher defensive firepower of the US bombers, which in any case proved somewhat less effective than pre-war US doctrine had presumed.[80] Both bombing offensives were slowly improving and the learning curve of the US forces was much steeper than its British counterpart, but by the end of 1942 little had been achieved that could be said to have noticeably influ-enced the course of the war, even including the much publicized 1,000 bomber raid on Cologne.

The Casablanca Conference of January 1943 sought to put the bomber offensive to the forefront of Allied strategy, but its directive was a fudge because Harris wanted to persist with the area strategy while Ira Eaker, the commander of the 8th Air Force, wanted to pursue the precision bombing policy. The conference, in effect, allowed both to go their own way, opaquely mentioning both morale and industry as the prime targets of the newly named combined bombing offensive.[81]

Efforts in 1943 again demonstrated an up-turn in the campaign. In July the RAF launched a major raid on Hamburg in which a high proportion of incendiary bombs (designed to burn rather than blast) were deployed. Due to the hot weather and dry conditions parts of Hamburg burned with such ferocity, possibly reaching temperatures of 1,000 degrees Celsius, that all the oxygen was used up and more was sucked in from outlying areas creating what became known as a "firestorm". The consequences were appalling with asphyxiation and incineration accounting for many of the 30,000–40,000 dead. The firebombing of Hamburg caused considerable consternation in Germany, with Albert Speer's comment that six more raids of that nature and the war would have been over being the most interesting, though he was later to moderate his statement.[82] The RAF was improving its accuracy and navigational prowess with the introduction of the latest electronic technology such as *Oboe*, *Gee*, and H_2S, while the excellent Avro Lancaster heavy-bomber began to constitute the backbone of the command's strength. Short term advantages were also gained by the deployment of aids such as *window*, which consisted merely of metal foil strips cut to the appropriate length to blind German radar. However, Harris' greatest effort, the attempted destruction of Berlin over the winter of 1943–4, resulted in excessive casualties to his command and failed to cripple Germany as he had hoped. The US 8th also failed in its disastrous double raid on the ball bearing factory at Schweinfurt in August and October. Marked out as a crucial chokepoint in the German economy, the US bombers suffered grievously in their attempts to destroy the complex. Some success was achieved but not even the USA could endure casualty rates of over 68 per cent.[83]

Eaker had already indicated that he believed that the destruction of the *Luftwaffe* and the gaining of air supremacy over Europe was the key to success: hence the *Pointblank* directive of May 1943 which called for the persistent targeting of the German aero-industry. However, he failed to appreciate the significance of his bombers' vulnerability to German interceptors, unless escorted by Allied fighters. This was to prove the breakthrough in the combined bomber offensive and was to have major consequences beyond the direct bombardment of Germany itself. The doctrine of the USAAF had been founded on the notion that the bomber would always get through. In any case, it was argued, fighters simply did not have the endurance to allow them to escort bombers over any great distance. Attempts to create long-range fighters had always foundered, resulting in low performance, heavy, twin-engine fighters, such as the *Luftwaffe*'s Bf 110, a design quite unable to cope with enemy high-performance single-engine fighters. However, it was clear to General "Hap" Arnold (Commander-in-Chief, USAAF) by the middle of 1943 that the only way the *Luftwaffe*'s fighter strength could be neutralized was by sending US escort fighters to do battle around the bomber formations as they travelled to and from their targets. The key to this was finding a fighter that would be able to fly to Berlin and back.[84]

Although the P-47 Thunderbolt was the first to give the *Luftwaffe* a nasty shock in July 1943 by operating with fuel-filled drop-tanks well inside Germany, it was the P-51 Mustang design that was to transform the air war over Europe. Simple improvements to the internal fuel capacity, as well as the addition of drop-tanks, enabled the high-performance Mustang, along with the Thunderbolt and the twin-engine Lightning, to fly into German airspace with the US 8th's bombers and begin tackling the German fighter arm in a series of bloody attritional battles. In January 1944 USAAF policy was altered to put their escort fighters on an offensive footing. It was their job to seek out the *Luftwaffe* while escorting the bombers and to do battle with them. Conversely, at the same time Goering ordered his fighter arm to take up a more careful and defensive posture when confronted by Allied escort fighters, to keep losses down. Adolf Galland, the *Luftwaffe* fighter commander in western Europe, later claimed that this was a considerable error in judgement.[85]

The breakthrough in the air campaign came in late-February 1944 in what was later titled "Big Week". A period of clear weather allowed the USAAF to begin a series of substantial raids on German aircraft production plants, which continued into March and then switched to targeting oil production before being used to support the Normandy landings. The *Luftwaffe* was forced to come up and fight and, although they inflicted heavy losses on the US bomber fleet (some 20 per cent were written-off in February), the cost to the German fighter arm was immense.[86] By attempting to intervene and engage the USAAF in air superiority battles the *Luftwaffe* opened itself up to heavy "imposed" attrition, attrition which the USAAF could cope with but with which the Germans could not. Moreover, the P-51 was greatly superior to the German interceptors, many of which had been slowed down by the addition of heavy armaments to increase their effectiveness against large bombers.

With US fighters arriving in ever growing numbers and beginning to shoot the *Luftwaffe* out of the skies, realization dawned that control of German airspace was being lost. Albert Speer recorded that Goering had always claimed that Allied fighters would never be able to reach Germany. When they did, it was clear the war was lost.[87] As loss rates soared, the growing problem of replacing the pilots, even more than their aircraft, began to appear insurmountable. Between January and May 1944 the *Luftwaffe* lost the equivalent of its entire fighter pilot strength, meaning that replacements could only just keep up with losses. Thus, no expansion of the fighter arm could take place at the very time the Allied air forces were encroaching ever further and in greater numbers into German airspace. While Milch and Speer made exceptional efforts to increase aircraft production, although largely

Table 6.3 – German fighter pilot loss rate, January 1942–May 1944

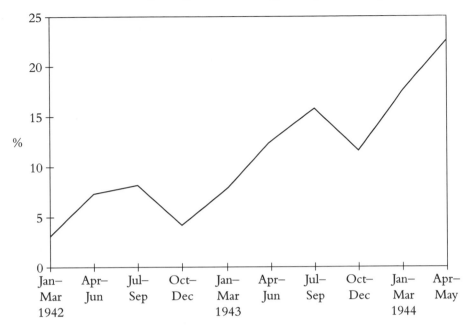

Source: Murray, Luftwaffe, pp. 310–11.

consisting of single-engined fighters, little could be done to prevent the haemorrhaging of trained *Luftwaffe* aircrew. Pilot training was hit particularly badly by the bombing raids on oil production and by 1944 German pilots had less than half the length of flying time prior to being thrown into the fray than their American and British counterparts. In the months leading up to the Normandy landings the *Luftwaffe* suffered grievous losses to its fighter arm, some 3,278 aircraft being lost resulting in a 78 per cent decline in strength. The battle for air supremacy over Europe had been won and the Allied air forces were able, once they had fulfilled their commitments to D-Day, to pick and choose their targets over Germany at will. For the Germans, rapid defeat came, not as a result of events in 1944, but in part because of the failure to increase production and training programmes in 1940–42. The crucial nature of attrition and industry to air campaigns in total war was no better illustrated than the battle for air supremacy over Europe in 1944, and the investment in long-term air power expansion made by the Allies some years before paid huge dividends.[88]

   In retrospect, it seems strange that it took until mid-to-late 1943 for the Allies to accept that the only way to press home their bomber offensive effectively was to seize control of the airspace over Germany by force. Yet

Table 6.4 – Flying hours in training programmes, 1939–45

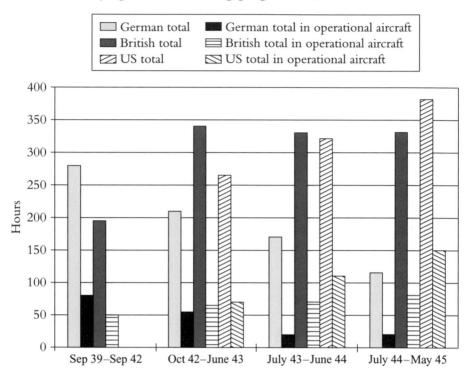

Legend:
- German total
- British total
- US total
- German total in operational aircraft
- British total in operational aircraft
- US total in operational aircraft

Y-axis: Hours

X-axis categories: Sep 39–Sep 42, Oct 42–June 43, July 43–June 44, July 44–May 45

Operational flying hours refers to fighter programme.
Source: Murray, *Luftwaffe*, p. 314.

the USAAF had a clear doctrine when they began their raids in 1942 and it was the failure of the heavily armed bomber formations in 1943 that convinced them that another solution was required. It was testament to the Allies' technical and productive capabilities that the P-51 Mustang, especially, could be adapted in such a short space of time, a feat that would have been quite beyond the capacity of the German aero-industry. It was also true that the introduction of the long-range escort brought the Combined Bomber Offensive more into line with Allied grand strategy. By attacking the *Luftwaffe* systematically, the USAAF's policy brought huge advantages in other areas of the war, such as the elimination of the *Luftwaffe* in France. This was because Goering had had to deploy what was left of the *Luftwaffe*'s fighter strength to defend Germany itself, thus depriving Rundstedt and Rommel of any kind of credible air support in the crucial campaign in Normandy in 1944.

The later stages of the bombing offensive in many ways caused the greatest controversy. First, Allied policy in the autumn of 1944 emphasized the value and importance of targeting oil production in Germany, which was viewed as a critical chokepoint in the German war machine. Considerable success was achieved in this area, but criticism was and has been levelled at Arthur Harris that he did not prosecute the campaign as fully as he might have because he did not believe it to be effective. Throughout the war he had argued that "panacea-mongering" would not solve anything. The only way to achieve results was to concentrate on area bombing. On many occasions he had been proved right, not least over the USAAF's Schweinfurt disaster, but on the oil offensive even Harris accepted after the war that he may have underestimated the effectiveness of the campaign.[89] At the time, although he opposed the principle of the policy, he did grudgingly carry it out, contrary to the popular perception that he ignored direct orders from above. Recent research has shown that RAF Bomber Command could have contributed little more than it actually did in the winter of 1944–5 to the oil offensive.[90]

However, the controversy that has overshadowed all others concerning the bomber offensive in World War II in Europe was that surrounding the Dresden raid of February 1945. The firebombing of the city by the RAF and the USAAF in which tens of thousands, perhaps as many as 100,000, perished in a firestorm akin to that which had gutted Hamburg in 1943 and was later to devastate Tokyo, caused a storm of protest then and has continued to do so ever since. Whatever the justification for area bombing in the war hitherto, the destruction of a city with little industrial plant, filled with fleeing refugees, at a time when the war was all but over, seemed little more than senseless slaughter. Many arguments have been offered, including: that the raid was a warning to demonstrate to the Soviets the strength of Allied air power; or that Harris was determined to prove that area bombing could have won the war; or that the military technology was available so had to be used to justify the investment.

None of these are in themselves an explanation. For example, far from being a purely political act, the Dresden raid was requested by the Soviets to cause the more rapid collapse of German resistance on the Eastern Front, though indeed some in Allied command may have considered the psychological value of a massive raid on the advancing Red Army. Again, although Harris still firmly believed in the area bombing policy, he was not directly responsible for the Dresden raid: this was merely the continuation of a policy in place for three years and which had been reaffirmed by the chiefs of staff only weeks before the attack on Dresden itself. The strategy remained what it had been since 1942 and the issue is not whether an active decision should have been made to destroy Dresden, but whether and if, there should have been a decision not to. Nobody in power considered such a revision of policy necessary until *after* the raid, and by then the achievements of RAF Bomber Command in particular had been tarnished.

Moreover, the selection of targets in the eastern sector was taken over Harris' head. He was merely directed to attack them when possible. It is also worth noting that in January and February 1945, the war was still being fiercely contested by the German armed forces. Although the final outcome may not have appeared to be in doubt, the cost of finishing the war was still high. The Red Army suffered 1,000,000 casualties in its winter/spring offensive to capture Berlin, and the western Allies had only recently fought off the German attack through the Ardennes that was to become known as the Battle of the Bulge. In addition, all the Allies were becoming increasingly concerned about the lack of troop replacements arriving in their front-line units. Loss rates remained excessively high as the Germans continued to resist with determination. Quite simply, there was an understandable desire to end the war as quickly as possible to save Allied lives.

What marks out the Dresden raid was the excessive brutality of its prosecution, which in the aftermath made even the Allied leadership flinch and made the protagonists seek a scapegoat. Harris, with his curious political *naïveté*, was the willing fall guy as, to his credit, he stuck to his principles, however questionable they may have been, when others turned their backs, including Churchill. In contrast, the US 8th carried out a largely successful whitewash of its role in the Dresden raid, repeatedly playing the precision bombing card in the post-war years to prove its innocence. The reality was that the USAAF was following its late-war psychological knockout blow policy worked out back in 1942 and, in any case, in the prevailing poor European weather the USAAF was often less accurate in its bombing than the RAF which had been developing radar assisted bombing for low/non-visibility operations since 1940/41. In many cases, the USAAF resorted to bombing what it euphemistically phrased "marshalling yards", which in truth meant area bombing.[91] What the Americans did well was to distance themselves from the policy of area bombing in a way that Harris never even attempted.

In many ways the Dresden raid has coloured the post-war view of the effectiveness of the bomber offensive. Yet, the impact of strategic bombing on the outcome of the war was immense, on three counts: first, the direct impact on the German economy caused by the physical damage of bombing; secondly, the massive redeployment of resources by the Germans to counter the bombing raids; and thirdly, the imposed attrition on the *Luftwaffe* caused by the bomber offensive, especially from the spring of 1944 onwards.

Table 6.5 – Allied bomb tonnage dropped on Europe, 1940–45

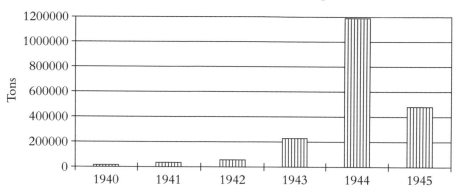

Source: Overy, *The air war*, p. 120.

The area of the debate which has caused most controversy has been that of what the bombing actually did to the German economy and consequently what it contributed to the outcome of the war. Steven Garrett has offered the most recent damning indictment of the strategic bombing campaign, and the RAF's area offensive in particular.[92] In essence, his criticism centres on the two points that German morale never came close to cracking under the weight of the bombing offensive, and more importantly that German war production increased dramatically from 1942 to 1944 in spite of the bombing offensive. Indeed, Garrett argues that bombing probably increased German industrial efficiency by forcing it to pull itself together. There is no doubt that the German war economy did expand significantly following Albert Speer's appointment as Reichsminister of Armaments, but it is spurious to argue that because production increased then bombing had no real impact. As Garrett also argues, there was considerable slack in the German economy that was not taken up until Speer's appointment and it was this, in conjunction with the major reorganization of German industry that brought about the increase in production. Strategic bombing acted as a braking effect on this increase, hampering attempts to expand output by disrupting and crippling the industrial infrastructure of Germany. As Richard Overy has put it, during the last two years of the war the German manager had two battles to fight: one to increase production, the other against the chaos and disruption caused by precision and area bombing.[93] Tank and aircraft production for 1944 was around a third lower than planned and the denial of such resources to the German armies dramatically aided the efforts of the advancing Allied armies. German production targets for 1945 aimed at manufacturing 80,000 aircraft, but dispersal and bombing had reduced the 1944 level

165

to 36,000, just 8,000 more than the Japanese, who did not suffer serious bombing or disperse their industry until late 1944. Bombing clearly kept the expansion of German industrial output to manageable proportions for the Allies.[94]

In addition, the impact on the morale of the German workforce is often overlooked. Around a third of the urban population under threat of bombing had no protection at all during raids, and in major cities they saw some 55–60 per cent of their homes destroyed by the Allied air forces. Mass evacuations were a partial answer for some six million civilians, but this had a severe impact on morale as families were split up and forced to live in difficult and trying conditions for long periods of time. Consequently, morale in the working force exposed to constant bombing slumped as the war went on. By 1944, absenteeism rates of 20–25 per cent were not unusual and in post-war analysis 91 per cent of civilians stated that bombing was the most difficult hardship to endure and was a key factor in the collapse of their own morale.[95]

The debate as to what the offensive actually achieved will go on, but the weight of modern research and opinion appears to back the view that considerable damage was done to the German war economy, hindering output in a variety of ways and contributing to the Allied victory. However, it is also the case that the hope that air power alone would bring about the defeat of Germany was unattainable. Air power worked only when integrated into an overall strategy for the prosecution of the war.

Whatever the direct impact of strategic bombing on the German war economy, the diversion of scant resources to defend the air space over the Third Reich was a major effect of the bomber offensive. The allocation of vast numbers of men and equipment to mount the defence of Germany is all too often ignored by those seeking to criticize the impact of the strategic air offensive. The drain on resources increased significantly as the war went on, diverting in particular guns, ammunition and technical equipment from the front-line armies. By 1944, 33 per cent of artillery production and 20 per cent of ammunition was directed towards anti-aircraft activity, while between one and two million Germans were employed in countering the bombing offensive. In addition, the investment of technology in battling the Allied air forces was a distraction the already straining and disparate German war economy could do without.[96] The argument, often cited, that the resources allocated to the bomber offensive by the Allies exceeded those deployed by the German defenders against them, and therefore was strategically wasteful, is also flawed because the British allocated no more than 12 per cent to the bomber offensive (and probably much less[97]). More importantly, this line of reasoning neglects the fact that the Germans did not have the resources to spare whereas the Allies did. The strategic bombing offensive added a major drain on German resources and, by diverting guns, aircraft, men and technical equipment from the front-line, the strategic balance came down firmly in the Allies' favour.

The third impact of the strategic air offensive was the destruction of the *Luftwaffe*, already mentioned. Critics of the bombing offensive invariably ignore this crucial contribution to victory. Without the threat of the strategic offensive, the *Luftwaffe* would almost certainly have been available to prevent the Allied air forces from influencing the ground war in northwestern Europe to the degree that they did. In view of the decided deficiencies of the Allied armies when dealing with the *Wehrmacht* and the SS on the ground, the lack of such air supremacy could well have been catastrophic.

Linked to this debate, it is often argued that the Allies could have used their air power resources in other more effective ways. The defeat of the U-boats for example, could have been achieved much earlier than it was, if long-range bombers had been diverted to such operations in early 1942. This is certainly true, but the numbers required to close the mid-Atlantic air gap were tiny, and it was more single-minded myopia that allowed the air gap to remain open until Spring 1943. In addition, although the Atlantic could have been made secure a year earlier, this would have had little effect on the outcome of the war. The US had little else to ship across to Europe until 1943 anyway, by which time the Atlantic campaign had been won.[98]

Yet another argument is that significant damage could have been done to the German economy by fast precision raids by large numbers of smaller accurate bombers, such as the Mosquito. This is flawed on two counts. First, it is simply not logical to assume that the Germans would or could not mount an effective defence against such attack in the same way that they blocked the four-engined bombers for so long. Secondly, these bombing tactics would never have crippled the *Luftwaffe*'s fighter strength and, as has been argued, this was one of the most significant contributions to Allied victory.

Finally, it has been stated that the resources allocated to the strategic force would have been better employed in the tactical role, supporting ground offensives. Again this is open to question, as the Allies had complete air supremacy over northwest Europe from the spring/summer of 1944, and there was little else it could contribute – there were still limits to the capabilities of aircraft to intervene in the ground war. Generally, it was an example of the resource advantage enjoyed by the Allies that they were able to provide tactical air supremacy over Europe as well as conducting a major strategic bombing campaign and creating ground forces capable of mounting the D-Day landings. The "resource" argument holds only if another use for such resources could be found that would have contributed more significantly to a more rapid Allied victory than strategic bombing, and those cited arguably would not.

There is little doubt that the strategic bombing offensive contributed greatly to Allied victory in World War II. However, the debate is so wrapped up in ethical and moral issues that the reality has been clouded by post-war indignation, in particular over the bombing of Dresden, Tokyo and of course the atomic bombings of Japan. In isolation the deaths of half-a-million German civilians as a result of aerial bombing in World War II when the war had to be won by Allied ground forces anyway seems obscene. Yet, when the war as a whole is considered and the wider implications of the bomber offensive appreciated, the justifications offered for the actions of the RAF and the USAAF in aiding Allied victory and defeating the Nazi regime are understandable. In strategic terms, the necessity and value of the combined bombing offensive to Allied victory is irrefutable.

Conclusions

The Second World War was undoubtedly the high point of so-called "total war". More than any other conflict, the demands made of a nation's resources – industrial, scientific and indeed moral – between 1939 and 1945 were immense. The sheer scale of the war at first seems to be the cause of its totality, with 40 million people dead, whole nations devastated and the end of the European order being some of the illustrations. However, in addition to the size of the conflict, the Second World War was total because of the nature of the fighting, and perhaps the single most important change was brought about by the coming of age of air power. Brutal and bloodthirsty war had long been known, but the depth and impact of air war went much further in striking at the heart of western society both in a physical and psychological manner. Air power demanded mass mobilization of economies, industries and scientific establishments to a degree hitherto unknown. As a measure of a state's ability to wage total war, air power was by far the most useful yardstick, as only a few were able to meet the challenge of fusing technical know-how with mass production in this most demanding of fields. By 1945, it was clear that the USA had all the necessary strengths and capabilities and, of the other powers, only Britain and the USSR had to lesser degrees kept up. Germany and Japan had most obviously failed not only to mobilize their resources effectively to meet the challenge of this new type of war, but had also failed to appreciate the impact air power could have on the conduct of war. The consequences of their myopia were profound: by the middle of the war, air power was becoming the key weapon in the effective application of resources to strategic ends. In contrast, the Allies, both at strategic and tactical levels, had developed such awesome air potential that they became able to exercise crushing battlefield superiority, in the western Allies' case making good considerable ground force deficiencies. One only has to read the accounts of German generals, desperately fighting constant rearguard actions, to understand what the surrendering of air supremacy to the Allies meant.

However, in the strategic air war over Germany, the Allied victory by spring of 1944 brought not only tremendous military advantage, but also perhaps the pinnacle, if it can be called that, of total war. War had reached a new level: with the ability to destroy almost at will, not only the enemy's military capability, but also the enemy state itself, had come deep ethical problems. To Clausewitz, the guru of modern western military thought, restraint in war was both dangerous and counterproductive. Yet he was writing in and for an age when war could never be truly total in the modern industrial sense and, notably, in an age when war was two dimensional. The "creation of Armageddon" had changed war in an irrevocable fashion and to such a degree that, as the Allies began the task of rebuilding Germany and witnessed at first hand the power that they possessed with their vast strategic bombing fleets, the age of total war started to pass into history. In the ensuing years the development of widespread mass destructive power in nuclear bomber fleets and, latterly, ballistic missiles reached such a point that total war became redundant, and air power was once again to be the key.

Chapter Seven

The war in the Far East, 1937–45

During the war in Europe, air power became a crucial and integral part of the mix of forces required to prosecute modern war. Moreover, the strategic bombing offensives and the depth of mobilization required to maintain air power effectiveness reached such proportions that if total war ever truly existed, many would argue it was during the war against Germany. However, the war that broke out between the Allies and Japan in the Far East and raged for almost four years could in many ways be said to have epitomized some aspects of total war even more, displaying such extremes as kamikaze suicide attacks and the atomic bombings. More than the war in Europe, the Pacific War, as it is often known, demonstrated an even greater reliance on air power both at tactical and strategical levels. The war was dominated by maritime operations and naval forces were the means by which offensive activity was carried out. More specifically, the arbiters of success or failure throughout the war were aircraft carriers. Surface combat vessels such as battleships and cruisers became secondary to the new flat topped capital ships and the projection of air power emerged as the key to effective operations. By the end of the war, the US Navy could call upon a huge fleet of fast, modern carriers all equipped with the latest aircraft, while the battleship had been reduced to a support or land-bombardment vessel. The transition was most clearly demonstrated when the epitome of the big gun battleship and the largest such ship ever built, the Japanese *Yamato,* was sunk by aircraft of the US Navy in 1945.

Air power also came more into its own because of the geography of the war. Whereas the war in Europe had been for the most part a continental based effort with vast armies deciding the final outcome, in the Pacific War, the campaigning took place over enormous expanses of ocean with small clusters of islands being the prizes. The usual way to capture such bases was to launch amphibious assaults and, of course, such maritime forces were highly vulnerable to air power. Consequently, maritime operations spearheaded by air power were the key to success in the war against Japan. Although land based campaigns did take place in southeast Asia and China, Japan was defeated by US drives across the Pacific, the so-called island hopping offensives, offensives dominated by air power to a degree unknown in Europe.

Additionally, air power continued unabated in the acceleration towards total war. Indeed, the two aspects of total war brought about by air power, as previously discussed, were emphasized yet further in the war against Japan. First, the degree and prosecution of the strategic bombing offensive against Japan from 1944 to 1945 reached proportions and levels of savagery unknown in Europe. General Curtis Le May's "torching of Japan" witnessed the abandonment of any qualms the USAAF may have had regarding the indiscriminate bombing of civilians. The systematic destruction and levelling of Japanese cities was on an unprecedented scale and, of course, culminated in the atomic bombings of Hiroshima and Nagasaki in August 1945. If the totality of war was ever brought home to civilian populations it was during the strategic bombing offensive against Japan, perhaps even more so because Japan never had any effective defence against such an assault.

Still further, the air war against Japan demonstrated, more emphatically than the war in Europe, the burgeoning demands made on economies, populations and industries by air campaigns and the consequences of not meeting the challenge. Even more so than Germany, Japan had little concept of what modern industrial war was and, as a result, air power was the first armed force to decline once the USA had dragged Japan into a gruelling war of attrition. The disparity in the respective approaches to war between the USA and Japan was illustrated by the growing gap between the air forces of the two combatants, from late 1942 onwards. The US was fully appreciative of the demands made on economies by modern war, while Japan was to suffer from many of the productive and mobilization problems that beset Nazi Germany, indicative of a less sophisticated and more martially oriented approach to war. The Pacific War was also another clear indication of the growing divide between the first rate and the secondary air powers. Japan failed, not only because of organizational problems, but because she simply did not have the capacity and resource base to match the USA. The sophisticated and modern economy of the Americans dwarfed the Japanese industrial base both in size and prevailing levels of technology. It was a gap that could have been narrowed by more effective use and husbanding of resources, but ultimately, Japan was simply not capable of meeting the demands of a protracted air power campaign against a foe the size of the USA.

Therefore, arguably, the Pacific War was to be the epitome of many aspects of total war in ways that were never experienced in Europe, both from the western viewpoint, and in the desperation demonstrated by the Japanese as they resorted to premeditated and co-ordinated suicide attacks. However, the scope and scale of technological and industrial war, of which air power was the most obvious manifestation, was such that Japan was even less well equipped to deal with it than Germany, and thus the limits and excesses of total war were ruthlessly demonstrated by the Allies as they swept away Japanese resistance from 1942 onwards.

Air power and the Far East, 1937–41

Japan had been the pace-setter of Asian air power since the earliest days of flight and both the army and navy air arms were considerable forces by the era of Japanese expansion in the 1930s. Japan had sought to create its own aero-industry in order to abandon reliance on western powers and, by the 1930s, both the army and navy air forces were operating capable indigenous designs. In 1931, with no other serious native aerial opposition the Japanese air forces were quickly able to establish air superiority over the Chinese air forces, such as there were, in the invasion of Manchuria. In the wake of this success, Japan began a major expansion and re-equipment programme for its air forces and, when the war with China broke out proper in 1937, both army and naval air units were relatively well prepared.[1]

The next four years proved to be a training ground for the Japanese air forces, and they honed their capabilities against the Chinese, while enduring difficulties against the Soviets. The conflict between China and Japan illustrated much of what was to come in the Second World War with long-range trans-oceanic strategic operations between mainland China and Japan, battlefield air support and air strikes launched from Japanese carriers against mainland targets.[2] The Japanese endeavoured to eliminate Chinese air forces both in northern and southern China with the army taking responsibility for the former and the navy for the latter. The Japanese were able to call upon 451 aircraft to support the invasion of China, with the Imperial Japanese Navy (IJN) carrying the brunt of the early fighting and the early losses. The lessons of the China Incident (as it was euphemistically labelled in Tokyo) were applied in aircraft design and organization by Japan, as the advocates of fast monoplane aircraft prevailed over the supporters of slower but more manoeuvrable biplanes,[3] and began a programme to procure a fast attack aircraft, the Ki-51.[4]

172

However, limitations on Japanese aerial capabilities were soon illustrated and, despite the propaganda, the Chinese air forces were never eliminated or put to the sword in the 1937–41 war. Since the debacle of 1931 the Chinese warlords and Chiang Kai-shek had been desperately trying to raise a viable air force, demonstrating the importance they now attached to air power. By 1937 the Chinese had developed basic aerial capability, based on foreign imports of pilots, aircraft and advisors. Indeed, the Chinese had curried favour with the Soviets and the Americans and both were to take part in combating the Japanese. Many of the Chinese air forces were equipped with obsolete aircraft and their organization and command structure left much to be desired. However, the Japanese could not gain air supremacy, nor decisively influence the outcome of the campaign, despite resorting to what were considered for the period quite brutal and indiscriminate city bombings.[5] It is clear that despite protestations and claims to the contrary by the Japanese, the Chinese air forces continued to provide opposition throughout the period and Japan's air forces were never allowed a free hand to operate at will. Again, it can be seen that denying air supremacy or contesting air superiority was enough to reduce drastically the degree to which air power could influence the outcome of land campaigns.

However, Japanese air power was to suffer quite badly at the hands of the Soviet Union's air forces (the VVS) in the so-called Nomonhan Incident between May and September 1939. The Japanese and Soviet forces had clashed before in 1938 at Changkufeng, but only the Soviets employed air forces and these were small in number. The following year, however, despite the mauling received by the Japanese at Changkufeng , hostilities broke out again. The Japanese units suffered heavily under attack from the Soviet forces, which employed combined arms tactics, supported by artillery and aerial bombardment. Any initial Japanese aerial success was quickly overcome by the superior strength in depth of the Soviets. Gradually air superiority switched to the VVS and against large numbers of I-15 and I-16 fighters the Japanese could only deploy older Kawasaki Ki-10 biplanes and small numbers of Nakajima Ki-27 monoplanes. Whereas the Soviets had Spanish Civil War veterans to call upon and a large pool of trained aviators and equipment, the Japanese had little in the way of reserves and were forced to pull pilots and aircrew out of the China War to deploy against the USSR.

By September the two powers had negotiated a peace settlement but, Nomonhan had been a rude awakening for the Japanese and had convinced them that war with the USSR must be avoided for the foreseeable future.[6] It was notable that Japanese attention turned decisively to the south and war with the West only when the USSR became embroiled in the struggle against Germany in June 1941. For the Japanese Army Air Force the experience of Nomonhan had indicated that Japan lacked adequate reserves of aircraft, supplies and most importantly, pilots. Whereas the VVS had been able to absorb losses relatively easily, the Japanese had not. Although air expansion schemes continued, Japanese training programmes for pilots and aircrew remained the most exhaustive and wasteful in the world, more so in the Imperial Japanese Navy (IJN). It was an issue that was to undermine Japanese air efforts once war had broken out with the USA, perhaps more than any other issue.

From 1938 onwards, the Japanese endeavoured to isolate China from western and Soviet aid once it had become clear that a short term decisive victory had been denied. Although by the end of 1938 the Japanese controlled many of the key areas of China, they had not achieved victory, and lacking the capacity and capability to maintain a high degree of military effort, the war degenerated into a stalemate, with little territory changing hands between 1938 and 1945. Japan's long-term strategy became one of blockade and isolation of China.

The years prior to Pearl Harbor had proved an excellent training ground for Japanese air forces, both army and navy, and much had been learnt in the way of operational and tactical know-how. However, the wider issues of attrition and depletion rates within air forces were glossed over, as were the demands made on armed forces by protracted and aggressive war of the sort Japan endured in China. Yet, having become embroiled in such a conflict, Japan had to find a way out of the predicament especially with the USA becoming more belligerent in its dealings with the Japanese government.

For the Allies, the lessons of the years up to 1941 were either ignored or could not be acted upon. Despite evidence to the contrary many intelligence sources in the West reported that Japan had a poorly equipped and trained air force. Nevertheless, the British, especially after 1939, were determined to avoid antagonizing the Japanese. They realized the parlous state of their own defences in Asia. When war came to the Pacific, the Americans were still expanding and re-equipping while the Europeans had little deployed in Asia and around the Indian Ocean due to the ebb and flow of the war in Europe.

Japanese strategy and air power

To students considering the Pacific War after the passing of over five decades, Japan's decision to attack the USA, China, Britain and the Commonwealth simultaneously seems tantamount to strategic suicide. How could

Japan hope to prevail against such combined strength, even if early seizures of territory and resources were possible? Indeed, whatever the outcome of events in the Pacific in 1942, with the eventual collapse of Germany three years later, Japan's fate would have been sealed in any but the most extreme of circumstances as the combined resources of the western world would have been turned against her.

However, Japanese strategy for the conduct of the war against the USA was the subject of much debate and conjecture in the period leading up to Pearl Harbor. Traditional Japanese thinking, based on a long established defensive strategy, was in fact abandoned by Admiral Isoroku Yamamoto in favour of more offensive planning in the years leading up to the war, and some regard this as being a principal reason for Japan's defeat. Since the Washington Naval Treaty of 1921–2 which had set a ratio of ten to six on naval strength in favour of the USA and Britain, Japan had been forced to plan for "defensive" war against the US Navy because of the imposed 40 per cent degree of material inferiority.[7] The only way to defeat the larger US Navy was, therefore, to lure it into a place of the IJN's choosing, weaken it with submarine attack, exhaust it, and only when the balance had swung more evenly in Japan's favour would the crushing of the US Navy take place in a massive set piece battle, dominated by battleships. Again, to make up the deficiency in numbers the IJN would rely heavily on tactical superiority forged from drill and training. As air power came to prominence in the late 1920s and early 1930s, the defensive plan was updated and air strikes were included as a means of weakening the US fleet. Both carrier aviation and land based air power were added to the Japanese battle plan, contributing to the growing belief in the IJN that victory over the USA was likely and almost inevitable.

However, the appointment of Admiral Yamamoto as Commander-in-Chief of the Combined Fleet in 1939 resulted in a widespread revision of Japanese strategy, despite the fact that Yamamoto himself was opposed to any war with the USA on the grounds of industrial inferiority.[8] Nevertheless, recognizing war as a likelihood, Yamamoto switched from a defensive footing to an offensive plan of action based around air power. The starting point of any war against the USA was now to be a surprise air strike against the US Navy's Pacific Fleet, based by May 1940 at Pearl Harbor in the Hawaiian Islands. This was not a new idea and many eager naval students had advanced the notion in the past, only to be castigated for not adhering to Japan's defensive strategy.[9] However, new doctrinal thinking concerning carrier battle-groups had been crystallizing in the IJN under the aegis of Commander Minoru Genda (see Chapter Five), and Yamamoto saw the use of carrier air power as a means of seizing the initiative in the early stages of a campaign against the USA. The Pearl Harbor attack was born out of a recognition in certain parts of the IJN of the potential of air power to influence maritime operations decisively. It is crucial to note that the principal targets of the Pearl Harbor raid were the US Navy's aircraft carriers, not the battleships which were in fact to bear the brunt of the attack. Once the carriers were eliminated, Yamamoto believed, the US Navy would be unwilling to venture forth into seas dominated by Japanese air power whether land or carrier based. While the US Navy rebuilt itself, the Japanese would be able to occupy the resource rich areas of southeast Asia and organize the so-called Greater East-Asia Co-Prosperity Sphere – essentially a Japanese Empire. When the US Navy returned, probably in 1943, the Japanese would be prepared to engage and defeat them in battle in a similar scenario to the old defensive strategy, with reliance again placed on land and carrier based air power, to weaken the Americans preparatory to a huge surface engagement in which the US Navy would be crushed and the US government forced to come to terms acceptable to Japan.

Japan's plans were riddled with flaws and misconceptions, but post-war criticism of Yamamoto's Pearl Harbor strategy is perhaps unfounded. He recognized the importance of carrier air power and that the destruction of the US carriers in the early stages of the war was essential to Japan maintaining the offensive long enough to capture the Co-Prosperity Sphere. The fact that the US carriers were absent from Pearl Harbor on 7 December unhinged the plan and eventually resulted in the need for the Midway operation. Once again, it is clear that gaining air supremacy was considered essential to offensive operations in modern war and, while the US carriers were at large, the threat to Japanese maritime forces would remain high. Midway was necessary because of the pivotal role that air power was playing in the Pacific Campaign. The fact that at the Coral Sea battle the IJN had lost a small carrier and had two fleet carriers knocked out of action resolved the issue. Yamamoto could not afford to risk the continued exposure of his fleet to surprise carrier strikes. Midway was therefore essential.

Further criticism of Yamamoto has been levelled because of the nature of the Midway plan which separated the Japanese fleet into small groups and effectively used the IJN's carrier force (temporarily reduced from six to four carriers because of the Coral Sea battle) as bait. The plan degenerated into disaster for many reasons but the basic principle of Yamamoto's thinking was sound. Indeed, victory at Midway and the destruction of three US carriers would have given the IJN air supremacy and a free hand for operations for one, possibly two years. This would probably not have saved Japan from ultimate defeat but it did demonstrate the crucial and decisive nature of air power to the conduct of operations in the Pacific campaign. Arguably, the loss of all four carriers at Midway merely hastened Japan's defeat. Japan enjoyed massive success in the wake of the Pearl Harbor raid until the catastrophe at Midway but, as has been suggested, the roots of Japan's decline were already embedded.

The essence of the IJN's decisive battle philosophy illustrated all too clearly a fundamental weakness of the Japanese war machine. The Great War had demonstrated to the world that modern war made heavy and exhausting demands of modern societies and economies, especially in air power terms, and that the much sought after decisive battle, both on land and at sea, had proved frustratingly elusive. Yet Japan's entire strategy for war against the USA was predicated on achieving just such a decisive victory. Concepts of long attritional war, although acknowledged by pre-war planners, took second place to tactical and operational considerations, that is making the Pearl Harbor raid and the subsequent battle of annihilation feasible.[10]

For example, rather than creating a reserve in depth for the IJN's aviators as preparation for the expected long war, the training programme used by the Japanese navy centred on the pursuit of excellence in very small numbers. The IJN's aircrew were drilled ruthlessly in the years leading up to Pearl Harbor and were without doubt the finest examples of naval aviators in the world in 1941. However, the drop-out and attrition rates in achieving such quality were enormously wasteful. In 1937, only 70 out of 1,500 applicants were accepted at Tsuchiura naval air training school near Tokyo. After the ten month programme only 25 remained. Indeed, as few as 100 pilots per year completed their training for the IJN, which simply did not allow for the creation of a trained reserve.[11] The naval air crew proved their worth in the early stages of the Pacific Campaign but, once they were lost in the carrier battles over Coral Sea, Midway and the Solomons, the effectiveness of the Japanese naval air arm diminished rapidly. By the final carrier battles of the war in 1944, the IJN's aircrew were poorly trained, suffering from 50 per cent operational loss rates.[12]

Another crucial factor in the demise of Japan was a lack of attention paid to trade defence. Once the resource rich areas of southeast Asia had been seized it was essential for Japan's long-term viability that the newly acquired raw materials be shipped back to Japan to facilitate the necessary increase in military output to compete with the USA. However, although such a task was crucial to Japan's war effort, it did not take place to any significant degree. The importance of trade defence to an island nation had been illustrated all too dramatically during the First World War when Britain had come close to defeat at the hands of the German U-boat fleet. Although the British were to repeat many of the mistakes of 1914–18 in the Second World War they, and their Allies, realized that success against the submarine was the first step on the road to victory. Japan's real failing was in not establishing such a priority. Trade defence operations were considered "defensive" and not fitting for warriors. The aeroplane, a key component in trade defence, was never deployed in any large numbers to defend the sea communications route from southeast Asia to Japan, and between 1942 and 1945 the American submarine fleet devastated the Japanese merchant marine. In total some 8,000,000 tons of Japanese shipping were lost in combat during World War II, of which 4,765,000 were destroyed by Allied submarines.[13] Perhaps the most significant consequence of this was that, of the 19,165,000 tons of oil produced in occupied territories less than 25 per cent ever got back to Japan. One of the most important reasons for the decline in Japan's fighting ability was its lack of fuel oil for operations and training, a crippling disadvantage in the latter half of the war, and always a concern throughout.[14] The British had proved that air power was arguably the most important factor in defeating submarine based merchant raiding, but the Japanese, wanting to concentrate on front-line battle effectiveness, allowed the life blood of the Japanese economy to haemorrhage in favour of a concentration on "offensive" aerial duties.[15]

The decisive battle philosophy, one deliberately eschewed by the US Navy once the war had broken out, continued to plague Japanese thinking, even Yamamoto's. The perception that the IJN was a true air power navy does not stand close scrutiny. Even as they were creating a highly efficient carrier arm they were also producing the largest battleships ever built in preparation for the expected decisive surface engagement with the US battlefleet. Moreover, Japanese destroyers were designed for fleet actions, not escort and trade defence duties, and Japanese submarines were expected to act in direct support of the battlefleet. Even Yamamoto's Midway plan was to culminate in a major surface action in which the remnants of the US fleet would be annihilated by the battlewagons of the IJN.

Nevertheless, in the early stages of the war the IJN enjoyed staggering success and seemed to be demonstrating a clear and prescient understanding of maritime air power philosophy. Following on from the Pearl Harbor raid, Japanese air forces quickly suppressed aerial resistance over the US, held Philippines preparatory to invasion, sank the Royal Navy's token Asian force of the battleship *Prince of Wales* and the battlecruiser *Repulse* with air strikes alone, this time while the ships were at sea, and spearheaded the occupation of the Dutch East Indies. In the Pacific itself, Japanese air power was the key to the seizure of many vital US and Allied island bases such as Guam and Wake.

It is true that the air forces arrayed against them were largely obsolete and inadequate, but the remorseless efficiency of the Japanese assault stunned the Allies. By the spring of 1942, Japanese carrier aircraft had raided Ceylon and

Australia and had driven the Royal Navy back to East Africa, clearly demonstrating the superiority of carrier based naval power over surface fleets. However, once the carrier fleet had been crippled at Midway, the IJN demonstrated its lack of understanding of the true role of air power in Pacific operations by frittering away its highly trained naval aviators in a gruelling series of duties around the Solomons in late 1942 and early 1943. First Yamamoto and then his successor Admiral Koga deployed naval aviators on ground bases to support operations in the southern Pacific. Over two-thirds of the fleet air forces were lost in this manner, and by the end of 1943 the Japanese had sacrificed more than 7,000 aircraft and aircrew.[16] With no effective means of replacing these losses, Japanese naval air power declined rapidly. Already outnumbered by early 1943, Japanese air power was swamped by odds of some five to two by January 1944.[17] By the time of the Battle of the Philippine Sea in June 1944, and despite considerable effort, the IJN's carrier force was, comparatively, a pale shadow of its former self, consisting of nine carriers (of which only five could be classed as fleet carriers) and 450 aeroplanes, many of which were obsolete and with pilots who lacked proper training. In stark contrast the US Navy could call upon 15 fleet aircraft carriers and over 900 modern carrier aircraft. Once again illustrating its lack of appreciation of anti-submarine warfare, the IJN lost two priceless carriers to US submarines, but of more significance was the enormous gap that had opened up between Japanese and US carrier air power. During the battle, on 19 June 1944, in what the American navy christened the "Great Marianas Turkey Shoot", US naval interceptors downed over 300 aircraft in a day for the loss of just 31. Follow up counter attacks reduced the Japanese carrier arm still further and the IJN's air power was to play no further significant role in the Pacific War.[18]

By the time of Leyte Gulf, the invasion of the Philippines in November 1944, the Japanese were resorting to a yet more extreme tactic, that of the *kamikaze*. It had become clear to the Japanese commanders that conventional air attacks were totally ineffective in the face of such overwhelming US superiority. Thus Admiral Onishi of the First Air Fleet devised the plan of using aircraft in a suicide attack role, which would rely on notions of the superiority of the Japanese spirit. The sacrificial attacks offered many advantages. Clearly, *kamikaze* pilots need not be particularly experienced and their attacks had to be completely wiped out by the Americans, rather than just driven off. Moreover, the loss of a few pilots and aircraft against the potential damage caused to a carrier or battleship was a reasonable trade off. The first strikes came as a rude shock to the Americans and set the scene for the closing stages of the war when US fleets would have to endure countless suicide attacks, a form of assault completely alien to western mentality. In the earliest encounters around the Philippines, the carriers *Santee* and *Suwanee* were damaged while the *St Lo* was sunk, all with heavy loss of life. During the closing stages of the war, and particularly in the campaigns around Okinawa, the threat of *kamikaze* attacks rose to serious proportions and the US forces were grateful for the arrival of Task Force 57, a modern Royal Navy fleet equipped with armoured carriers rather than the wooden topped designs used by the US Navy. During the months of the *kamikaze*, the Japanese launched over 3,000 suicide attacks in which some 49 ships were sunk, including three carriers, while 280 ships were damaged of which 44 were carriers.[19]

Although the *kamikaze* attacks presented a new and extreme kind of problem for the Allies, ultimately it was no answer to the vast superiority in numbers held by the western forces. Moreover, the usual perception of the *kamikaze* pilots as brainwashed fanatics seeking a glorious afterlife is inaccurate. Most were not soldiers but students, who were motivated by notions of honour and pride in the traditions of their families and country. Nevertheless, the *kamikaze* strategy illustrated all too vividly the differing attitudes of Japan and the West to modern war .[20]

The Japanese predilection with "offensive" duties manifested itself in other ways which impinged on air power performance in the war. The IJN, like other Japanese military institutions, emphasized heavily the role of *élan*, or military spirit in warfare, mirroring European thought, especially that of the French, on the eve of the Great War in 1914. The First World War proved, however, that technology, of which air power was a prime example, was a more than important factor in the conduct of modern warfare. Japan was yet to accept this, despite the lessons of the skirmishes with the technically superior Soviet armed forces in the late 1930s. Consequently, Japan went to war with a narrow view of the requirements for military success, and technology was an area that suffered from some neglect. However, these failings should not be overstated as the Japanese had relatively efficient radio detectors and in certain frontline battle type technologies they were ahead of the USA on the outbreak of war, for example in some areas of aircraft and torpedo design.

Nevertheless, in general the Japanese military eschewed the "boffin" and technical war much loved by the western powers. The lack of radar in the early stages of the war was a serious disadvantage and was largely responsible for the IJN carrier fleet being caught unawares at Midway. The failure of Japanese cipher technology was again a cause of defeat and poor radio security plagued air power efforts throughout the war, most notably at the Battle of the Philippine Sea when US radio operators listened in as the Japanese attack co-ordinator directed the doomed assault on Task Force 58.[21]

Duties such as radar and intelligence operations were considered unworthy of true fighting men and thus, only those unfit for much else were placed in backroom duties, and such activities suffered from inadequate and incapable personnel.

It is clear that Japanese air power strategy failed in World War II, and not just because the war was lost. Although the IJN had illustrated all too graphically what maritime air forces were capable of, they did not fully understand the implications of their discovery. In contrast to the European theatre, the defensive capability of air power was severely limited by the strictures of the geography of the Pacific campaign. Mobile, not static, air power was the key to victory in the campaign and Japan's carrier fleet was simply not up to the task once it had been fatally compromised in the battles of 1942. Island groups were easily isolated and had their small pockets of static air power reduced by surprise raids, such as those conducted by US Task Force 58 prior to the Philippine Sea engagement. Yet Japan continued to rely on such penny packets of dispersed air forces to support their mobile fleet because they still expected the war to be decided by a surface engagement, and also because their own carrier force was, after 1942, inadequate in terms of training and numbers. The whole basis of Japan's pre-war "defensive" strategy relied on the combined use of land and carrier based air forces to deplete an advancing US fleet as it approached Japanese-held waters. However, the war demonstrated that this strategy was untenable. Once this started to become apparent it was too late for Japan to adjust.

Reliance on superior fighting capability and the dominance of "decisive battle" mentality created a Japanese military structure akin to an inverted pyramid, with the upper half representing the military fighting capability, and the lower half the supports for the continuing effort. Once the front-line force had been reduced by a series of attritional battles, the weak and flimsy supports for the Japanese war machine were unable to provide adequate replacements. Moreover, once the USAAF began the systematic strategic bombardment of Japan in 1944 the whole basis of the Japanese war effort crumbled. The inability of Japanese air power, either land or carrier based, to prevent this was the fundamental reason for Japan's defeat.

Industry, mobilization and technology

It is clear that Japanese air power declined markedly relative to Allied air strength as the Second World War progressed and a key factor in this demise was the failure of the Japanese economy to meet the demands made of it by the war. Mirroring the failure of German aircraft production, Japan's aero-industry suffered from a lack of central direction until it was too late, poor levels of state and private mobilization and shortages brought about by blockade and bombing. Moreover, the Japanese military forces imposed themselves forcefully on the means of production, distorting and hindering the process still further. In addition, and unlike the European Axis nations, the Japanese suffered from the rivalry of two air forces – the army's and the navy's – compounding the problems by duplicating the interference.

This latter issue manifested itself in a number of areas. For example, the IJN and the army failed to co-ordinate procurement policies, thus resulting in a large number of aircraft types being adopted, all requiring different support services and spare parts. During the war, the Japanese produced 53 basic naval aircraft types (with 112 variations) and 37 army designs (with 52 variations). In contrast, the USA deployed 18 models for the army and navy combined, thus allowing much simpler logistical support and enhancing the concentration of production.[22] In addition, the army and navy could not agree on types of electrical equipment and components, forcing industry to produce double the number of jigs and tools for production.[23] Still further, the navy and army, conscious of the scarcity of resources, even in the early stages of the war, established links with their own suppliers and tapped sources of raw materials which they guarded jealously from each other, to the point of hoarding surplus materials even when desperately required by the other service. Interference in the production process by the military was common, as it was considered that manufacturers and capitalists were not to be trusted, and in any case the opinions and ideas of those at the front-line were of more value. Consequently, production was continually disrupted to incorporate new ideas and modifications.

However, of more significance was the lack of central planning and organization in the Japanese aero-industry. Demonstrating once again the lack of understanding of the demands and nature of modern industrial war, the Japanese had no considered plan for the expansion and organization of aircraft production after 1941. Only steady expansion of aircraft output had been underway during the 1930s with a 300 per cent increase between 1931 and 1936, and a 400 per cent increase between 1936 and 1940, and was slowing down.[24] Levels of aircraft production in 1940 for the navy and the army combined were 4,768, while by 1941 the figure was 5,088.[25] However, these levels of increased output, where the concentration had been on the quality of the air forces through training rather than accelerated production, failed to lay the foundations for wartime expansion. In the years 1939 to 1941, US aircraft production had increased by approximately 500 per cent and British by 250 per cent, whereas Japan, supposedly preparing for war of

Table 7.1 – Available air strength, 1943–5

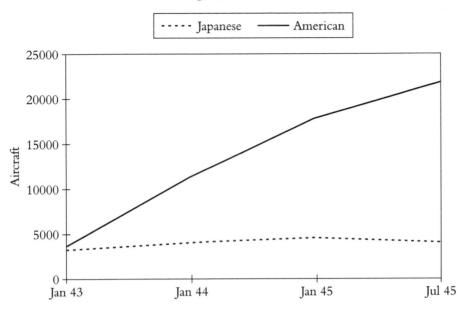

Source: Cohen, *Japan's economy*, p. 233.

some kind against the USA and the West, saw a rise of a little over 10 per cent.[26]

Once the war had degenerated into a long attritional affair by 1942, Japan's inadequacies in long-term planning and pre-war mobilization became clear. Japanese industry was primitive by western standards being based on many small scale operations which hindered co-ordination and organization. To make matters worse, for over a year little was done to adapt the Japanese aero-industry to the demands of war. The military remained too powerful and the civilian government too weak until as late as November 1943 when the Ministry of Munitions was established to try and pull the disparate parts of the Japanese economy together.[27] It was determined that the aero-industry was capable of producing 53,000 aircraft per year, although the raw materials did not exist to reach such a figure.[28] Therefore, it was considered that increased efficiency was of paramount importance, not expanded plant, thus illustrating the underlying problems of the sector.

By 1943 it was clear that US air power was starting to swamp Japanese front-line air strength and levels of attrition were threatening to hand air supremacy to the Americans. The Munitions Ministry set in motion plans to increase output to 97,000 aircraft between January 1944 and August 1945, although this was reduced on reflection to 66,000 and only some 40,000 were actually constructed.[29] With front-line casualties increasing, Japanese output barely covered losses and, with no reserves and little or no effective training, Japanese air strength fell qualitatively and quantitatively. Moreover, in the same way that the *Luftwaffe* had been distorted in Europe by the increasing need for fighters at the expense of bombers, so too were the Japanese air forces obliged to abandon their army and navy support operations in favour of contesting air superiority. In 1941 fighters made up 21 per cent of output while bombers constituted 29 per cent. By 1945, these figures had shifted to 49 per cent and 17 per cent respectively, severely restricting the ability of Japan's air forces to intervene in an effective manner in front-line operations. The problem was compounded by the growing need in late 1944 to deploy fighters in Japan itself to combat the menace presented by the US 20th's strategic bombing campaign, and in the last year of the war the number of fighters deployed as strategic interceptors doubled.[30]

Attempts to introduce new types of aircraft designs into front-line service repeatedly failed and new models were often little better than their predecessors. Squabbling permeated even this area and the replacement for the famous Mitsubishi A6M Zero fighter, the A7M Reppu, was continually delayed because the navy and the designer could not agree on the best engine for the aircraft.[31] Other new designs, such as the Raiden and the Shiden, which came to be respected by Allied pilots, also suffered from production failings and latterly from the exigencies of the blockade and the bombing campaign.

Problems persisted for much of the war in a number of areas of production. First, Japanese capitalists and businessmen were unwilling to switch production *en masse* to less profitable military output, while central government maintained surprisingly low levels of taxation on private income and wealth.[32] Labour mobilization was also a significant area of confusion. Initially, manufacturers had to find their own workers, with no help from the navy or the army.[33] Labour dilution did take place on a massive scale as the war progressed but the armed services repeatedly drafted even senior skilled workers into the army and the navy and by 1945 the ratio of skilled to non-skilled labour was one to two thousand. Such low levels of supervision and expertise resulted in around 33 per cent of engine parts output being unusable, further hindering serviceability and production levels.[34]

However, the two most important factors in the attrition of Japan's aero-industry in the latter half of the war were the submarine blockade and the bombing offensive. US submarines took a heavy toll of Japanese merchant shipping severely restricting production, training and combat effectiveness. As has been stated above, the diminishing supplies of fuel oil severely restricted training and engine testing such that in the latter stages of the war only 10 per cent of engines were tested prior to delivery.[35] The blockade also led to shortages of cobalt, nickel, chromium, molybdenum and tungsten – all essential in the production of alloys for aero-engines.[36] Engine production fell away with about a 50 per cent shortfall in meeting production targets. The engine to airframe ratio fell from 2.3:1 in 1941 to 1:1 by 1945 resulting in there being no reserve of engines or spare parts, thus curtailing operational readiness and training.[37] By the closing stages of the war, airframes were lying about unused because there were no engines to power them.

The effects of the bombing of Japan were also profound and seriously undermined all the efforts of the Munitions Ministry to increase production. The United States Strategic Bombing Survey (USSBS), conducted after the war, estimated that some 43 per cent of engine production and 18 per cent of airframe construction was lost in Japan between December 1944 and July 1945 as a direct result of the bombing campaign. Absenteeism increased dramatically as workers fled to the countryside to escape the bombing and to search for food. Spring 1945 saw the loss of some 20–25 per cent of productive personnel hours.[38]

One of the counters to the US bombardment was the dispersal of Japanese industry away from easily targetable cities to underground plants – mines, quarries, railway tunnels and so forth – and into the countryside. New tunnels were dug and by the end of the war some 100 underground plants were in various stages of construction and the expectation was that aircraft production would have been totally subterranean by December 1945. However, the dispersal programme came too late, its introduction being postponed in 1944 so as not to interfere with production levels. The navy and army claimed that maximum output was required to fight the expected decisive battles of that summer and autumn, the campaigns which were to become the Philippine Sea and Leyte Gulf. Only if production would not be compromised would they agree to the dispersal programme, and it could not. The emphasis on output at all costs up to October 1944 resulted in the wearing out of production tools and jigs and stalled the introduction of dispersal, thus making the aero-industry highly susceptible to sustained heavy bombing which began in November. Panic dispersal began as a result and the passing of the "Urgent Dispersal of Plants Act" only partly alleviated the problem.[39] By the last six months of the war, production was falling away under the weight of aerial bombardment and blockade.

It was in many ways a remarkable achievement that, from a much weaker base than their Axis partners in Germany, the Japanese managed to maintain the levels of production that they did. In 1944, the first full year of mobilization, production of airframes, engines and propellers increased by 69 per cent, 63 per cent and 70 per cent respectively and overall Japan manufactured

28,180 aircraft, approximately 75 per cent of Germany's output from an industrial base one-third the pre-war size.[40] Nevertheless, Japan suffered from many problems similar to those encountered in the expansion of the German aero-industry. Lack of co-ordination, poor planning, and military interference all undermined Japanese efforts which were further damaged by the highly effective blockade and the increasing ferocity of the bombing offensive in the last year of the war. Ultimately, like Germany, Japan was ill-equipped and in many ways unwilling to adapt her economy and industry to "total" industrial war, and when confronted by an enemy such as the USA whose style epitomized the productivist approach to war, both in economic mobilization and strategic thinking and planning, the Japanese could not hope to prevail for any length of time.

US/Allied air strategy and the conduct of the Pacific War

The importance of air power to the USA in the conduct of any future war had already been established prior to 1941 and the Roosevelt administration had invested heavily in the development of the American air forces since the Munich crisis (see Chapter Five). Well before the Pearl Harbor raid, it was considered that air power would be a crucial element in any war against Japan, and indeed the Pacific War proved that air superiority and even air supremacy were not only crucial but indeed decisive and fundamental to US victory. Louis Allen has even gone so far as to state that the only campaign which really mattered in the war against Japan was the US Navy's drive across the Central Pacific to the island bases such as Saipan which allowed the USAAF systematically to flatten all but one of Japan's cities in the most ferocious and one-sided strategic bombing offensive ever seen.[41] This view can be refined by adding the submarine offensive which throttled Japan's industrial production, but the pivotal nature of the aeroplane to US strategy in the war against Japan is irrefutable. Clearly the aircraft was the only weapon capable of covering the vast expanses of the Pacific effectively. It was the US Navy's attainment of air superiority over the Central Pacific which spearheaded America's war effort, and ultimately it was air power which delivered the final *coup de grâce* to Japan in August 1945. The USA's view of the nature of air war was more refined and in line with the demands of modern war. The attainment of air superiority was, by necessity, to be a long drawn out campaign of attrition in which Japanese air power would be whittled away preparatory to the US offensive. Notably, and in stark contrast to the Japanese plan of war, the USA never expected a single battle to be decisive. The war against Japan was to be a remorseless series of engage-ments on a variety of fronts and media, supported by a massive mobilization of industrial capacity.

The European powers however, had little answer to the Japanese on-slaught in the first few months of the war and were quickly driven back to India and Australia. In what was essentially a ground war, air power played only a limited and supportive role, and the Allied air forces struggled to assert themselves in southeast Asia due to a lack of resources and strategic necessity. The attainment of air superiority allowed innovatory measures to be undertaken, notably the air supply of Chinese forces now cut off by the loss of the Burma road, and later, by the use of Orde Wingate's chindits – troops airlifted behind enemy lines and supplied by air drops. These were partially successful and, like other airborne operations, had limited flexibility, but they illustrated what could be possible with air-mobile troops if air superiority could be seized.[42] The resupply of troops operating in China was also limited in impact. A little over 300,000 tons of equipment and fuel was flown "over the hump" into China prior to 1945 and most of this went to Chennault's US air units or to support operations into northern Burma from China. Little, therefore, went to aid the Chinese struggle against the Japan-ese, and the airlift was largely symbolic of US aid to China rather than of much material value.[43]

The role of air power in the strategic planning for the Pacific war prior to 7 December 1941 was still a matter of some debate. It has already been outlined that the US Navy was agonizing over the true role of maritime aviation, although the expansion of the US carrier fleet was underway in 1941 to such a degree that Japan could not possibly keep up. Indeed Japan's perception of a marked inferiority in carrier aviation which was likely to emerge by the middle of the 1940s, was one of the causes of the outbreak of war. Nevertheless, the US Navy itself was not entirely convinced that the aeroplane was now the decisive weapon in naval warfare and the notion of a decisive Jutland style engagement still pervaded US Naval planning.[44] US naval expansion for the 1940s was aimed at creating a balanced fleet for surface engagements – battleships and aircraft carriers – although the notion of operating carriers in independent task forces was starting to take root.

Pearl Harbor and the months which followed were to change all of that. With their battleships at the bottom of Pearl Harbor or sufficiently damaged to put them out of action for the foreseeable future, the US Navy was forced into adopting a more carrier based strategy. Admiral Chester Nimitz, Commander-in-Chief of the Pacific Fleet, pursued a policy of using his carriers to harass the Japanese, without overly risking his now most vital commodity. With only small numbers of carriers and no other offensive

Table 7.2 – Frontline carrier tonnage, 1930–44

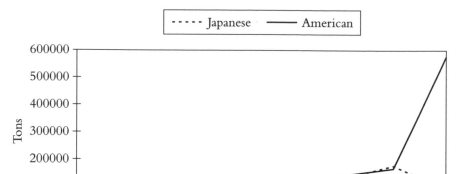

potential the US fleet would not be ready for anything else until late 1943, and the first priority in 1942 was to blunt the Japanese offensive and grind down its carrier air arm wherever possible. The crushing victory at Midway in June 1942 evened up the carrier fleets and severely restricted Japanese offensive capability and the attritional battles of late 1942 and early 1943 saw the Pacific naval campaign reduced to a virtual stalemate. That is, until the output of the US economy started to pour forth carriers, aircraft and supplies in mid-1943.

The outpost of US power in Asia and the Pacific, the Philippines, had for much of the interwar period been identified as indefensible. *War Plan Orange*, America's long-standing strategy for war with Japan, had until the late 1930s worked on the assumption that the Japanese would be able to seize the Philippines in the early stages of a war.[45] This was tacitly accepted in the *Rainbow 5* plan, which superseded *Orange*, and was to form the basis of US strategy in World War II, along with agreement with the British that Germany was a greater threat than Japan and that a "Germany first policy" was to be adopted on the outbreak of any global war.[46] The only alteration to the US plan was the move by General Douglas MacArthur to offer a viable defence of the Philippines by the expansion of the Filipino army and with the allocation of extra US support, principally increased numbers of aircraft, in the period leading up to the outbreak of war. A force of B-17 four engined heavy-bombers, the US Army's great hope, was to be sent to the Philippines where, it was hoped and believed, it would be able to drive off any enemy naval force.[47] However, on the outbreak of war, MacArthur's training and expansion scheme was still incomplete and only 35 B-17s were in place. In any case the performance of the B-17 in maritime operations was to be a profound disappointment throughout the war and even a much greater force of such aircraft would probably have been unable to intervene decisively against the Japanese invasion. Surprise Japanese air raids quickly reduced American air strength and MacArthur's whole plan soon unravelled. The US Army and the Marines Corps were driven back to Australia and the South Pacific as the Philippines and a variety of island bases rapidly fell to the Japanese offensive. However, with the defeat of the Japanese carrier fleet at Midway, the US Army was able to halt the Japanese advance through the Solomons at Guadalcanal, and by early 1943, along with the navy, the US Army and the marines were ready to go onto the offensive.

It is testament to the mismatch in resources between the USA and Japan that the Americans were able to turn the tide in the Pacific as early as 1943 with only some 15 per cent of their war effort given over to the task.[48] Moreover, US resources were further divided by the two-pronged strategy adopted by the Joint Chiefs of Staff for the re-conquest of the Pacific and the defeat of Japan. In an effort to placate both the army and the navy lobbies, the US Navy under Admiral Nimitz was to drive across the Central Pacific towards the Marianas and southern Japan, while MacArthur and the army were to advance along the islands of the south Pacific, with the aim of re-capturing the Philippines and Formosa. The fact that the Americans were able to support both of these offensives again demonstrated the odds the Japanese were up against.

To support the expanding resources at their disposal the US forces now had to develop the means with which to prosecute their largely air oriented strategies. US air support for ground operations in the Pacific was forged in the fierce fighting at Guadalcanal and later at Bougainville where, once again, the importance of first gaining air superiority was proven to be crucial in facilitating the effective use of ground support air forces. In the fighting in New Guinea, Japanese forces feared artillery and mortar attack far more than air assault, but by Bougainville in December 1943 this had changed and air power posed the greater threat. The experience in the southern Pacific formed the basis of air support for US amphibious and marine ground forces for the rest of the war and into the post-war era.[49]

US Naval air doctrine and capability quickly developed after Midway, although the carrier fleet endured a difficult learning experience in and around the Solomons during 1942 and 1943, which saw the loss of two fleet carriers, the *Hornet* and the *Wasp*. However, whereas the Japanese could not so easily replace their losses, the USA could, and by the middle of 1943 the next generations of carriers were arriving – the *Essex* and the *Independence* classes. With them came vast numbers of new Grumman F6F Hellcat fighters and TBF Avenger torpedo-bombers, while the Curtiss SBC Helldiver dive-bomber offered an alternative to the ageing but popular Douglas SBD Daunt-less. All of these aircraft, along with new land-based types, were superior to their Japanese adversaries and were of course available in much larger num-bers. Perhaps equally importantly, during the period after Pearl Harbor, the direction of Pacific naval operations had fallen to the air admirals, much to the chagrin of the battleship men. The developing war clearly proved that the carrier was the most important weapon and during this time, despite the reinforcement of the surface fleet, the carrier admirals won control of the US Navy.[50] During the debates with the army over which service should spear-head the drive towards Japan, one of the misgivings of MacArthur and his staff had been the supposed vulnerability of carriers. The loss of two carriers in late 1942 around the Solomons had seemed to underline this point. The US Navy therefore worked hard on developing fleet doctrine to deal with the issue. The result was the multi-carrier task force, escorted by surface vessels capable of providing anti-aircraft, anti-submarine and gunnery sup-port. The battleship began a new career as an anti-aircraft gunnery platform with the large primary guns being used for amphibious assault support and to provide protection against any enemy surface vessels which evaded detection and got too close to the carriers. Such a large and multi-faceted force would dominate the central Pacific to such an extent that it would be capable of meeting a land based as well as a carrier based air assault, defeat it and offer more or less continuous support to amphibious landings.

The primary function of this large fast carrier/fast battleship task force would be to gain air supremacy, or at least air superiority, over any given area. The small scale carrier groups of 1942, which relied on stealth and surprise to avoid destruction, were to be replaced, partly at the strong behest of Admiral Ted Sherman, with larger self-contained multi-carrier forces. The doctrine for the creation and use of such a force was developed under the tutelage of Admiral John Towers following his arrival in the Pacific as Commander, Air Force Pacific Fleet in October 1942. Nimitz was initially cool to Towers but was won over by the work done by the new appoint-ment and his staff in 1942–3, especially in helping to frame "PAC 10", the doctrine which was to form the foundation of later US Naval success.[51] By early 1944, Admiral Towers had been appointed Deputy Commander-in-Chief, Pacific Fleet and Task Force 58 had been created comprising all the various carrier divisions under the command of Marc Mitscher, a noted air admiral. It was Task Force 58, either under the command of the Fifth Fleet's Admiral Raymond Spruance or the Third Fleet's Admiral William "Bull" Halsey (when it became Task Force 38) which was to destroy Japanese naval aviation in 1944.

Clearly by 1944, the US Navy was an air navy in the true sense of the term. Air power dominated operations in the Pacific and in the war against Japan. The Americans had placed the aeroplane at the heart of their strategy for the prosecution of the war. With the Marianas captured, prior to the Battle of the Philippine Sea in June 1944, the second role of air power in the Far Eastern war was about to be significantly stepped up: the so-called torching of Japan.

The "torching" of Japan

During the final year of the Second World War, the USAAF launched what could be regarded as the campaign which epitomized total air war more than any other, the strategic bombing offensive against Japan. In the space of nine months the US 20th Air Force, and principally XXI Bomber Command, burned out dozens of Japanese cities in a series of ferocious and arguably barbaric firebombing raids. Against little or no opposition, the Americans razed city after city to the ground killing hundreds of thousands of Japanese and concluded with the atomic bombings of Hiroshima and Nagasaki in August 1945. Without doubt, the ability of air power to inflict a punishing degree of industrial and machine war was proven in the months of the so-called "torching" of Japan and the apogee of total war had been reached. Such was the destruction and indeed the revulsion in many quarters that although the bombing offensive ended the war against Japan without the need for an amphibious invasion, the cost in ethical and moral terms had been heavy and quite possibly excessive.

Curiously, the USA had been particularly critical of indiscriminate bombing in the years leading up to World War II and in Europe had attempted, certainly until the closing stages of the war against Germany, to pursue a policy of precision bombing of industrial and military targets. Not for them was the indiscriminate area bombing adopted by the RAF's Bomber Command, or so they claimed.[52] In fact, the desire to end the war quickly in the winter of 1944–5 when weather and operating conditions precluded precision raids, led the US 8th Air Force to move towards more area bombing (although they euphemistically called it bombing of "marshalling yards"). The new tactics improved efficiency and clearly contributed to the collapse of the German state in 1945, but it was at the cost of lingering qualms about surrendering the moral and ethical high ground that the US had tried to stake out for itself.[53] In the Far East, with racism and barbarity on both sides, there were far fewer concerns about killing Japanese civilians in the first place, but with the USAAF following an incremental path towards "total war" the final step to indiscriminate area bombing in March 1945, although there were still reservations, was a small one.

Planning for the bombing of Japan had begun back in the 1930s when it had been agreed that the USA would need a very-long-range bomber for any campaign against the Japanese homelands owing to the vast distances involved. Planning for the bomber dated back to 1937, but design work on the aircraft which became the B-29 Superfortress began in 1940.[54] The USAAF had already ordered 250 straight off the drawing board while the aircraft was still in development but, after testing in September 1942, a major crash programme was initiated to mass produce the B-29, which it was now recognized could outperform by some distance any other bomber then in existence.[55] The B-29 was considerably faster than its contemporaries and importantly for the vast distances involved in Pacific operations, had a range double that of the B-17 and the Lancaster. The bomber also had remote controlled gun turrets and pressurized cabins, both of which represented yet further leaps forward in the technology of air power and mass destruction.

However, the earliest bombing campaigns launched from China and India against a variety of targets in southern Japan and southeast Asia respectively, enjoyed only limited success. Even when the Marianas were occupied in June 1944, allowing the US 20th Air Force to begin operating B-29s against Japan's major cities and industrial centres by November, difficulties were still encountered. Brigadier-General H. Hansell, an advocate of precision bombing with European experience, was appointed to the XXI Bomber Command in the Marianas to launch the final aerial assault on Japan. Many had staked their reputations on the success of the offensive, General Arnold included, but they were soon to be disappointed. The B-29 had been rushed into service and its engines were still unreliable, resulting in high abort and accident rates. Moreover, the first crews deployed in the Marianas had been trained in night-time radar bombing for duties in India and China. Such tactics were quite unsuitable for operations over Japan, while the tactics of high altitude day-time precision bombing proved fraught with practical difficulties. Most importantly, the weather caused significant problems, with vast cloud fronts disrupting formations and high tail winds creating ground bombing speeds of 550 knots, quite beyond the technology and training of bomb-aiming equipment and bombardiers respectively.[56] The bombing attacks caused little damage to Japanese industry and the whole programme seemed on the point of collapse.

For the USAAF and General Arnold, aiming in the long-term to gain an independent US Air Force, the failure presented real political difficulties.

The B-29s might easily be given to the army and the navy for operational support at the direction of MacArthur or Nimitz, both of whom had already expressed reservations about the validity of bombing Japanese cities. Indeed, the whole basis of strategic air war was under threat. In January, Hansell was replaced and Arnold consolidated all B-29 forces (XX and XXI Bomber Commands) in one group with General Curtis LeMay as commander. A tough and efficient leader, LeMay, in a similar fashion to Harris with Bomber Command in 1942, pulled the US forces together with reshaped operational practices and a major shake up in personnel. Initially, however, he encountered the same problems that had confounded Hansell, and although morale in his force had improved, results remained disappointing.

The move towards area bombing with incendiaries, which transformed the whole campaign, was to come largely at the prompting of LeMay himself, even though Arnold remained committed to precision raids on Japanese aero-industry plants. Recognizing the need for a change and being aware of Arnold's incapacity to intervene quickly due to ill-health, LeMay gambled with new tactics. For *Operation Meetinghouse*, the first mass-firebombing raid on Tokyo in March 1945, LeMay switched to night-time area attacks at low-level with reduced defensive armament, to increase payload. Moreover, following encouraging reports of incendiary raids in February, LeMay switched to using firebombs *en masse*. It had long been accepted that Japanese cities, constructed of highly combustible materials, would burn easily. The new tactics reduced wear and tear on the B-29's still temperamental engines and, importantly, exploited deficiencies in Japanese low-level anti-aircraft defences and the lack of suitable night-time interceptors. Although the stated aim was to attack industrial and strategic targets, this in reality equated to area bombing of urban areas in similar fashion to the RAF's bombing of Germany.[57]

The results were both appalling and spectacular. In the firebombing of Tokyo around 100,000 died in quite the most awful circumstances, with many suffocating from the lack of oxygen or dying from the intense heat caused by the firestorm. Others tried to escape by jumping into rivers, but quite often the water itself was boiling, resulting in further grisly carnage. American crews were shocked and repulsed by the sight of people being incinerated by napalm, and many wore their oxygen masks to escape the sickening stench of burning flesh. The attack proved all too vividly what the USAAF could do as Tokyo was devastated and one million people made homeless.[58] To compound the disaster, the Japanese were totally incapable of combating such raids and by early June, Nagoya, Kobe, Osaka, Yokohama and Kawasaki had followed Tokyo into ashes. Over 40 per cent of the urban areas of these cities were devastated and during June, July and August many minor Japanese cities went the same way.

There was no real attempt to rein in LeMay, even when General Spaatz was sent to the Pacific to command the 20th Air Force. The programme was well established and had been fully endorsed by Arnold and the USAAF staff in America. Justification was based on military expediency and, according to LeMay and his supporters, when confronted with industrial dispersal and a militarized society it was the only way to force Japan to surrender. In later raids US aeroplanes dropped leaflets warning civilians to leave urban areas as they were now potential targets, but the primary aim was to bludgeon Japan into surrender before growing war-weariness in the USA prompted a nego- tiated rather than an unconditional surrender. There was certainly concern over projected friendly casualties if US forces had to carry out *Operation Olympic*, the invasion of Japan, in November 1945. The fanatical resistance of the Japanese in the final island campaigns on Okinawa and Iwo Jima had demonstrated the willingness of the emperor's armed forces to fight on. In spite of the appalling suffering caused by the firebombings and with military production all but extinguished, still the army was determined to fight to the bitter end. Arguably, the limits of conventional bombing had been met and against a determined and fanatical foe it was perhaps not as decisive as had been hoped. Indeed, it was to take a number of further body blows in August to convince the Japanese to end the war, although it was the atomic bombings in particular of 6 and 9 August that delivered the *coup de grâce*.

The atomic bombs

No single act in the history of air power has epitomized the so-called degeneration into "total war" more vividly than the dropping of the atomic weapons on Japan in August 1945. The programme to develop the bomb had been underway for years and once again demonstrated that only the most technological and thoroughly organized of states could now attain the higher levels of military status. Indeed, by the end of World War II, only the USA could be considered a first class air power in strategic terms because only it had nuclear capability. The first atomic bomb was dropped by the B-29 *Enola Gay* on August 6 and 80–100,000 people perished. Thousands more were to die from burns and radiation poisoning in the days, months and years following. Three days later, and one day after the Soviet declara- tion of war with Japan, Nagasaki was destroyed by a second bomb which killed 35,000. The Japanese surrendered, though it should be noted that many still wanted to fight on and a last minute coup to prevent the transmis- sion of the emperor's call to lay down arms had to be averted. The escalation of war was in many ways complete and the atomic bombings elided with the fire bombings to open a new chapter in conflict. However, it could also be judged that what the US 20th air force achieved in the spring and summer of 1945 was exactly what had been considered before the war by theorists and air power advocates – surely this was Douhetism at its most intense?

Such was the impact of the atomic bombings that many post-war analysts have attributed, without question, a higher degree of decision making than was apparent at the time to those who decided to drop the bomb. Contemporary reservations were voiced, but such qualms had been aired over the fire bombings and rejected by those seeking to end the war as quickly as possible. Moreover, there were many who simply considered the atomic bomb to be just another, if more extreme, air weapon. As in the case of the Dresden raid, it was more of a question of why the USAAF should *not* drop the atomic bomb, rather than why they should. Moreover, the critical argument of those in power in 1945 was how they were to end the war as quickly as possible.

However, it would be disingenuous to argue that the atomic bombs did not represent something new, even though the Tokyo firebombing raid killed similar numbers to Hiroshima and considerably more than Nagasaki. In both cases vast numbers of people died and whether it was by one bomb or hundreds of bombs is to a certain degree a moot point. Yet somehow there is a difference in the minds of many and this has been exaggerated to such an extent that the firebombing of Japan has receded into the background. When one examines such issues it is essential to note that for the vast majority of contemporaries, the atomic bombings were just further steps along the road to victory.

However, the fact that the atomic bombs were and are viewed as a major escalation in air war has opened a whole debate as to why the bombs were ever dropped. In the post-war years nuclear weapons became political and diplomatic tools and many have viewed the atomic bombs, retrospectively, in the same way. The revisionist school of historians, principally spearheaded by Gar Alperovitz, has argued that the bombs were dropped for political reasons, primarily to intimidate the Soviets, and as such can be viewed as the first major act of the Cold War. The argument rests on the point that the political aspects of the decision to drop the bomb predominated over military considerations. It is claimed that Japan was about to surrender anyway, that the bombs were unnecessary to end the war and indeed that the US government prolonged the war in order to use the weapon to wring concessions out of Stalin.[59]

While these arguments probably attest a level of significance to the atomic bombs that was not so obvious at the time, it is clear that some in power did consider the bombs to be a new extreme in war and as such they could be used for broader political aims. However, this does not support the argument that such considerations predominated. The most significant argument revolves around whether or not Japan was about to surrender and, although there is evidence that the Japanese government was looking to end the war, it was on nothing approaching terms acceptable to the USA.[60] The fact that the Japanese were still vacillating after Nagasaki suggests that prior to the events of 6–9 August there was little likelihood of a realistic surrender being negotiated. Consequently the USA was liable to use all reasonable methods to end the war. The atomic bombings can therefore be viewed as another measure, following on from the fire bombings, towards forcing the Japanese surrender and as such in the context of the time can be viewed as "necessary", especially with the spectre of thousands of US casualties looming if *Operation Olympic* had to be carried through.

Much of the post-war debate has been fuelled by US army generals and navy admirals claiming, largely for political reasons, that the bombs were unnecessary to end the war.[61] The USSBS (Unites States Strategic Bombing Survey) claimed that Japan would have surrendered by November 1945 anyway, without the atomic bombings, the Soviet declaration of war or the intended *Operation Olympic*. This view has been recently questioned, however, as the basis of the survey's assumptions were founded on flawed post-war interviews. Moreover, the USSBS had certain institutional views, most notably that the conventional bombing campaign had been the key to US success.[62] However, it is difficult to accept that conventional methods could have ended the war with fewer casualties than the atomic bombings and certainly not with less Allied loss of life.

Perhaps the most obvious point is that the US forces and the US government wanted to end the war as quickly as possible, that they desperately wanted to avoid the carnage of invading Japan itself, and that this more than anything convinced the Americans to carry on the policy of pummelling Japan into surrender. This is not to argue that political considerations did not flow from that decision, but there is no effective evidence to support the contention that it prompted it.[63]

Conclusion

The war against Japan demonstrated more forcefully than ever that the ability to wage modern war rested on industrial capability and mobilization and that such utilization of resources was necessary for the deployment of effective air forces more than for other arms. Air power was now clearly the dominating factor in maritime war and, ultimately, it was air power that decided the outcome of the Pacific war in strategic as well as operational terms. Not only were Japan's armed forces swept aside because they could not compete in the air, but the whole structure of Japan was also threatened in the last year of the war by the USAAF's strategic bombing fleet in an entirely novel manner. Clearly, the demands of total war, of which air power continued to be a significant measure, were beyond Japan on economic, strategic and political levels and her failure in the air war was the most vivid example of what that failure, in the age of strategic bombers, could mean for the home population.

Ultimately, the atomic bomb had heralded a new age in warfare, an age in which air power was the final arbiter of conflict. The final years of World War II proved that air power was not only indispensable to the conduct of ground and maritime war, it now had the power to wreck cities in an instant and to incinerate whole populations in seconds. Yet, at the very moment when air power seemed to have vindicated the prophets of the interwar years, and indeed before, civilization looked into the abyss of truly total war and hesitated.

Chapter Eight

Air power and the post-war world

As the world came to terms with the impact of six years of global war, many political and military commentators and leaders were already wrestling with the new strategic scene and, indeed, had been since the closing stages of the conflict with the Axis nations. However, the emergence of the Cold War and the bi-polar world order, dominated by atomic and nuclear weapons, was by no means pre-ordained or obvious in 1945, although with the benefit of hindsight it may appear to have been so. The Soviet Union was exhausted by four years of savage conflict, Britain though wishing to pursue a world role was economically crippled and the USA had yet to develop a fully fledged international profile. The incremental slide into the Cold War was of course eventually to result in superpower confrontation, although never in open military conflict, and for this many have claimed that the fear of nuclear warfare was crucial. Politicians, especially when deflecting the arguments of the nuclear disarmament lobby, all too readily argued that nuclear weapons had kept the peace in Europe for decades and that an era of almost "total peace" had superseded the age of total war. Could it be therefore, that air power, the ultimate embodiment of total war had, when coupled with nuclear weaponry, attained such a level of sophistication and potential that full scale war was no longer a viable political option? Whereas direct military confrontation between the superpowers was to be rendered highly unlikely by the late 1950s and 1960s with the acceptance, if only implicitly by the USSR, of deterrence and mutually assured destruction (MAD), it was certainly not the case in the 1940s and early 1950s that strategic atomic weapons had that power. Moreover, the impact of the determination to develop such capability in strategic air power was to have serious repercussions on tactical and conventional air power, which consequently quickly declined in the post-war era, only to re-emerge in the 1980s as an important strategic level weapon.

The nature of modern air power

Many of the trends established in the interwar period continued into the post-1945 era, most notably air power's impact on the wider world. The creation of the global village, begun back in the 1930s, accelerated in the years after 1945 to the extent that by the late 1950s and early 1960s jet air travel had become readily accessible to mass populations in the industrial world. The development of jet airliners and a fully integrated world air travel network owed much to military advances in the wake of World War II, and jet technology, which supplanted piston-engined aircraft in the decade following 1945, built on the pioneering work of the wartime German scientists in particular. New developments and the pushing back of the boundaries of speed and endurance in air travel, fired by military activity, also filtered through to civil aviation. Notably, and in contrast to the interwar period, it was military aviation which led the way in the development of aerotechnology. Moreover, this trend manifested itself in other ways, the most important example being the input of the military into the early stages of space exploration.

The rate and level of technical advancement accelerated dramatically after 1945, raising unit costs and further dividing the dwindling band of first rate air powers from the rest. The post-war period has seen the development, for example, of V/STOL (vertical or short take-off and landing) aircraft, supersonic fighters, radar technology and missile systems (guided, surface-to-air, precision guided munitions and heat seeking, to name but a few). Indeed, some innovations have changed the nature of conflict quite significantly. The helicopter has offered tremendous flexibility to ground and logistical support operations, while perhaps the most revolutionary change to command and control of air war has come through the creation of AWACS (airborne warning and control system) aircraft, such as the Boeing E-3. Moreover, mid-air refuelling and stealth technology have provided the USA with enormous superiority over rival powers and an almost unchallenged capability to intervene anywhere on the planet. The increasing accuracy and ability to avoid euphemistically titled "collateral damage" has also enhanced the acceptability of intervention. One estimation of growing capability has argued that during the Gulf War, to destroy a target which previously took

4,500 B-17 or 95 F-105 sorties, now required just one F-117 (stealth bomber).[1] The political advantages of such "clean" actions, however artificial the circumstances may have appeared in the war against Iraq, are clear.

Although the development of ballistic missile technology by the late 1950s and early 1960s (ICBMs and SLBMs for example) seemed to undermine the development and role of air power, by taking away the strategic aspect of air forces, the importance of air power to military strategy and thinking remained. Indeed, during the arms reduction and limitation talks of the 1970s and 1980s, the respective levels of certain types of aircraft (the "Backfire" bomber for example) stayed at the forefront of negotiations. Moreover, in the post-Cold War world, where the tactical and operational aspects of conflict have, temporarily at least, eclipsed intercontinental strategic power, air forces have returned to prominence in military thinking. Clearly the importance of "cutting edge" military technology to major powers has resulted in new developments in the relationship between government, industry and the military. The growth of powerful aero-industries and the formation of the so-called "military-industrial" complex has been a source of much debate. The issue has arisen that governments have been forced or persuaded to buy the latest military technology by a combination of industrial profiteers and rampant militarists. Undoubtedly, the desire to maintain parity or to better the enemy was a major aim during the Cold War, and the demands of air power were at the forefront of this drive, but it is arguably the case that the heads of the aero-industries in the aftermath of the Second World War did not want to become too entangled and reliant on government financing. Circumstances dictated otherwise, and the perception that the USA and the USSR constantly had to compete with each other was one predicated on many beliefs and policies.[2] Nevertheless, it is clear that the demands of technological improvement and refinement have played a major part, more so than in the interwar era, in shaping the development of air power in the post-war world.

The end of totality

The impact of air power on the development of total war was profound, as has been explored, but, in the post-war world, certain aspects of this interaction have obviously altered significantly. With the emergence of potential nuclear destruction, the likelihood of long, drawn out attritional wars between major powers has all but been eliminated, certainly since the middle of the 1950s, and thus the widespread mobilization of national resources and the concomitant demands made by air power during wartime has, for the major powers, ceased to be an issue.

However, the depth of technological mobilization, even in peace time, has been maintained and almost certainly increased, with critical repercussions. Whereas the investment in new technology, in the USA prior to 1941, was in profitable capital goods, after 1945, it has been argued, the military persisted in focusing the development of new technology on the arms race and in particular on nuclear and air power weapons. The impact of this has been lower levels of investment in non-military high technology and the surrendering of the lead in this field to nations such as Japan.[3] Ultimately, the need to maintain technological parity and, if possible, superiority, has become vital and, arguably in the closing stages of the Cold War, decisive. Moreover, it has been argued that the inability of the Soviet Union to meet the technological demands of NATO's 1980s policy of the air-land battle and Follow-On Forces Attack (FOFA), which appeared to undermine significantly the Warsaw Pact's superiority in ground forces, was a key reason in the shift and ultimate collapse of Soviet defence policy.[4] Therefore, air power in the post-war era, and certainly in the past 20 years, has made a more focused and specific demand on aero-industries, but in its way it is arguably more total. Consequently, both superpowers, and to a lesser extent the medium powers, have made continuing and strenuous efforts to maintain the heavy technological commitment to air power, be it manned or missile based.

The totality of air power's impact on civilian populations has also developed in the post-war world. Although nuclear weapons arguably reduced the likelihood of Armageddon being visited upon them, populations have had to accept that they have become priority targets and if war did come it would almost certainly be total in its impact and destruction. Unlike the popular perceptions prior to World War II, when it was expected that air bombardment would take days or even weeks to bring about the destruction of urban life, in the age of the four minute warning and when nuclear holocaust threatened civilization itself, the totality of the threat increased dramatically. The notion of nuclear destruction seared itself into popular culture in all manner of ways. A wide variety of films, literature, music and peace movements are clear examples of the feared repercussions of mismanagement of the world situation. Films such as *The War Game*, *On the Beach*, and *Dr Strangelove* are perhaps the most famous examples. Although this was a continuation of a trend dating back to the late nineteenth century novels of Verne and Wells, the gravity of the situation from the late 1950s onwards was such that its impact was much more profound. Air power and nuclear weapons had brought about new perceptions of war in the popular consciousness, and the constant repressive fear of the "total" threat to civilization lingered for decades.

The limitations of post-war air power

Although some viewed air power as the ultimate weapon in the post-war period it was to transpire that air power had serious shortcomings and was not to dominate the military landscape of the world in the manner envisaged and which seemed to have been indicated in the closing stages of World War II.[5] Strategic and nuclear equipped air forces were not to play a major role in determining superpower policy until the mid-to-late 1950s, and only then did they exert the kind of restraining deterrent effect that emerged with the adoption of MAD. However, even when nuclear bombers and missiles were available in significant quantities they did not provide the level of deterrence expected. The USA and the USSR continued to be embroiled in indirect confrontation and, moreover, it was to become apparent that in anything other than *direct* confrontation, nuclear attack was neither credible nor realistic. The threat of nuclear annihilation, which was to be largely responsible for the obsolescence of total war by the late 1950s, did not prevent the Cold War from breaking out in other areas of the globe and on different levels and thus the notion that strategic air power had brought in an era of total peace cannot be accepted.

Conventional air power was also rendered relatively ineffective in the post-war world and this was perhaps more surprising. In no serious conflict were the western powers able to deploy conventional or tactical air power with any degree of decisiveness, that is, until Saddam Hussein offered an obliging target in 1991. Indeed, the predilection with strategic air power and the move to non-conventional forms of conflict repeatedly undermined the role air power could play in the post-war era.

Clearly, the development and trends in air power since 1945, certainly on the largest scale, have been away from total war and towards maintenance of peace and low-level conflict, and in the former case strategic nuclear air power has been successful. Not only has major war become politically unacceptable and hence unlikely, the speed with which it has been widely accepted that full scale war would escalate into a nuclear confrontation has meant that mobilization of industries and economies onto a total war footing has equally become unthinkable and pointless. The war would be over long before this was possible or indeed necessary.

In addition, the deployment of conventional air power on a scale large enough and total enough to reach levels similar to World War II has not occurred, for a number of reasons. First, western air powers have been confronted with non-conventional or low-intensity wars, such as Vietnam and Afghanistan, in which the full array of air power has not, and could not, be used for political reasons and was, in any case, found to be wanting when employed in peoples' wars. Moreover, unless an enemy power has been willing to fight an open, full scale conflict the effectiveness of air power has fallen away dramatically. The Gulf War proved what air power is technically capable of, but in confrontations in Afghanistan, Somalia and Bosnia, major powers were either unwilling or unable to utilize air power to the full.

However, where air power has been utilized by minor powers, further restraints have become apparent, underlining trends in the development of the nature of air power. Minor powers, unless backed by client superpowers, as in the case of Israel and the USA, have been unable to deploy air power with any degree of decisiveness because of the huge demands made of them by sustained air conflict. The Iran–Iraq war for example, illustrated that neither state was capable of maintaining a credible air power offensive because of the costs and levels of attrition involved. This resulted in the lowering of the level of technology deployed to reduce costs and maintain belligerency, thus decreasing effectiveness. The ability of a state to sustain air war probably now only rests with the major powers, and possibly only with the USA. Clearly the gap between the first rate military powers and the others has grown steadily since the late nineteenth century and, as we move into the new millennium, the rise in individual unit costs of aircraft has reached such levels that for the first time medium powers such as Britain and France, previously considered first rate air powers, have begun to adopt new methods of maintaining leading air power status, such as collaborative international development programmes and the possibility of accepting lower levels of technical proficiency to increase available numbers.

Therefore, far from emerging from the ruins of World War II as the supreme and omniscient force, air power has struggled to assert itself and its impact has been patchy and far short of what many in 1945 might have expected. It could be argued that air power as a pivotal weapon of total war had clearly proved its case during the Second World War, but from 1945 onwards, in many ways, it has failed to adapt to an age when total war has become less and less likely.

The rise of strategic nuclear air power

The most significant development in air power in the post-war world was undoubtedly the rise of the nuclear bomber and the ballistic missile. The emergence of a force with the capacity to raze cities to the ground with one bomb elevated, or degenerated, war onto a different level. The management and handling of this new weapon was to dominate not just air power but theories and strategies for the conduct of war as a whole in the post-war period. Ultimately, air theorists and strategists were to spend the next 40 years considering how to use nuclear weapons on a variety of levels, such as political, diplomatic and strategic, to the detriment of most other forms of air power and rarely with any degree of major success. Curiously however, less consideration was given to how to use nuclear weapons in a military sense. A sophisticated approach to targeting and planning was often lacking.

The primary concern of air power strategists, and indeed most military thinkers between 1945 and the early 1990s, was the confrontation between the USA and the USSR, with other minor nuclear powers only playing a limited role. The interaction between air power and this confrontation was essentially two way: air power dictated what was theoretically feasible, and thus at times drove policy, while peculiar political and economic forces drove air power development in certain directions to meet specific strategic requirements.

Perhaps the most significant theorist in the early era of nuclear strategy was Bernard Brodie who quickly recognized certain axioms of the future of air power, and indeed of national strategies. Brodie identified that atomic weaponry had in fact proved to be the salvation of strategic air war, because the reality was that no state would in the future be able to mount such a ruinously expensive war of attrition to gain command of the air as had been conducted by the USAAF and the RAF over Germany between 1940 and 1945. Only then had strategic bombing really started to prove decisive. This passes over the indirect yet crucial impact of the strategic air war on Germany, but the point was well made. The atomic bomb negated the need for a massive air superiority campaign, for one aircraft with one atomic bomb could do the task of a whole fleet of conventional strategic bombers in one mission. Although Brodie was critical of Douhet in other ways, he acknowledged that with the atomic bomb, the principles of Douhetism had, by a combination of events that the Italian could not possibly have foreseen, come to fruition.[6] The future of war was therefore to be radically different. Rather than planning to win wars, the need was now to prevent them and thus the policy of deterrence began to develop. Despite the claims of others, such as Edward Earle,[7] that strategic air power was now far too destructive and had to be negotiated into oblivion, Brodie argued that strategic atomic warfare had to be dealt with as a reality – it could not be "uninvented". The eventual and expected emergence of the long-range missile equipped with a nuclear warhead would indeed compound the problem still further.

A variety of air force generals were espousing similar thinking, though they were initially unwilling to accept the replacement of manned bombers with pilotless missiles.[8] In the USAAF, General Hap Arnold and his successor, Carl Spaatz, both talked of swift surprise attacks from the air being the only conceivable threat to the USA itself, and that the best form of defence was to develop the capability to strike back at potential enemies with equal or preferably greater force: in other words, atomic based strategic deterrence. Moreover, and like their pre-war forerunners, the arch advocates of air power again began claiming that air power had rendered land and maritime based forces largely redundant.[9] As the USA wrestled concurrently with the problems of mass demobilization and the deterioration of East–West relations, so atomic based strategic thinking began to embed in the US armed forces' theorizing or, more accurately, in the ideology of the newly created US Air Force (USAF – formed in 1947). However, such strategies were not incorporated into US strategy until the Cold War began to freeze with the blockade of Berlin and the outbreak of the Korean War.[10]

Indeed, during the late 1940s US atomic capability was decidedly limited. In 1946, the stockpile of atomic bombs numbered nine and the assembling of more would take three days with yet more time required to transport them to the operational bases.[11] Moreover, in early 1947 the US Strategic Air Command (SAC) had only six technicians available to arm such bombs and only ten B-29 bombers and 20 trained aircrews to deliver them. Still further, no air force A-bomb assembly teams would be available until the end of 1947 to replace their civilian predecessors.[12] Nevertheless, the strategic aim of US atomic forces was in theory already crystallizing and was based around the notion that 80 per cent of the USSR's industrial centres were within range of B-29s based in western Europe and the Middle East.[13] Clearly however, SAC was in no fit state to carry out such a plan and, in any case, the fusing of air power potential and national strategy was yet to occur. Clearly Harry Borowski's claim that US strategic air power in the late 1940s was merely a hollow threat rings true.[14]

The rise to prominence of nuclear based strategy occurred over the period between 1947 and 1954 when the USA's world position clarified and certain key events propelled the US government in the direction of deterrence and a defence policy reliant on nuclear arms. Although atomic bombing had been included in US strategic thinking since 1947, it was never central, partly because Truman had grave reservations about deploying them.[15] Moreover, by the time the Korean War broke out in 1950, the USSR had surprised the US by exploding its own atomic bomb, and the political scenario effectively precluded the early use of nuclear weapons by the Americans. Despite the calls by MacArthur for the use of atomic bombs, it took until the closing stages of the war for the US government to go as far as intimating that they might be used, and even then, it has been argued, the impact of the threat on the North Koreans and their supporters was overestimated.[16]

However, the Korean War was a key turning point. The success of the UN operation was tempered by the prohibitive cost of deploying large scale conventional forces, and ultimately, or so it seemed, the issue had been decided by the threat of nuclear force. Moreover, although the supremacy of the USAF's nuclear forces had been undermined by the arrival of the Soviet atomic bomb, new developments were already underway to strengthen the American position and regain temporary nuclear superiority.[17] Most notably this included the development of the hydrogen bomb, which was viewed by the US government as a measure to create a short term defensive deterrent which would allow the USA to build the expanded conventional forces required for the new world role the Americans had created for themselves, and which the Korean War had clearly demonstrated the West was lacking.[18]

For SAC, the war was timely to say the least. General Curtis LeMay's appointment as commander of SAC in 1948 had seen the beginning of a process of change and modernization, with LeMay determined not to allow the strategic air force to be caught unprepared and unawares as it was in 1942 over Germany.[19] Clearly much had to be accomplished and the USAF was horrified by its inability to offer an alternative during the Berlin Crisis of 1948–9, as the European based atomic forces were inadequate and effectively ignored by the Soviets.[20] The Korean War proved to be a major boost, therefore, by precipitating the injection of resources to allow the USAF to carry out a nuclear role if need be, something that clearly did not exist prior to 1950. To prevent this impotence occurring again it was accepted that a standing ready force for use in crisis situations was necessary. It was not acceptable to wait for a war to break out before strategic forces could be expanded to meet any threat developing from the war. Therefore, in 1952 the USAF argued for the creation a strong strike force capable of delivering an early knockout blow to act as a deterrent and to offer the USA a viable offensive strategic policy.[21]

By the time that Eisenhower became president in 1953, US defence policy was resting, albeit temporarily, on nuclear armed strategic air power while conventional forces, allowed to decline markedly since 1945, were rebuilt. The incoming administration rapidly reassessed the situation and moved strategic air power to the centre-stage even more, on the grounds of the exorbitant costs of developing a whole new generation of ground and tactical forces. The British were also moving in this direction. In order to maintain a world role, they would have to rely on the supposed deterrent and threat of nuclear weapons even more than the Americans. For the relatively impoverished Britons, who were unable to contemplate the massive expansion of their conventional forces, the nuclear option, even if it lay some way off, was crucial to sustaining superpower status, if only temporarily and with little basis in reality.[22] Eisenhower's thinking was based on a number of assumptions. Primarily, the new president was concerned about the long-term economic stability of the USA, which was central to the viability of any defence strategy. Any new policy would have to be based on solid fiscal foundations, and clearly the aspiration of the Truman administration, as stated in the NATO Lisbon goals, of wanting to create new conventional forces to make the western world defensible without recourse to nuclear arms, was financially ruinous and untenable.[23] Eisenhower was also convinced that any war in Europe would rapidly escalate to a nuclear war, and thus such weapons were a viable and acceptable part of the strategic environment in which the USA was situated. The best way to prevent such a war was to base defence on a clear and solid policy of deterrence through strong nuclear forces.

During the summer of 1953 *Project Solarium* was carried out to establish the USA's new defensive thinking, eventually being formalized in NSC (National Security Council) 162/2 in October 1953. In this so-called "New Look" strategy, future emphasis was to be placed on the use of nuclear weapons to deter further Soviet aggression, and SAC's capability was to be the cornerstone of the policy. Any major act of Soviet aggression was to be met with the threat of a massive nuclear attack by the USA's strategic air forces. However, SAC was still in no fit state to meet this demand and would not be until the middle of the 1950s, and therefore USAF's slice of the defence budget was to be increased to 46 per cent, considerably more than either the navy or the army, clearly emphasizing the status of air power in US defence planning.[24] Moreover, to make good continuing deficiencies in conventional forces in Europe it was accepted that tactical nuclear weapons would be used to supplement conventional NATO forces in order to defeat the superior Eastern Bloc ground forces.[25]

Eisenhower's long-haul strategy of creating a solid defence policy based on lower costs resulted in $8.4 billion dollars being shaved off the defence budget – clearly a "bigger bang for a buck" as was stated by one defence secretary.[26] The policy was underpinned by a speech made by Secretary of State John F. Dulles in January 1954, in which he claimed that US defence policy was now predicated upon an instant and "great capacity to retaliate" to Soviet aggression.[27]

Thus was born the notion of massive retaliation, a frequently misquoted and misunderstood stratagem. All too readily, commentators perceived that the USA was setting up a trip wire policy in which any act by the USSR, or indeed acts believed to be backed by the Soviets or China, would be met by a huge nuclear strike by SAC.[28] This of course was patently untrue. The USA maintained flexibility in its approach and it was never accepted policy that a minor war in a remote part of the globe against communist insurgents would result in the devastation of Moscow or Peking, as Dulles made clear later in 1954.[29]

Nevertheless, flaws in the new air power based policy of national defence quickly emerged. The policy was accepted as being viable only as long as the USA could maintain significant nuclear superiority, but the savings made by relying on the New Look were considerable and it would take a strong and perhaps foolhardy US administration to revert to an expensive conventional defence policy in the future when the USSR caught up. In other words, a future US government would have to deal with the problem of either persevering with a weakened nuclear deterrent, or investing heavily in considerably expanded conventional forces. Ultimately, it could be argued, this is what the Reagan administration did from 1981 onwards. However, it took two decades for the USA to accept the problem that had been bequeathed to it by the switch to nuclear defence in the early-to-mid-1950s.

Massive retaliation also brought problems for NATO. In the 1950s the Europeans were struggling to expand their contribution to conventional defence and the emergence of nuclear deterrence in part allowed them, like the USA, to evade the question of dealing with such problems. Europe came to rely first on US strategic nuclear defence, and secondly, on the use of tactical nuclear weapons to deter or even defeat an Eastern Bloc invasion, even though this latter case was likely to embroil the USA in a nuclear war with the USSR. Although the Europeans were to remain nervous about US commitment to such a scenario, it proved difficult to wean them off reliance on nuclear defence at all levels.

Most importantly, however, massive retaliation was severely undermined by the rapid emergence of a viable Soviet nuclear arsenal, both strategic and tactical, in the years following the instigation of Eisenhower's New Look. The credibility of America's nuclear deterrent only existed while the USSR could not strike back in a similar fashion. Once this was no longer the case, the likelihood of the USA launching a massive nuclear strike against the USSR, and thus themselves suffering the consequences of a Soviet counter-strike, was slim. And by the middle of the 1950s the Soviet Union had such a capability.

The rise of Soviet strategic air power

Despite the blasé acceptance of the existence of the atomic bomb at the Potsdam meeting in July 1945, Stalin had been desperately driving forward a programme to build a Soviet atomic bomb to negate the threat of an American device. The level of the mobilization of a weakened Soviet economy in the post-war era is testimony to the importance attached to the acquisition of a comparable device to the American bomb. The demands made on Soviet investment at a time when reconstruction was urgently required fused with espionage to produce a plutonium atomic device by 1949, although it appears that the USSR would have had a bomb by 1951/52 without outside input anyway.

Stalin was conscious that a world where the USA had atomic weapons, and the USSR did not, would be unacceptable and a clear symbol of the superiority of the capitalist West over the communist East. Before the USSR had acquired atomic weapons, Stalin's policy was one of bluff, in which he pursued a belligerent foreign policy that belied his concern over the American atomic monopoly. By conducting the policies he did, for example over the Berlin crisis, Stalin attempted to convince the West that atomic weapons mattered little in foreign policy. Despite the heavy burden, Stalin determined to pursue the policy, even when others counselled a more conciliatory approach to East–West relations. The long term cost was the acceptance of a ruinous arms race with the USA, first to attain atomic capability, then thermonuclear weapons, followed by ballistic missiles, and ultimately the capacity for mutually assured destruction. Although Stalin died in 1953, he had already set in motion a policy that successive Soviet leaders could do little about. With the Cold War already deep and hostility and rivalry endemic, the moment to avert the arms race and the age of nuclear plenty had passed long before the middle of the 1950s. It must also be stated that the cost of conciliation with the USA in the late 1940s was one that few Soviets, and certainly not Stalin, would have been willing to accept.[30]

By the middle of the 1950s, the course and nature of the development of strategic air power in the era of the Cold War was set and, although manned bombers were to be replaced by intercontinental ballistic missiles (ICBMs) and submarine-launched ballistic missiles (SLBMs), the essence remained much the same, despite being intensified in the 1960s with the emergence of mutually assured destruction. One side's developments resulted in a counter by the opposition and a general unwillingness to accept any perceived vulnerability led to mistrust and antipathy. The arms race epitomized the perceived place strategic nuclear air power, be it bomber or missile based, had to play in international politics and strategy. The newly elected President

Kennedy came to believe that a budget deficit would not cripple the US economy and thus, in contrast to Eisenhower, was happy to expand the US defence programme along the lines urged by his military advisor, Maxwell Taylor. By the early 1960s, the USA held 1,000 Minuteman and 54 Titan ICBMs, 41 Polaris submarines, each with 16 SLBMs and a force of nuclear bombers, largely created in an effort to eradicate a perceived technological inferiority to the Soviet Union following the launch of Sputnik in 1957.[31] Soon after, the USSR launched a new expansion and development programme to make good a perceived deficiency supposedly exposed during the Cuban missile crisis of 1962. Still further, in the late 1960s, the USA developed multiple independently targetable re-entry vehicles (MIRV) to make up for an apparent inferiority in the respective numbers of missiles held by the superpowers.[32] Indeed, although US missile levels stayed at 1,750 from 1967 onwards the number of warheads carried expanded to a staggering 7,000, more than enough to destroy all Soviet cities many times over.[33]

Wholly new strategies were developed to control or deploy such weapons of mass destruction. The US policy of massive retaliation was completely undermined by the rise of Soviet strategic nuclear capability, and the consequent emergence of MAD was in essence a method of management, a tacit acceptance that nuclear weapons were no longer merely another weapon in the diplomatic war of international relations. There were concerns over the development of first strike capabilities and viable counter-measures were all viewed as potentially destabilizing effects, thus illustrating a crucial difference between the nuclear age and the age of conventional bomber deterrence of the 1930s when such deterrence was far less credible.[34] Nevertheless, the finely balanced nuclear deterrence held, largely because the consequences of failure were unthinkable. The search for first strike capability (the strategy of wiping out the enemy's nuclear strength in one surprise first attack) continually foundered because of technical failings and because of the basic underlying assumption that the risks of creating such a capability were too great. It was a tenet of nuclear strategy not to make opponents believe that they were vulnerable to a first strike because it might prompt them into rash preventative action of their own. The power and fear of nuclear weapons was such that direct and hostile confrontation between two similarly equipped powers was something to be avoided, and in this respect air power had reached its zenith in making mass war both unfeasible and unthinkable.

Yet for all that supposed power, in reality strategic nuclear weapons played a largely peripheral role in the conduct and development of Cold War strategies. Little of advantage was ever gained out of the possession of nuclear weapons, other than the avoidance of suffering the disadvantage of not possessing them. Even in the latter case, as existed in the late 1940s, the use of such power, even if the Americans had actually possessed it, was effectively unthinkable without considerable and direct military provocation. The use of military force has invariably rested on notions of proportionality and it would have been, and still would be, unthinkable for a state to respond to a minor skirmish or low intensity conflict with nuclear retaliation. It has been argued that the fire bombings of Dresden and Hamburg were disproportionately destructive when measured against the strategic and political benefits gained. That is an arguable case but a nuclear strike against Vietnam in 1968 by the USA, or by Britain against Buenos Aires in 1982, were not: both would have been politically unacceptable and both demonstrated the impotence of nuclear arms in confrontations with lesser powers, or indeed against any power in a low or medium threat scenario. This latter case was always the concern of NATO, for the nagging doubt remained that the USA would not risk, or offer a viable and credible threat of, strategic nuclear escalation to "save" Europe from a conventional Soviet attack.

Tactical and conventional air power

Therefore, by the early 1960s, strategic nuclear air power had reached an impasse and, since that time, the more interesting and far reaching air power developments have come in the tactical and, for the most part, conventional field. Ultimately, the perceived growth in the effectiveness of tactical air power in the 1980s was to have pivotal strategic consequences. However, in the two decades after World War II the decline in tactical air power capability was remarkable and, perhaps until the 1980s, only Israel, in peculiar circumstances, was able to marry air power to strategic national goals in an effective manner.

The Korean War exposed many failings in the tactical air forces of even the USA and the emphasis on strategic air power in the years after World War II had led to the clear neglect of other areas of air capability. General Weyland, the air officer commanding US Far East air forces, famously stated that what was remembered from World War II was not written down, or if written down was not disseminated, or if disseminated was not read or properly understood.[35] Tactical air power equipment had not moved on since 1945, and indeed was less plentiful, while more importantly the air forces lacked direction. Air superiority was roughly maintained throughout the conflict by the western forces but because there was no overall integration of air power into offensive land operations, tactical air forces achieved only a minimal impact. Interdiction of enemy supplies and movement was achieved but this in itself could not be enough, proving as World War II had, that there were limitations to tactical air power and its best use was in support of a concerted all arms operation.[36] Korea was a frustrating experience for the USAF which preferred to argue afterwards that such a campaign was most unlikely to occur again and resources should be concentrated on the confrontation with the USSR. Such thinking was to have a deleterious effect on the ability of US air power in Vietnam.

In other ways Korea was to be a watershed in the founding of the western alliance and NATO. The West's limitations were exposed in the Far East and plans were put in hand to remedy the situation with attention naturally being paid to Europe. The Lisbon discussions resulted in a target of 9,000 tactical aircraft being set in April 1953, but the degree of rearmament accepted in that year would have been similar in level to the British and French military expansion of the late 1930s. Although expansion did take place in the early 1950s the British were keen to promote the cheaper nuclear alternative, both at tactical and strategic levels.[37] Weyland, now Commander-in-Chief, Tactical Air Command, was also an advocate of tactical nuclear weapons as a means of balancing the Eastern Bloc's apparently overwhelming conventional forces advantage. Secretary of State Dean Acheson was surprised at the interest in what he described as "Buck Rogers" gadgets, but with the emergence of the New Look, NATO tactical air power developed a nuclear reliant doctrine for operations in Europe.[38] Clearly such a policy was cheaper, for the size of ground forces could be rationalized at lower levels than the Lisbon agreement had set. Moreover, the degree of training and sophistication of tactical aircraft need not be so high because the strength of the force was in the nuclear weaponry. Consequently, air superiority fighters, direct ground co-operation aircraft and training declined, as it was naturally assumed that a war in Europe would require NATO to deploy nuclear weapons with which it was difficult to miss. Again, the USAF was later to rue this policy when confronted with the Vietnam problem.[39]

There were of course drawbacks with NATO's new doctrine. First, the extra reliance on nuclear weapons for the defence of Europe both at strategic and tactical levels meant that it would be much harder in the future to draw the Western Alliance away from such a strategy because the alternative, major expansion of conventional forces, was financially unpalatable. Secondly, and perhaps more importantly, by the early 1960s the Warsaw Pact forces also had tactical nuclear weapons, undermining the deterrent effect that NATO's short-range nuclear weapons might have had.

By the late 1960s, NATO defence strategy was in a state of flux. Western Europe was in effect still depending for its defence on nuclear weapons and, in particular, the USA's massive intercontinental arsenal. This however, as has been explored, lacked credibility: the USA wanted to confine a war to Europe and at all costs aimed to avoid massive escalation which would result in a nuclear holocaust. The attempt in 1967 to adopt so-called "flexible response", in effect dealing with each problem as it emerged with a variety of forces, did little to solve the underlying issue that NATO was in no fit state to stop a Warsaw Pact attack by conventional means – at some stage nuclear escalation would be required.

In contrast, Warsaw Pact strategy was to rely on conventional forces and avoid nuclear escalation, for quite obvious reasons. Indeed, Soviet air power was more conventionally based, although tactical nuclear capability existed to be deployed if NATO escalated a confrontation, or if the situation warranted it. Soviet air doctrine was predicated on the axioms established during World War II and centred on the use of air forces to support any ground offensive in Europe. Much of Soviet air strength was intended to seize air superiority, or at least to eliminate the threat of NATO air power to Warsaw Pact ground forces.[40] To compound the problem for NATO, Soviet air forces obtained the lion's share of an overall four per cent per annum increase in Soviet defence expenditure between 1970 and 1978, and indeed the Soviet air force expanded by 50 per cent between 1967 and 1977.[41]

However, for perhaps the only time in the Cold War, air power was to have a pivotal impact on the development of events and not just the formulation of strategy. Arguably, strategic nuclear air power impacted little on the outcome of the Cold War. Paradoxically, it was to be NATO's development of a new tactical air doctrine that was to be the most significant effect air power had on the superpower relationship. That initiative was the concept of the integrated "air-land battle" and in particular the development of Follow-On Forces Attack (FOFA) in the early 1980s. For perhaps the first time, NATO began to wrestle with the problem of confronting a much larger Warsaw Pact ground force capability with non-nuclear forces. By utilizing the latest technology in communications, control, targeting and delivery systems, NATO aimed to develop the ability to break up Eastern Bloc attacks by halting enemy front-line attack units and then destroying "follow-on forces" as much as 100 miles into the rear zone of the Warsaw Pact area.[42] In many ways the development plan was to bring at least parity in conventional forces to NATO without recourse to massive increase in manpower. It was estimated that by placing greater emphasis on new technology the West would be able to steal a march on the East and lessen or eradicate the need to rely on nuclear weapons to meet a Soviet backed invasion of Germany.

The development of FOFA was a prime example of President Reagan's expansion of US defence forces in general to combat the so called "empire of evil" in the early 1980s. Indeed in many ways the development of FOFA was most important, for the aim was to negate the one significant advantage the Warsaw Pact had over the West – conventional forces. Although FOFA was a long-term aim and the capability did not exist in the middle of the 1980s to carry it out properly, the effect of this new programme on the Soviet hierarchy was marked. It was considered that, without a major re-organization of the Soviet defence and development system the USSR would not be able to meet the challenge. Far from just negating a perceived Soviet advantage, the West had set in motion the seeds of Gorbachev's reforms and the ultimate collapse of the Soviet empire.

Conventional air power outside Europe

Since 1945, air power has been used in a number of theatres away from direct superpower confrontations, often for colonial purposes, but invariably it has had limited effect. For the most part, air forces have been used in a supporting transport and logistical role and only on occasion have they been allowed to be deployed to their full potential. This certainly applied in French actions in Indochina and Algeria, and likewise to the British in southeast Asia. The concentration on strategic and Europe based air policies was to have serious consequences on US air capability away from its NATO commitments in the Cold War era. The failings, which had been in effect left unaddressed since Korea, were exposed in America's disastrous Vietnam escapade. During their long involvement in southeast Asia, America's air forces struggled to assert the authority they could and should have been able to command. The Second World War had supposedly proven that an enemy with no or little air support was at the mercy of a state with strong air capability and determined ground units. However, Vietnam was not the kind of conflict the USAF and the other US air forces had trained for, nor did they relish it. Indeed, both the limited nature and style of the war confronting the USA combined to dissipate the advantages air power might have brought.

Perhaps most importantly, the air forces were never allowed to impose themselves as they had in World War II, but in addition the terrain and the existing force structure of the US air forces helped to hinder their activities still further. The unwillingness of the US government, which controlled events and operations very tightly, to allow their forces to secure control of the air resulted in US aircrews having to operate under the threat of surface-to-air missile (SAM) attack. US air power losses to enemy action amounted to an incredible 2,561 aeroplanes and 3,587 helicopters.[43]

In essence, US air forces were deployed as political and diplomatic weapons and were only used in a stuttering and limited fashion, which in effect forced both Vietnam and the western forces to suffer a slow and lingering period of death and destruction. US B-52 bombers dropped around 3,750,000 tons of bombs on southeast Asia during US involvement in the region, but only some six per cent on the source of American concerns, North Vietnam. When finally unleashed in 1972, during *Operation Linebacker*, the US air forces were able to demonstrate their military effectiveness, in particular during *Linebacker II*, with over 700 B-52 sorties being undertaken over an 11 day period in December 1972.[44] However, the notion that the North Vietnamese were "bombed" back to the negotiating table is something of a myth. They were looking to talk anyway, aware as they were of the Americans' weakening resolve. Even if area bombing could have been deployed effectively back in 1965, the political ramifications and international condemnation would have been significant, again underlining the limited conditions in which air power could be properly used. The idea that the USA would have been justified in "carpet bombing" cities in support of a minor policing and support operation in 1965 is simply not tenable, in political and perhaps moral terms. Vietnam proved that air power was an excellent weapon of major war, but of limited use in supporting low-intensity conflicts restricted by political considerations.[45]

Afghanistan demonstrated again that without a clear long term goal and the freedom to achieve it, even superpower forces could come to grief. Air operations in Afghanistan centred on general air support and limited close support firepower sorties. Despite the hostile terrain and the general indecision of the campaign from a political perspective, the VVS (Soviet Air Force) carried out their tasks with low loss rates until the advent of US Stinger and British Blowpipe SAMs in the mid-1980s. With such weapons available, the *Mujahedin* were able to increase loss rates on Soviet air forces, dramatically curtailing the effectiveness of airborne operations, and thus overall Soviet effectiveness as their tactics were heavily reliant on air support. As in Vietnam, although outright military victory was never an option, the use of an attritional persisting strategy served the *Mujahedin* well. Air power was incapable of delivering much more to the Soviets than it did in the war. Indeed, whereas the Americans were eventually able to deploy air power to questionable strategic effect in 1972, the USSR did not have that option owing to the nature of the campaign. Air power was able to deliver a stalemate in Afghanistan but without recourse to a brutal and protracted ground campaign in which heavy losses would naturally have been incurred, outright military victory for either side was an unlikely option.[46]

The inability of air forces to impose themselves on non–standard conflicts has been illustrated many times in the post-war era, but Vietnam and latterly Afghanistan have been the most vivid examples. The attention paid to nuclear options in Europe has been partly responsible, but the most obvious reason for their failing has been the fact that air forces, by their very nature, can have only a limited impact in less than full scale war. Moreover, in the post-war world, actions have often taken place in the full glare of world attention and the acceptability of tactics used by the colonial powers was thus greatly reduced. In what amounted to policing or containment operations in the post-war era, air forces could play only a supportive role (for example, transport, reconnaissance and logistics). There are clear political and physical constraints on what air forces can do in such circumstances as was the case in Bosnia or Somalia, for example.

Maritime air power has suffered in the post-war world from the lack of a clearly identifiable enemy. The US Navy ended World War II as the most powerful, but maritime opponents have not emerged since 1945 to offer a viable threat. Only in the late 1960s did the USSR begin to develop significant surface naval power, but it was never even close to being a major threat, and nor was it particularly important to Soviet strategy. The dominance of air power in maritime strategy provoked questions in the post-war years over the validity of maintaining large carrier battle groups akin to those used to defeat Japan, as the peculiar circumstances which led to the nature of fighting witnessed in the Pacific War were highly unlikely to be repeated. Moreover, in the 1950s and 1960s, with nuclear considerations dominating, the value of investment in conventional carrier forces was seriously questioned, and indeed continues to be so.

In the context of the Cold War, and in a strategic sense, the US Navy's air-maritime forces played a limited role but, as a means of dominating a given area in a conventional manner, carrier battle groups and their air forces have proven effective, for example offering sustained support during the USA's involvement in Korea and Vietnam. The argument that such fleets are expensive white elephants has not really been sustained, especially when carriers offer a high degree of flexibility in a supportive, policing or low-intensity conflict scenario. Even medium powers such as France and Britain have maintained greater world roles by their ability to offer air support in a flexible manner from sea-based platforms. However, the US Navy considers that its carrier groups are not suited to full scale war environments and are best deployed as symbols of intent in low intensity situations. If so, questions regarding the returns on investments in such forces emerge if they are so limited. However, while it remains unlikely that an air–naval war between two major powers will occur, the real role of carrier groups has and will continue to be to offer a relatively secure, mobile and flexible military capability, as well as providing an important political and diplomatic weapon amid the confusion of threats and problems likely to emerge in the twenty-first century.[47]

Perhaps the most successful linking of conventional air power to national strategic goals occurred away from the superpower confrontation, in Israel, although as with all international affairs in the Cold War period the USSR–USA struggle had a peripheral influence. The survival of Israel in the post-1945 world has perhaps been the nearest approximation to a total war, though actual conflict has been sporadic and since the late-1970s the level of direct threat to Israel has receded. Nevertheless, Israel used air power to great effect to defeat her Arab adversaries and in doing so demonstrated what air power, in a true international war situation, was capable of.

However, caveats must be noted and not least the fact that these were conventional conflicts between states fought over open terrain. Moreover, although air power was crucially effective in 1967, it was less so in 1973 and in the Lebanon campaign of the 1980s the limits of an air force's ability to intervene in non-standard operations were again illustrated. In addition, although Israel has been able to link air power to clear national goals and strategies in a more effective manner than others, it must also be remembered that they have had a forgiving and generous sponsor in the USA from whom considerable resources have flowed to allow Israel to be aggressive with her air forces. Arguably, without such support and in a long and protracted campaign, Israeli air power would have declined in a similar manner to the air forces deployed by Iran and Iraq in the war of the 1980s.[48]

With the collapse of the Soviet Union, contemporary air power has been confronted with a radically altered environment and one in which two extremes of operations have been illustrated. First, throughout most of the 1990s, air power has been impotent in the Balkans, for many of the reasons that befuddled US involvement in Vietnam and Soviet intervention in Afghanistan. A lack of clear political goals, no identification of attainable military objectives and a hostile and volatile operating environment have all conspired to limit what air forces could offer. Clearly, air power has a significant role to play in such peacekeeping or low intensity campaigns, in terms of transport, air mobility, resupply and intelligence gathering. However, fire support in an environment such as Bosnia could only be limited, for political reasons. In sharp contrast, air power was heralded as the key factor in Allied victory in the Gulf War of 1990–91. There is little doubt that the ground force's job was rendered little more than a mopping up operation after the highly effective aerial bombardment both of Iraqi military and strategic metropolitan targets. If an example of Douhet's thesis was needed this was surely it, argued many air power advocates in the aftermath of the overwhelming success. However, neither Bosnia nor the Gulf have offered conclusive proof of anything. Iraq offered a conventional target in a helpful operating environment and the Allies held huge qualitative and quantitative advantages in equipment and personnel. Air supremacy was never in doubt and, with a relatively clear political objective and a mandate to use considerable force, the Allies were able to deploy conventional air power to the full. In other circumstances there is little evidence to support the notion that air power would be as decisive.

Future air power forces are clearly going to need a high degree of flexibility to meet requirements for operations as varied as Bosnia and the Gulf – both are possibilities in the twenty-first century. Moreover, strategic level nuclear forces have not been made redundant with the collapse of the Soviet Union, although their hold on military thinking and strategic thought has largely been broken.

Conclusions

There have been a number of changes in the relationship of air power to war, strategy and peace in the post-1945 era. Most notable has been the loosening of the grip of total war as the manner in which conflicts between major powers are ultimately resolved. The likely levels of destruction which would accrue from such a conflict in the age of nuclear weapons have meant that in many ways the links between air war and mobilization of economies and mass industries have been broken. The apogee of total war between 1939 and 1945 demonstrated that mass mobilization of a nation's, indeed many nations', resources were required to sustain an effective air war campaign. However, the post-1945 world has been very different. Not only did the spectre of nuclear holocaust emerge, but the technology of aircraft increased dramatically to such levels that mass mobilization and attritional campaigns were untenable. What became necessary in the Cold War world was not mass mobilization, but harnessing of specific parts of industry and the economy to meet the needs of air power. The technological aspects of this "war without fighting" made huge demands, however, and ultimately the USSR was unable to maintain parity. In contrast, the USA arguably devoted such resources to this war that by the late-1980s the industrial and technological lead forged out the Second World War had been frittered away in profligate and highly focused investment in non-productive military technology, allowing others such as Japan to catch up.

Clearly, although in many ways the age of total war had passed, the demands of air power on a nation's material and psychological resources remained. The threat of nuclear destruction hung constantly over the world for decades in a manner more intense than the fear of massed bombing attack in the 1930s, and while open war between the superpowers never broke out, conflict by proxy, through client states, continued right up to the collapse of the Soviet Union. In these instances air power was a key, factor, initially being the sole instrument of deterrent, and ultimately being a key factor in the technological escalation that precipitated the disintegration of the Eastern Bloc.

As the twentieth century draws to a close, the influence air power continues to exert over military activity, now more likely to be conventional and limited in aims and levels of intensity, remains crucial. Although the post-war years have again reiterated the point that air power cannot act alone and nor can it be the sole determining factor in the development of strategies, it has become abundantly clear that operations must be supported by effective and efficient air power. Even in confused scenarios such as Bosnia, air forces have a key role to play in offering flexibility and supporting firepower, and with the receding threat of nuclear war it is in the conventional field that air power will continue to play its most significant role.

Chapter Nine

Conclusions

Air power: a cause and measure of total war?

In just 50 years or so, air power developed from the first controlled flight to the level of destroying cities and whole societies with, by the 1950s at least, remarkably little effort. During this revolutionary period, the age of total war came and went as did, quite possibly, the apogee of air power. Certainly the kind of mass air power and total mobilization of effort seen in World War II will not be witnessed again in anything like the same manner: far too many economic, technological and political factors would preclude it. However, this is not to state that air power no longer exerts significant influence over military and political activity as it quite evidently does. But the nature and extent of air power born in the Great War, which struggled to assert itself in the interwar years, and then ultimately which played a crucial and arguably pivotal role in World War II, is now a phenomenon of the past.

Air power in the age of total war, as has been seen, changed both the "face" and the "body" of war. For those involved in the fighting, the harnessing of air power became fundamental to survival. Even in the Great War, failure to utilize air strength effectively could result in disaster and, by the Second World War, air power was critical to success. Indeed, much of Germany's achievement in the 1939–42 period rested on air superiority and the effective implementation of air doctrine developed in the interwar era. Although not the sole cause of Germany's defeat, it is no surprise that the *Luftwaffe*'s sharp decline coincided with Germany's failure and collapse from 1942 onwards, notably even when German ground forces maintained their unit-for-unit superiority over both Soviet and western Allied forces. Japan, similarly, slid to defeat: as initial air superiority was frittered away or sacrificed in attritional battles, so effective and sustained belligerency drained away and ultimately Japanese civilians and cities were to pay the price for such shortcomings.

By World War II, air power dictated the conduct of operations in almost all theatres of war. Only on the Eastern Front did aircraft play a supportive role, largely for economic and geographical reasons. Elsewhere, success was virtually unthinkable without air supremacy, or at least the ability to contest air superiority for a sustained period. Air power alone was not enough to win. It had to be integrated into an overall combined arms strategy. But it did more than any other arm to prepare and spearhead the road to victory.

However, air power did more than recast the face of battle. More than any other force, it impacted markedly on the nature of industrial war. Both world wars required massive mobilization and effort from the whole "body" of the nation, and aero-industries in particular, made specific and concentrated demands because of the high levels of attrition and particular types of resources required to maintain air campaigns.

For the western Allies, air strength was a measure of their success. In both world conflicts they realized more than Germany and her allies, that the route to victory lay in mass-production. In the interwar period, with war looming again, Britain and the USA built the foundations of their expanding aero-industries, in a way that Germany could and would not mirror. The Allies realized that "total war" made far greater and more specific requirements of an economy and, in particular, that air power made the greatest demands, not only in simple levels of resources, but also in the nature and type of technological, scientific and industrial effort required. The Allies, the Soviet Union included, understood what sacrifices would have to be made and accordingly built air strength of immense and overwhelming power by 1944. The consequences of failure for Germany were catastrophic and defeat came rapidly once air supremacy had been conceded.

The failure to contest control of air space over an industrial state resulted in disaster. Clearly of most significance to the civilian populations of Europe and the Far East was the threat and then the reality of aerial bombardment. Since before World War I, fear of this new weapon of war had loomed large over societies and governments alike. To mass populations nothing encapsulated modern war more than air raids and the panic and terror which ensued. The impact on cities and urban populations was huge, requiring a wholly new approach to war: civil defence, air-raid precautions, evacuation of non-essentials, dispersal of industry and much more. Equally, civilian populations became the targets of concerted military action for sustained periods for the first time, and the threat and experience seared itself onto the consciousness of the modern world.

Since 1945, the impact of air power on the conduct and planning of conflict has lessened, largely because mass industrial war has, in effect, become obsolete. Mass air power was first and foremost a weapon of "total war" and that age has gone. Nevertheless, air power, in conjunction with nuclear weapons, played a significant part in shaping the Cold War, forcing both sides, certainly by the 1950s, to re-evaluate their attitudes and approaches to war itself. War was not made obsolete by nuclear armed air forces, as some have argued, but it had become so potentially destructive that war had to be conducted by other means. When so constrained, air power has been less effective. Air strength is still crucial to traditional military success, but in order to be fully effective, restraints have to be removed and in limited war environments this cannot be the case. Moreover, new modes of conflict such as terrorism and guerrilla activity, to say nothing of peace enforcement and anti-drug trafficking duties, have offered new challenges to which air power has only slowly adapted. In the post-Cold War world these are the challenges which air power must now confront in a manner which arguably it did not in the period between 1945 and 1991.

There is little doubt that air power transformed warfare in the most revolutionary manner, quite possibly, since humankind first started organizing itself into antipathetic tribal groupings. The escalation of war into the skies was a culmination of the drive towards mass industrial war, a trend begun a century before as western civilization first started linking economic strength with military capability on an ever increasing scale. In addition, the impact on society was significant indeed, shaping and changing perceptions of the role and place of war in the modern world. By the 1914–1945 era, war had become "total" indeed, and the emergence of air power as a decisive force, and one which required vast economic resources, was a critical multiplying factor in this transformation. Thus, air power and total war were linked as both causes and consequences of each other, shaping and deepening the experience of war in the twentieth century to a degree unknown in modern history.

Notes

Chapter One

1. A good example being: E. Hobsbawm, "Barbarism: a user's guide", *New Left Review* **206**, July–August 1994.
2. The three key effects of strategic bombing can be found in: W. Murray, *Luftwaffe – strategy for defeat* (Washington: Allen & Unwin, 1983); R. Overy, *Why the Allies won* (London: Jonathan Cape, 1995); and S.L. McFarland & W.P. Newton, *To command the sky* (Washington: Smithsonian Institution Press, 1991).
3. S. Garrett, *Ethics and airpower in World War Two* (New York: St. Martin's, 1993), p. 167.
4. G. Best, *Humanity in warfare* (London: Weidenfeld & Nicolson, 1980), pp. 262–3.
5. D.C. Watt, "Restraints on war in the air before 1945", in *Restraints on war: studies in the limitation of armed conflict*, M. Howard (ed.) (Oxford: Oxford University Press, 1979); Best, *Humanity in warfare*; Garrett, *Ethics and airpower in WWII*; R. Saundby, "The ethics of bombing", *Air Force and Space Digest* **50**(6), 1967; R. Schaffer, "American military ethics in World War Two – bombing of German civilians", *Journal of American History* **47**, 1980; R.H. Wyman, "The first air rules of warfare", *Air University Review* **35**(3), 1984; W. Hays Parks, "Conventional aerial bombing and the law of war', *US Naval Institute Proceedings* **108**(5), 1982.
6. C. Barnett, *Engage the enemy more closely* (London: W.W. Norton, 1991), see the chapter entitled "The battle for the air" in particular.
7. L. Robineau, "French air policy in the inter-war period and the conduct of the air war against Germany from September 1939 to June 1940, in *The conduct of the air war in the Second World War*, H. Boog (ed.) (Oxford: Berg, 1992); P. Vennesson, "Institution and airpower: the making of the French air force", in *Airpower: theory and practice*, J. Gooch (ed.) (London: Frank Cass, 1995) for the alternative view.

8. R. Overy, introduction to Boog, *The conduct of the air war in WWII*.

9. M. Parillo, *The Japanese merchant marine in World War Two* (Annapolis: Naval Institute Press, 1993).

10. Ikuhiko Hata, "Admiral Yamamoto's surprise attack and the Japanese Navy's war strategy", in *From Pearl Harbor to Hiroshima: the Second World War in Asia and the Pacific 1941–5*, S. Dockrill (ed.) (London: Macmillan, 1994).

11. On this topic see A. Marwick, *The deluge* (London: Bodley Head, 1965); A. Marwick, *Britain in the century of total war* (London: Bodley Head, 1968); A. Marwick, *War and social change in the twentieth century* (London: Macmillan, 1974); G. Wright, *The ordeal of total war* (New York: Harper & Row, 1968); P. Calvocoressi & G. Wint, *Total war* (London: Allen Lane, 1972); A. Calder, *The people's war* (London: Jonathan Cape, 1969); B. Bond, *War and society in Europe 1870–1970* (London: Fontana, 1984); I.F.W. Beckett, "Total War", in *Warfare in the twentieth century: theory and practice*, C. McInnes & G.D. Sheffield (eds) (London: Unwin and Hyman, 1988).

12. U. Bialer, *The shadow of the bomber: the fear of air attack and British politics 1932–9* (London: Royal Historical Society, 1981).

13. T.L. Kraus, "Planning the defense of the atlantic 1939–41: securing Brazil," in *To die gallantly: the battle of the Atlantic*, T. Runyan & J.M. Copes (Oxford: Westview, 1994).

14. To emphasize the point, the title of "Hap" Arnold's autobiography was: *Global mission* (London: Harper & Bros., 1949).

15. M.S. Smith, *British air strategy between the Wars* (Oxford: Oxford University Press, 1984).

16. Steven Garret uses this argument to support the notion that strategic bombing was largely counter-productive in World War II in *Ethics and airpower in World War Two*.

17. See A. Calder, *The Myth of the Blitz* (London: Jonathan Cape, 1991).

18. J.M.A. Gwyer & J.R.M. Butler, *Grand strategy – Volume III: June 1941 to August 1942* (London: HMSO, 1964), pp. 21–48.

19. See D.R. Headrick, *The tools of empire: technology and European imperialism in the nineteenth century* (Oxford: Oxford University Press, 1981) for the broader arguments and, as an example, D.E. Omissi, *Air power and colonial control: the RAF 1919–39* (Manchester: Manchester University Press, 1990).

Chapter Two

1. R. Bilstein, *Flight in America 1900–1983* (Baltimore: The Johns Hopkins University Press, 1984), p. 12.

2. C.H. Gibbs-Smith, *Aviation: an historical survey* (London: HMSO, 1970), p. 4.

3. B. Collier, *A history of air power* (London: HMSO, 1974), p. 1.

4. *ibid.*, p. 3.
5. C.F.S. Gamble, *The air weapon* (Oxford: Oxford University Press, 1931), p. 27.
6. P. Mead, *The eye in the air* (London: HMSO, 1983), p. 13.
7. Collier, *A history of air power*, p. 8.
8. Collier, *A history of air power*, p. 9.
9. E.P. Alexander, "The great charge and artillery fighting at Gettysburg" in E.P. Alexander (ed.) *Battles and leaders of the Civil War – Volume III* (New York: Century, 1884), p. 358.
10. Gamble, *The air weapon*, p. 56.
11. Mead, *The eye in the air*, p. 16.
12. See T. Crouch, *A dream of wings – Americans and the airplane* (London: Smithsonian Institution Press, 1981), for the background to flight in the USA.
13. A. Gollin, *No longer an island* (London: Heinemann, 1984), pp. 26–9.
14. *ibid.*, p. 69.
15. Bilstein, *Flight in America 1900–1983*, pp. 14–5.
16. I.F. Clarke, *Voices prophesying war 1789–1984* (London: Oxford University Press, 1961), p. 6.
17. See M. Paris, *Winged warfare* (Manchester: Manchester University Press, 1991) for more on air power literature.
18. G. de Havilland, *Sky fever* (London: Hamilton, 1961), p. 46; P. Joubert de la Ferte, *The fated sky* (London: Hutchinson, 1952), p. 17; and W. Mitchell, *Winged defense* (London: Putnam, 1925), p. 26.
19. Paris, *Winged warfare*, p. 29.
20. *ibid.*, pp. 36–7.
21. H.B. Franklin, *War stars: the superweapon and the American imagination* (Oxford: Oxford University Press, 1988), pp. 81–90.
22. C. Christienne et al., *Histoire de l'aviation militaire Francaise* (Paris: Charles Lavauzelle, 1980), pp. 36–7.
23. Collier, *A history of air power*, pp. 35–6.
24. J.H. Morrow, *Building German air power 1909–14* (Tennessee: University of Tennessee Press, 1976), p. 17.
25. A. Gollin, *Impact of air power on the British people and their Government 1909–14* (London: Heinemann, 1989), pp. 309–11.
26. H.S. Villard, *Contact! The story of the early birds* (Washington: Smithsonian Institution Press, 1987), pp. 55–60.
27. Gollin, *Impact of air power on the British people*, pp. 309–12.
28. D.R. Jones, "The beginnings of Russian air power 1907–22, in *Soviet aviation and air power: a historical view*, R. Higham & J.W. Kipp (eds) (Boulder: Westview, 1977), p. 16.
29. *ibid.*, p. 14.
30. P. Facon, *L'Armee Francaise et l'Aviation 1891–1914* (paper presented to the Southern Historical Association, November 1985), p. 15, cited in J.H. Morrow, *The Great War in the air – military aviation from 1909–21* (Washington: Smithsonian Institution Press, 1993).

31. Morrow, *The Great War in the air*, p. 30.
32. L. Morgat, "L'aviation en Berry avant la Grande Guerre", *Revue Historique des Armees* **1**, 1980, p. 196.
33. Morrow, *The Great War in the air*, p. 36.
34. P. Fritzche, *A nation of fliers* (Harvard: Harvard University Press, 1992), Chapter 1.
35. Morrow, *Building German air power*, p. 28.
36. Morrow, *The Great War in the air*, p. 22.
37. Bilstein, *Flight in America*, pp. 26–31; A. Turnbull & C. Lord, *History of US Naval Aviation* (New Haven: Yale University Press, 1949), pp. 1–14; Morrow, *Great War in the air*, pp. 49–50; R. Futrell, *Ideas, concepts, doctrine: a history of basic thinking in the United States Air Force 1907–64 – Volume I* (Montgomery: Aerospace Studies Institute, Air University, 1971), pp. 13–5.
38. Morrow, *Building German air power*, pp. 108–14; Morrow, *The Great War in the air*, pp. 45–7; E. Peter, *Die k.u.k. Luftschiffer und Fligertruppe Osterreich-Hungarns 1794–1919* (Stuttgart: Motorbuch Verlag, 1981), pre-war chapters.
39. See M. Paris, "The first air wars – North Africa and the Balkans", *Journal of Contemporary History* **26**, 1991, pp. 97–109.
40. P. Vergnano, *Origin of aviation in Italy 1783–1918* (Genoa: Intyprint, 1964); A. Lodi, *Storia delle origini dell'aeronautica militare 1884–1915 – Volume 2* (Rome: Edizioni Bizzarri, 1977); Morrow, *Great War in the air*, pp. 48–9.
41. Jones, *The beginnings of Russian air power* Chapter 2; R. Kilmarx, "The Russian Imperial Air Forces of World War One" *Airpower Historian* **10**, 1963.

Chapter Three

1. D. Lloyd-George, *The great crusade: extracts from speeches delivered during the war* (New York: Harper, 1923), p. 212.
2. M. Paris, *Winged warfare* (Manchester: Manchester University Press, 1992), p. 7.
3. L. Goldstein, *The flying machine and modern literature* (London: Macmillan, 1986), p. 89.
4. Compiled from J.H. Morrow, *The Great War in the air* (New York: Smithsonian Institution Press, 1993), p. 476.
5. R. Higham, *A concise history of air power* (London: St. Martin's, 1972), pp. 28–9.
6. D. Winter, *The first of the few* (London: Penguin, 1982), p. 36.
7. Paris, *Winged warfare*, p. 8.
8. Morrow, *The Great War in the air*, p. 346.
9. The Italian War Effort, AIR 1/684/21/13/2237. (London: Public Record Office).
10. D.R. Jones, "The Beginnings of Russian Air Power" in *Soviet aviation and air power: a historical view*, R. Higham & J.W. Kipp (eds) (Boulder: Westview, 1977), pp. 21–5.

11. P. Mead, *The eye in the air* (London: HMSO, 1983), p. 76.

12. See T. Travers, *The killing ground* (London: Allen & Unwin, 1987); G.D. Sheffield "Blitzkrieg and attrition: land operations in Europe 1914–15" in *Warfare in the twentieth century: theory and practice*, C. McInnes & G.D. Sheffield (eds) (London: Unwin & Hyman, 1988); L. Kennett, *The first Air War 1914–18* (New York: Free Press, 1991), pp. 220–1.

13. Mead, *The eye in the air*, pp. 53–7.

14. Kennet, *The first air war*, p. 23.

15. *ibid.*, p. 25.

16. Mead, *The eye in the air*, pp. 104–5; also see Chef de Bataillon Renaux, "L'Aerostation d'observation dans l'Armee allemande pendant la guerre 1914– 18, *Revue de l'aeronautique militaire* March-April, 1922.

17. L. Crosara, *Gli aerostieri, notizie storiche degli aerostieri militari dal 1793 al 1919* (Rome: Intyprint, 1924), pp. 41–3.

18. Kennett, *The first air war*, p. 31.

19. *ibid.*, p. 33.

20. See A.H. Carlier, *La Photographie aerienne pendant la Guerre* (Paris: Charles Lavauzelle, 1921).

21. G.P. Neumann (ed.), *Die deutschen Luftstreikrafte im Weltkriege* (Berlin: Mittler und Sohn, 1920), p. 490.

22. Mead, *The eye in the air*, p. 46.

23. A.H.G. Fokker & B. Gould, *Flying Dutchman: the life of Anthony Fokker* (New York: University of Nebraska Press, 1931), pp. 122–7; J.H. Morrow, *German air power in World War One* (Nebraska: University of Nebraska Press, 1982), pp. 40–1.

24. Kennett, *The first air war*, p. 70.

25. F. von Bulow, *Geschicte der Luftwaffe* (Frankfurt: Moritz Diensterweg, 1937), pp. 65–71.

26. J. Blanc, *L'Aviation de chasse Francaise 1916–18* (Paris: University of Paris, 1982), pp. 2–4.

27. Kennett, *The first air war*, pp. 71–3.

28. R. Higham, *A concise history of air power*, p. 36.

29. G.P. Neumann (ed.), *Die Deutschen Luftstreikrafte im Weltkriege* (Berlin: Mittler und Sohn, 1920), p. 472.

30. R.P. Hallion, *Strike from the sky* (Smithsonian: Smithsonian Institution Press, 1989), introduction.

31. *ibid.*, p. 21.

32. R. Muller, "Close air support: the German, British and American experiences, 1918–41", in *Military innovation in the interwar period*, W. Murray & A.R. Millett (eds) (Cambridge: Cambridge University Press, 1996), pp. 146–7.

33. W. Raleigh & H. Jones, *The war in the air – Volume 4* (Oxford: Oxford University Press, 1922), p. 166.

34. B. Greenhous, "Close support aircraft in World War One: the counter anti-tank role", *Aerospace Historian* **21**, 1974.

35. J.R. Cuneo, "Preparations of German attack aviation for the offensive of March 1918", *Military Affairs* **7**, 1943, pp. 68–70.

36. J.S. Corum, "The Old Eagle as Phoenix: the Luftstreitkrafte creates an operational air doctrine", *Air Power History* **14**, 1992.

37. General Voisin, *La Doctrine de l'Aviation francaise de combat* (Paris, 1932), pp. 127–30.

38. Greenhous, *Close support aircraft in WWI*, pp. 87–93.

39. See Higham, *A concise history of air power*, pp. 41–3; and Hallion, *Strike from the sky*, pp. 30–8.

40. Kennet, *The first air war*, p. 188.

41. J. Terraine, *Business in great waters: the U-boat wars 1916–45* (London: Cooper, 1989) is the best single volume survey of this topic.

42. J. Buckley, "Failing to learn from the past", *The War Studies Journal* **2**, 1996.

43. J. Killen, *A history of maritime air power* (London: Muller, 1969).

44. G. Till, "Adopting the aircraft carrier: the British, American and Japanese case studies", in *Military innovation in the interwar period*, W. Murray & A.R. Millett (eds) (Cambridge: Cambridge University Press, 1996), pp. 194–5.

45. L. Kennett, *A history of strategic bombing* (New York: Scribner, 1982), p. 19.

46. Kennett, *The first air war*, p. 43; P. Pletschacher, *Die Konigliche bayerischen Fliegertruppen 1912–19* (Stuttgart: Schoen, 1978), p. 30.

47. D. Robinson, *The Zeppelin in combat: a history of the German Naval Airship Division 1912–18* (Seattle: Foulis, 1980), pp. 77–8.

48. F. Porro, *La Guerra nell'aria*, 2nd edn (Milan: Corbaccio, 1935), p. 110.

49. Kennett, *The first air war*, p. 59.

50. E. Angelucci, *The world encyclopaedia of military aircraft* (London: Jane's, 1981), pp. 70–8.

51. Higham, *A concise history of air power*, p. 52.

52. T.D. Biddle, "British and American approaches to strategic bombing: their origins and implementation in the World War Two combined bomber offensive", in *Airpower: theory and practice*, J. Gooch (ed.) (London: Frank Cass, 1995), pp. 92–4; D. Divine, *The broken wing: a study in the British exercise of air power* (London: Hutchinson, 1966), pp. 142–3.

53. Kennett, *A history of strategic bombing*, pp. 29–32.

54. *New York Times*, October 14th, 1917.

55. *ibid.*, p. 25.

56. W. Raleigh & H. Jones, *The war in the air* (Oxford: Oxford University Press, 1922–37), Appendices Volume, appendix 35.

57. C. Christienne et al., *Histoire de l'aviation militaire Francaise* (Paris: Charles Lavauzelle, 1980), pp. 156–7.

58. G.W. Mixter & H.H. Emmons, *United States Army aircraft production facts* (Washington: Government Printing Office, 1919), p. 5.

59. Morrow, *The Great War in the Air*, p. 364.

60. *ibid.*, pp. 370–1.

61. J.H. Morrow, "The German aircraft industry in two World Wars", in *The conduct of the air war in the Second World War: an international comparison*, H. Boog (ed.) (Oxford: Berg, 1992), pp. 37–9.

62. Morrow, *German air power in World War One*, pp. 186–93.

63. *ibid.*, p. 190.

64. Christienne, *Histoire de l'aviation militaire Francaise*, pp. 176–7.

65. Morrow in H. Boog, *The conduct of the air war in WWII*, p. 47.

66. C.H. Gibbs-Smith, *Aviation – an historical survey* (London: HMSO, 1970), p. 178.

67. E.C. Johnson, *Marine corps aviation: the early years 1912–1940* (Washington: Government Printing Office, 1977), p. 63.

68. R. Blunck, *Hugo Junkers: ein leben fur technik und luftfahrt* (Frankfurt: Econ-Verlag, 1934), p. 89.

69. E. Heinkel, *Sturmisches leben*, Jurgen Thorwald (ed.) (Stuttgart: Mundus-Verlag, 1953), p. 69.

70. A. Eteve, *La victoire des cocardes* (Paris: Charles Lavauzelle, 1970), p. 302.

71. G. Wissmann, "Imperialistischer krieg und technisch-wissenschaftlicher fortschritt", *Jahrbuch fur wirtschaftgeschite* **2**, 1962, pp. 145–58.

72. Morrow, *The Great War in the air*, pp. 374–5.

Chapter Four

1. R. Higham, *Air power: a concise history* (London: St. Martin's, 1972), p. 31.

2. L. Kennett, *A history of strategic bombing* (New York: Scribner, 1982), pp. 42–3.

3. F. Ferber, *L'aviation: ses debuts. Son developpement. De crete a crete. De ville a ville. De continent a continent* (Paris: Ader, 1908), p. 159.

4. The potential effects of such a decisive blow against Paris were the subject of speculation by a Belgian officer, Poutrin, in June 1911 in *Revue generale de l'aeronautique miliaire*. (Quoted in Kennett, *A history of strategic bombing*, p. 43.)

5. C. Ader, *Aviation militaire* (Paris: Ader, 1909), p. 29; R. Scott, "Can the Panama Canal be destroyed from the air?", *Sunset*, April 1914, p. 784.

6. C. Ader, *Aviation militaire* is perhaps his most notable work. Lord Montagu of Beaulieu predicted the same in 1909, quoted in Kennett, *A history of strategic bombing*, p. 43.

7. F. Sykes, *From many angles* (London: Harrap, 1942), pp. 558–74.

8. Kennett, *A history of strategic bombing*, p. 55.

9. R. Higham, *The military intellectuals in Britain 1918–39* (New Jersey: Rutgers University Press, 1966), p. 259; see also the D. Ferrari translation of Douhet's 1927 volume *The command of the air* (New York: Faber & Faber, 1942).

10. D. MacIsaac, "Voices from the central blue: the air power theorists", in *Makers of modern strategy*, P. Paret (ed.) (Oxford: Oxford University Press, 1986), p. 630.

11. References for Douhet's thinking come from the 1942 Ferrari translation of *The command of the air.*

12. The role of the Italian aircraft manufacturer Caproni in supporting Douhet should be noted. It could be argued as some have that Douhet was merely a willing mouthpiece for Caproni who sought a support for his heavy-bomber designs.

13. The 1942 Ferrari translation of Douhet, *The command of the air.*

14. T. Mason, *Air power: a centennial appraisal* (London: Brassey's, 1994), p. 45.

15. Higham is quite adamant on this point in *Military intellectuals.*

16. L.E.O. Charlton, *War from the air* (London: T. Nelson and sons, 1935), pp. 127–34.

17. R. Saundby, *Air bombardment: the story of its development* (London: Chatto & Windus, 1961), pp. 34–5.

18. A. de Seversky, *Victory through air power* (New York: Simon & Schuster, 1942). See also the famous Disney cartoon of the same title made to illustrate de Seversky's arguments.

19. C.S. Segre, "Giulio Douhet: strategist, theorist, prophet?", *Journal of Strategic Studies* **15**(3), 1992, p. 352.

20. Kennett, *A history of strategic bombing*, p. 57.

21. On the role of Trenchard, see T. Davis Biddle "British and American approaches to strategic bombing: their origins and implementation in the World War Two combined bomber offensive" in *Airpower: theory and practice*, J. Gooch (ed.) (London: Frank Cass, 1996), but also see Kennett, *A history of strategic bombing.*

22. Biddle, in Gooch (ed.) *Airpower: theory and practice*; W. Murray, "Strategic bombing: the British, American and German experiences", in *Military innovation in the interwar period*, W. Murray & A.R. Millett (eds) (Cambridge: Cambridge University Press, 1996).

23. Biddle, in Gooch (ed.), *Airpower: theory and practice*, pp. 106–8.

24. Murray, in Murray & Millett (eds), *Military innovation in the interwar period*, pp. 122–5.

25. Biddle, in Gooch (ed.), *Airpower: theory and practice*, pp. 110–4; Murray, in Murray & Millett (eds), *Military innovation in the interwar period*, pp. 124–6.

26. T. Greer, *The development of air doctrine in the army air arm 1917–41* (Washington: Office of Air Force History, 1985) gives a clear outline of Chennault's arguments.

27. Murray, in Murray & Millett (eds), *Military innovation in the interwar period*, pp. 124–6.

28. J.S. Corum, *The roots of blitzkrieg* (Kansas: University of Kansas Press, 1992), pp. 144–7.

29. J.S. Corum, "From biplanes to blitzkrieg: the development of German air doctrine between the wars", *War in History* **3**(1), 1996, p. 89.

30. W. Murray, "A tale of two doctrines: the *Luftwaffe*'s 'Conduct of the Air War' and the USAF's Manual 1–1", *Journal of Strategic Studies* **6**(4), 1983; also,

W. Murray "The *Luftwaffe* before the Second World War: a mission, a strategy", *Journal of Strategic Studies* **4**(3), 1981.

31. M. Cooper, *The German Air Force 1933–45: an anatomy of failure* (London: Jane's, 1981), pp. 34–43.

32. J.S. Corum, *The Luftwaffe: creating the operational air war, 1918–40* (Kansas: University of Kansas Press, 1997), pp. 281–3.

33. Murray, in Murray & Millett (eds), *Military innovation in the interwar period*, pp. 130–3.

34. R. Muller, *The German air war in Russia* (Annapolis: Naval Institute Press, 1992), pp. 151–2.

35. P. Vennesson, "Institution and airpower: the making of the French air force", in Gooch (ed.), *Airpower: theory and practice*; L. Robineau, "French air policy in the inter-war period and the conduct of the air war against Germany from September to June 1940", in *The conduct of the air war in the Second World War: an international comparison*, H. Boog (ed.) (Oxford: Berg, 1992).

36. L. Ceva & A. Curami, "Air army and aircraft industry in Italy 1936–43", in Boog, *The conduct of the air war in WWII*, pp. 85–91.

37. K.R. Whiting, "Soviet aviation and air power under Stalin 1928–41", in *Soviet Aviation: a historical view*, R. Higham & J.W. Kipp (eds) (Boulder: Westview, 1977), pp. 51–2 and 58.

38. A. Milward, *The German economy at war* (London: Athlone Press, 1965); R. Overy, "Hitler's war and the German economy: a reinterpretation", *Economic History Review*, 2nd series, Vol. XXXV, no. 2.

39. Corum, *The roots of blitzkrieg*, pp. 144–55; Corum, "From biplanes to blitzkrieg", p. 89.

40. M. Forget, "Co-operation between air force and army in the French and German Air Forces during the Second World War", in Boog (ed.), *The conduct of the air war in WWII*, pp. 422–4.

41. Corum, "From biplanes to blitzkrieg", pp. 96–8.

42. Forget, in Boog (ed.) *The conduct of the air war in WWII*, pp. 424–6.

43. Corum, "From biplanes to blitzkrieg", pp. 97–8.

44. R.R. Muller, "Close air support: the German, British and American experiences 1918–41", in *Military innovation in the interwar period*, W. Murray & A.R. Millett (eds) (Cambridge: Cambridge University Press, 1996), p. 161.

45. *Ibid.*, p. 162.

46. Forget, in Boog (ed.) *The conduct of the air war in WWII*, pp. 416–22.

47. P. Vennesson, "Institution and airpower: the making of the French Air Force", in *Airpower: theory and practice*, J. Gooch (ed.) (London: Frank Cass, 1995), pp. 49–51.

48. E. Cohen & J. Gooch, *Military misfortune: an anatomy of failure in war* (London: Macmillan, 1990), p. 227.

49. P. Mead, *The eye in the air* (London: HMSO, 1983), pp. 147–8.

50. Muller, in Murray & Millett (eds) *Military innovation in the interwar period*, pp. 163–8.

51. See B. Bond & M. Alexander, "Liddell-Hart and De Gaulle", in Paret (ed.), *Makers of modern strategy*, Chapter 20.

52. R. Hallion, *Strike from the sky: the history of battlefield air attack 1911–45* (Washington: Smithsonian Institution Press, 1989), pp. 51–3.

53. J. Slessor, *The central blue* (London: Cassells, 1956), pp. 659–60.

54. See W.F. Craven & J.L. Cate (eds), *The army air forces in World War Two – Volume VI* (Chicago: University of Chicago Press, 1955), pp. 221 onwards; also L. Kennett, "The US Army Air Forces and tactical air war in the Second World War", in Boog (ed.), *The conduct of the air war in WWII*, pp. 458–561.

55. Muller, in Murray & Millett (eds), *Military innovation in the interwar period*, pp. 173–6.

56. N.M. Heyman, "NEP and the industrialization to 1928", in Higham & Kipp (eds), *Soviet aviation and air power*, p. 41.

57. N.M. Heyman, "NEP and the Industrialization to 1928" and K.R. Whiting, "Soviet aviation and air power under Stalin 1928–42" both in Higham & Kipp (eds), *Soviet aviation and air power*.

58. G. Till, "Adopting the aircraft carrier: the British, American and Japanese case studies," in Murray & Millett (eds), *Military innovation in the interwar period*, p. 194.

59. D. MacIsaac, "Voices from the central blue: the air power theorists", in Paret (ed.), *Makers of modern strategy*, pp. 630–1.

60. W. Mitchell, *Winged defence* (London: Putnam, 1925), pp. 64–6; I.D. Levine, *Flying crusader*, (London: Peter Davies, 1943), pp. 181–8.

61. See G. Till, *Air power and the Royal Navy 1914–45: a historical survey* (London: Jane's, 1979).

62. *ibid.*, pp. 197–8.

63. J. Buckley, *The RAF and trade defence 1919–45: constant endeavour* (Keele: Keele University Press, 1995), Chapters 1–4.

64. C.G. Reynolds, *The fast carriers – the forging of an air navy* (New York: McGraw Hill, 1968), pp. 14–5.

65. E.S. Miller, *War Plan Orange: the US strategy to defeat Japan 1897–1945* (Annapolis: Naval Institute Press, 1991).

66. Reynolds, *The fast carriers*, p. 18.

67. Ikuhiko Hata, "Admiral Yamamoto's surprise attack and the Japanese navy's war strategy", in *From Pearl Harbour to Hiroshima: the Second World War in Asia and the Pacific 1941–5*, S. Dockrill (ed.) (London: Macmillan, 1994).

68. J.H. Belote & W.M. Belote, *Titans of the sea* (New York: Harper & Row, 1975), pp. 22–3.

69. Reynolds, *The fast carriers*, pp. 6–9.

70. Reynolds, *The fast carriers*, Chapter one; Saburo Toyama, "Lessons from the past", *US Naval Institute Proceedings*, September 1982.

71. M. Parillo, *The Japanese merchant marine in World War Two* (Annapolis: Naval Institute Press, 1993), Chapter one for the doctrinal failings.

Chapter Five

1. J.H. Morrow, *The Great War in the air: military aviation from 1909–21* (Washington: Smithsonian Institution Press, 1993), pp. 350–6.
2. J.S. Corum, *The roots of blitzkrieg* (Kansas: University of Kansas Press, 1992), p. 149.
3. *ibid.*, pp. 160–3.
4. R.P. Hallion, *Strike from the sky: the history of battlefield air attack* (Washington: Smithsonian Institution Press, 1989), pp. 55–8.
5. N.M. Heyman, "NEP and the industrialization to 1928", in *Soviet aviation and air power: a historical view*, R. Higham & J.W. Kipp (eds) (Boulder: Westview, 1977), pp. 41–2.
6. M. Maurer, *Aviation in the US army 1919–39* (Washington: Office of Air Force History, 1987); J.B. Rae, *Climb to greatness: the American aircraft industry 1920–60* (London: MIT Press, 1968), p. 3; see also W. Biddle, *Barons of the sky – from early flight to strategic warfare: the story of the American aerospace industry* (New York: Henry Holt, 1991).
7. C. Christienne et al., *Histoire de l'aviation militaire Francaise* (Paris: Charles Lavauzelle, 1980), pp. 213–28; Morrow, *The Great War in the air*, p. 357.
8. Morrow, *The Great War in the air*, p. 358.
9. J. Ferris, "The theory of a French air menace, Anglo-French relations and the British Home Defence Air Force programmes of 1921–5", *Journal of Strategic Studies* **10**, March 1987.
10. *ibid.*
11. J. Ferris, *The evolution of British strategic policy 1919–26* (London: Macmillan, 1989).
12. D.R. Headrick, *The tools of empire: technology and European imperialism in the nineteenth century* (Oxford: Oxford University Press, 1981).
13. D.E. Omissi, *Air power and colonial control: the RAF 1919–39* (Manchester: Manchester University Press, 1990), pp. 9–11.
14. *ibid.*, p. 24.
15. *ibid.*, p. 37.
16. *ibid.*, p. 35.
17. *ibid.*, Chapter 3; also J. Buckley, *The RAF and trade defence 1919–45: constant endeavour* (Keele: Keele University Press, 1995), Chapter 1.
18. J. Buckley, "Failing to learn from the past: air power and trade defence 1917–43", *War Studies Journal* **2**(1), 1996, pp. 1–16.
19. Hallion, *Strike from the sky*, pp. 67–9.
20. Christienne, *Histoire de l'aviation*, pp. 231–4.
21. R. Sherrod, *History of marine corps aviation in World War Two* (Washington: Combat Forces Press, 1952), pp. 1–23; Hallion, *Strike from the sky*, pp. 71–4; R. Muller, "Close air support: the German, British, and American experiences, 1918–41", in *Military innovation in the interwar period*, W. Murray & A.R. Millett (eds) (Cambridge: Cambridge University Press, 1996), pp. 176–7.

22. Hallion, *Strike from the sky*, pp. 79–88.
23. C.H. Gibbs-Smith, *Aviation: an historical survey from its origins to the end of World War Two* (London: HMSO, 1970), pp. 185–6.
24. A good example can be found in M.L.J. Dierikx, "Struggle for prominence: clashing Dutch and British interests on the colonial air routes 1918–42", *Journal of Contemporary History* **26**, 1991, pp. 333–51.
25. E.L. Homze, *Arming the Luftwaffe: the Reich Air Ministry and the German aircraft industry 1919–39* (Nebraska: University of Nebraska Press, 1976), p. 32.
26. Higham, *A concise history of air power* (London: St. Martin's, 1972), pp. 75–7.
27. S. Ritchie, *Industry and air power: the expansion of British aircraft production, 1935–41* (London: Frank Cass, 1997).
28. E. Angelucci, *World encyclopaedia of civil aircraft* (London: Jane's, 1984), pp. 111–7.
29. Higham, *A concise history of air power*, p. 79.
30. Compiled from E. Angelucci, *World encyclopaedia of civil aircraft*. Although there are examples of faster aircraft prior to the late 1930s, they are the exception rather than the rule.
31. R. Overy, "Air power in the Second World War: historical themes and theories" in *The conduct of the air war in the Second World War: an international comparison*, H. Boog (ed.) (Oxford: Berg, 1992), p. 20.
32. *ibid.*, p. 12.
33. The best survey of this air fear factor is found in: I.F. Clarke, *Voices prophesying War 1763–1984* (London: Oxford University Press, 1966); also M. Cooper, *The German Air Force 1933–45: an anatomy of failure* (London: Jane's, 1981), pp. 38–9; the impact of air-mindedness on the Nazi regime is covered in P. Fritzche, *A nation of fliers* (Cambridge, Mass.: Harvard University Press, 1992), Chapter 5.
34. U. Bialer, *The shadow of the bomber: the fear of air attack and British Politics 1932–9* (London: Royal Historical Society, 1980).
35. Air Ministry paper to CID, 1928 quoted in R. Overy, "Air power and the origins of deterrence theory before 1939", *Journal of Strategic Studies* **15**(1), 1992, pp. 78–9.
36. *ibid.*, pp. 80–1.
37. Cooper, *The German Air Force 1933–45*, p. 35.
38. W. Murray, *Strategy for defeat: the Luftwaffe 1933–45* (Washington: Allen & Unwin, 1983), pp. 6–10.
39. M. Smith, *British air strategy between the wars* (Oxford: Oxford University Press, 1984).
40. Overy, "Air power and the origins of deterrence theory before 1939", p. 74.
41. P. Facon, "The high command of the French Air Force and the problem of rearmament 1938–9: a technical and industrial approach", in Boog, *Conduct of the air war in the Second World War*, pp. 154–8.
42. O.H. Bullitt (ed.), *For the President: personal and secret. Correspondence between Franklin D. Roosevelt and William C. Bullitt* (Boston: Andre Deutsch, 1972), p. 288.

43. Cooper, *The German Air Force 1933–45*, Chapters 1 and 2; D. Wood & D. Dempster, *The narrow margin – the battle of Britain and the rise of air power 1930–40* (London: Hutchinson, 1961).

44. N. Gibbs, *Grand strategy I* (London: HMSO, 1976), pp. 558–99; Murray, *Strategy for defeat*, pp. 113–6; Homze, *Arming the Luftwaffe*, pp. 264–7.

45. Homze, *Arming the Luftwaffe*, pp. 244–5.

46. K. Middlemass & J. Barnes, *Baldwin: a biography* (London: Weidenfeld & Nicolson, 1969), p. 736.

47. RAF Expansion Scheme K, AIR 8/226 (London: Public Record Office).

48. RAF Expansion Schemes, AIR 8/249 (London: Public Record Office).

49. W. Murray, "Strategic bombing: the British, American and German experiences", in *Military innovation in the interwar period*, W. Murray and A.R. Millett (eds) (Cambridge: Cambridge University Press, 1996), pp. 102–3.

50. Angelucci, *World encyclopaedia of civil aircraft*, p. 361.

51. Facon, in Boog, *Conduct of the air war*, pp. 158–65.

52. Murray, *Strategy for defeat*, p. 9.

53. Cooper, *The German Air Force 1933–45*, pp. 61–4.

54. *ibid.*, p. 14.

55. *ibid.*, pp. 12–3.

56. Murray, in Murray & Millett (eds), *Military innovation*, pp. 110–1.

57. Homze, *Arming the Luftwaffe*, pp. 223–4.

58. K.R. Whiting, "Soviet aviation and air power under Stalin 1928–41", in Higham & Kipp (eds), *Soviet aviation*, p. 51.

59. *ibid.*, pp. 62–3.

60. L. Ceva & A. Curami, "Air Army and Aircraft Industry in Italy 1936–43", in Boog (ed.), *Conduct of the air war*, pp. 85–97.

61. A.D. Coox, "The rise and fall of the Imperial Japanese Air Forces", in *Air power and warfare – proceedings of the Eighth Military History Symposium, USAF Academy, 1978*, A.F. Hurley & R.C. Ehrhardt (eds) (Washington: Office of Air Force History, 1979), pp. 86–92.

62. R.E. Bilstein, *Flight in America 1900–83* (New York: Johns Hopkins University Press, 1984), p. 126.

63. M. Maurer, *Aviation in the US Army 1919–39* (Washington: Office of Air Force History, 1987), pp. 136–7.

64. C.G. Reynolds, *The fast carriers: the forging of an air navy* (New York: McGraw Hill, 1968), pp. 19–20.

Chapter Six

1. J.S. Corum, *The Luftwaffe: creating the operational air war 1918–40* (Kansas: University of Kansas Press, 1997), pp. 5–7, offers a clear view of this enduring myth.

2. *ibid.*, pp. 281–3.
3. W. Murray, "The Luftwaffe before the Second World War: a mission, a strategy?", *Journal of Strategic Studies* **4**(3), 1981, p. 263.
4. R. Hallion, *Strike from the sky: the history of battlefield air attack 1911–45* (Washington: Smithsonian Institute Press, 1989), p. 131; W. Murray, *Strategy for defeat: The Luftwaffe 1933–45* (Washington: Allen & Unwin, 1983), p. 30.
5. R. Muller, "Close air support: the German, British and American experiences 1918–41, in *Military innovation in the interwar period*, W. Murray & A.R. Millett (eds) (Cambridge: Cambridge University Press, 1996), pp. 181–3.
6. W. Murray, *German military effectiveness* (Baltimore: Nautical and Aviation Publishing Company of America, 1992), pp. 229–43.
7. M. Cooper, *The German air force 1933–45: an anatomy of failure* (London: Jane's, 1981), pp. 97–9.
8. F. Heiss, *Der Sieg im Osten* (Berlin: Schoen, 1940), p. 3.
9. Hallion, *Strike from the sky*, p. 133.
10. C. Bekker, *The Luftwaffe Air Diaries* (London: Macdonald, 1967), p. 50.
11. *ibid.*, p. 139.
12. Cooper, *German air force 1933–45*, p. 112.
13. Corum, *Luftwaffe*, pp. 276–8.
14. Murray, *Strategy for defeat*, p. 38; see also W. Swint, "The German air attack on Rotterdam", *Aerospace Historian* **21**, 1974.
15. Murray, *Strategy for defeat*, p. 39.
16. Cooper, *German air force 1933–45*, p. 121.
17. Murray, *Strategy for defeat*, pp. 46–7.
18. A term used by Murray in *Strategy for defeat*.
19. Murray, *Strategy for defeat*, pp. 55–6.
20. Cooper, *German air force 1933–45*, pp. 218–9.
21. Murray, *Strategy for defeat*, p. 81; Hallion, *Strike from the sky*, p. 229; V. Hardesty, *Red phoenix: the rise of Soviet air power 1941–5* (Washington: Smithsonian Institution Press, 1982), p. 61.
22. Hardesty, *Red phoenix*, p. 72.
23. Hallion, *Strike from the sky*, p. 237; Murray, *Strategy for defeat,* p. 88.
24. Cooper, *German air force 1933–45*, p. 225.
25. P. Deichmann, *Spearhead for blitzkrieg: Luftwaffe operations in support of the army 1939–45*, A. Price (ed.) (London: Greenhill, 1996), pp. 152–3; R. Muller, *The German air war in Russia* (Annapolis: Naval Institute Press, 1992), pp. 151–2.
26. Hallion, *Strike from the sky*, p. 250.
27. Murray, *Strategy for defeat*, pp. 94–6; Muller, *German air war in Russia*, p. 183.
28. *ibid.*
29. See C. Barnett, "The battle for the air" in *Engage the enemy more closely* (London: W.W. Norton, 1991); and J. Buckley, *The RAF and trade defence: constant endeavour* (Keele: Keele University Press, 1995), Chapter Five.
30. Murray, *Strategy for defeat*, pp. 238–9.

31. W.F. Craven & J.L. Cate (eds), *The army air forces in World War Two, Volume VI* (Washington: University of Chicago Press, 1983), p. 278.

32. Suchenwirth, *The development of the German Air Force 1919–39* (USAF Historical Study **160**, 1983), pp. 23–4.

33. B.A. Carroll, *Design for total war* (London: Mouton, 1968), pp. 172–9.

34. R. Overy, *The air war* (London: Macmillan, 1980), pp. 177–9.

35. *ibid.*

36. *USSBS Report No. 4*, pp. 45–6 (Washington: Government Printing Office, 1945–9).

37. W.A. Boelcke, "Stimulation and attitude of the German aircraft industry during rearmament and war", in *The conduct of the air war in the Second World War: an international comparison*, H. Boog (ed.) (Oxford: Berg, 1992), p. 75.

38 . "V weapons campaign", *USSBS Report No. 60* (Washington: Government Printing Office, 1945–9).

39. Hardesty, *Red phoenix*, pp. 250–1.

40. E. Angelucci, *Encyclopaedia of military aircraft* (London: Jane's, 1981), pp. 233–4.

41. See R.W. Clark, *The rise of the boffins* (London: Phoenix House, 1962); S. Zuckerman, *Scientists and war* (London: Hamish Hamilton, 1966).

42. See H. Hansell, *The airplan that defeated hitler* (Atlanta: Aerospace Studies Institute, Air University, 1972); and Craven & Cate (eds), *Army air forces in WWII*, Volume II, pp. 348–70.

43. D. Fleming & B. Bailyn (eds), *The intellectual migration: Europe and America 1930–60* (Cambridge, Mass.: Harvard University Press, 1968).

44. Overy, *The Air War*, pp. 187–91.

45. Hardesty, *Red phoenix*, p. 217.

46. *ibid.*, p. 252.

47. J.T. Greenwood, "The great patriotic war 1941–5", in *Soviet aviation and air power: a historical view*, R. Higham & J.W. Kipp (eds) (Boulder: Westview, 1977), pp. 127–9.

48. See J. Erickson, "Red army battlefield performance, 1941–5: the system and the soldier", in *Time to kill: the soldier's experience of war in the West*, P. Addison & A. Calder (eds) (London: Pimlico, 1997).

49. Hallion, *Strike from the sky*, p. 160.

50. J. Terraine, *The right of the line: the Royal Air Force in the European war 1939–45* (London: Hodder & Stoughton, 1985), pp. 356–7.

51. Hallion, *Strike from the sky*, p. 157.

52. B.H. Liddell-Hart, *The Rommel papers* (New York: Harcourt, Brace and Co., 1953), pp. 285–6.

53. Hallion, *Strike from the sky*, p. 163.

54. US War Department, *Field Manual FM 100–20* (Washington: Government Printing Office, 1943).

55. W.F. Craven & J.L. Cate (eds), *The army air forces in World War Two, Volume II* (Chicago: University of Chicago, 1949), pp. 486–7.

56. Quoted in J. Slessor, *The central blue* (London: Cassells, 1956), p. 566.
57. Murray, *Strategy for defeat*, pp. 223–32; Hallion, *Strike from the sky*, p. 189.
58. H.H. Arnold, *Second report of the Commanding General of the USAAF* (Washington: Government Printing Office, 1945), p. 36.
59. W.R. Carter, "Air power in the battle of the Bulge: a theater campaign perspective", *Air Power Journal*, **3**(4), 1989, pp. 21–3.
60. For details on these preparations see L.F. Ellis, *Victory on the West – Volume I* (London: HMSO, 1962), Chapter Five.
61. Encapsulated effectively by T. Copp, " 'If this war isn't over, and pretty damn soon, there'll be nobody left, in this old platoon . . .': First Canadian Army, February–March 1945", in Addison & Calder (eds), *Time to kill*.
62. S. Hart, "Montgomery, morale, casualty conservation and 'Colossal Cracks': 21st Army Group's operational technique in North West Europe, 1944–5", in *Military power: land warfare in theory and practice*, B.H. Reid (ed.) (London: Frank Cass, 1997).
63. An excellent example of this is found in M. Hastings, *Das Reich: the march of the 2nd SS Panzer Division through France* (London: Joseph, 1983).
64. W.F. Craven & J.L. Cate (eds), *The army air forces in World War Two*, Volume III (Chicago: University of Chicago Press, 1949), pp. 190–3.
65. See I. Gooderson, "Allied fighter-bombers versus German armour in North-West Europe 1944–5: myths and realities", *Journal of Strategic Studies* **14**(2), 1991; also see I. Gooderson, *Air power at the battlefront: allied close air support in Europe 1943–5* (London: Frank Cass, 1998).
66. A concerted armoured offensive east of Caen in July 1944, aimed at bleeding German reserves and resources and possibly leading to a breakout from the Normandy beachhead area.
67. *Operation Cobra* was the codename for the successful breakout of the US 12th Army Group from the Normandy beachhead just after *Goodwood*.
68. See I. Gooderson, "Heavy and medium bombers: how successful were they in the tactical close air support role during World War Two?", *Journal of Strategic Studies* **15**(3), September 1992; also see Gooderson, *Air Power at the Battlefront*.
69. J. Ellis, *The sharp end of war* (London: Newton Abbott, 1982), pp. 175–89.
70. Some recent examples are, R.A. Pape, *Bombing to win: air power and coercion in war* (New York: Cornell University Press, 1996), pp. 311–13; J. Ellis, *Brute force: allied strategy and tactics in the Second World War* (London: Andre Deutsch, 1990), pp. 213–21; and S. Garrett, *Ethics and airpower in World War Two* (New York: St. Martin's, 1993).
71. J.R.M. Butler, *Grand strategy – Volume II: September 1939 to June 1941* (London: HMSO, 1957), pp. 343–5; J.M.A. Gwyer & J.R.M. Butler, *Grand strategy – Volume III: June 1941 to August 1942* (London: HMSO, 1964), pp. 21–48 and pp. 349–52.
72. W.S. Churchill, *The Second World War – Volume II* (London: Cassells, 1949), p. 567.

73. R. Sherwood, *The Whitehouse papers of Harry L. Hopkins – Volume II* (London: Eyre & Spottiswood, 1949), p. 585. See also J.S. Underwood, *The wings of democracy: the influence of air power on the Roosevelt administration 1933–41* (Texas: Texas University Press, 1991), Chapters Eight and Nine.

74. W.A. Harriman & E. Abel, *Special envoy to Churchill and Stalin* (London: Hutchinson, 1976), pp. 150–7. See also R. Beaumont, "The bomber offensive as a Second Front", *Journal of Contemporary History* **22**, 1987; R. Overy, *Why the Allies won* (London: Jonathan Cape, 1995), Chapter Four.

75. Overy, *Why the Allies won*, pp. 109–10.

76. C. Webster & N. Frankland, *The strategic air offensive against Germany – Volume I* (London: HMSO, 1961), pp. 150–1.

77. *ibid.*, Volume II, p. 22.

78. See R. Davis, "Operation Thunderclap: the US Army Air Forces and the bombing of Berlin", *Journal of Strategic Studies* **14**(1), March 1991.

79. T.D. Biddle, "British and American approaches to strategic bombing: their origins and implementation in the World War Two combined bomber offensive", in *Airpower: theory and practice*, J. Gooch (ed.) (London: Frank Cass, 1995), pp. 118–20.

80. I.B. Holley jnr., "The development of defensive armament for US Army bombers, 1918–41: a study in doctrinal failure and production success", in Boog (ed.), *The conduct of the air war*, pp. 131–47.

81. Webster & Frankland, *The strategic air offensive against Germany – Volume II*, pp. 28–9.

82. A. Speer, *Inside the Third Reich* (London: Weidenfeld & Nicolson, 1970), pp. 388–9.

83. Biddle, in Gooch (ed.) *Airpower*, p. 121.

84. S.L. McFarland, "The evolution of the American strategic fighter in Europe 1942–4", *Journal of Strategic Studies* **10**(2), 1987.

85. *ibid.*, p. 196.

86. Murray, *Strategy for defeat*, pp. 226–41.

87. Speer, *Inside the Third Reich*, p. 290.

88. Murray, *Strategy for defeat*, p. 241.

89. S. Cox's introduction in A.T. Harris, *Despatch on war operations: 23rd February 1942 to 8th May 1945* (London: Frank Cass, 1995).

90. *ibid.*

91. W.H. Park, "Precision bombing and area bombing: who did which and when?", in Gooch (ed.), *Airpower*.

92. Garrett, *Ethics and airpower in WWII*, particularly Chapter Six.

93. Overy, *Why the Allies won*, pp. 130–1.

94. Murray, *Strategy for defeat*, p. 240.

95. Overy, *Why the Allies won*, p. 131; O. Groehler, "The strategic air war's impact on the German civilian population", in Boog (ed.), *Conduct of the Air War*, pp. 284–90; "Effects on German Morale", *USSBS Report 64B* (Washington: Government Printing Office, 1945–9).

96. Overy, *Why the Allies won*, p. 131.
97. R. Overy, *Bomber Command 1939–45* (London: Harper Collins, 1997), p. 200.
98. See M. Milner's chapter in Gooch (ed.), *Decisive campaigns of the Second World War.*

Chapter Seven

1. R.J. Francillon, *Japanese aircraft of the Pacific War* (London: Putnam, 1970), pp. 30–1.
2. R.P. Hallion, *Strike from the sky: the history of battlefield air attack 1911–45* (New York: Smithsonian Institute Press, 1989), p. 117.
3. J.H. Belote & W.M. Belote, *Titans of the seas* (New York: Harper & Row, 1975), pp. 21–2.
4. Hallion, *Strike from the sky*, p. 118.
5. C.J. Argyle, *Japan at war 1937–45* (London: Barker, 1976), pp. 2–4.
6. A.D. Coox, *Japan against Russia 1939*, two volumes (Palo Alto, California: Stanford University Press, 1985); see also A.D. Coox *The Anatomy of a small war: the Soviet–Japanese struggle for Changkufeng/Khasan 1938* (Westport, Connecticut: Greenwood, 1977).
7. The best one volume examination of this issue is *The Washington Conference 1921–2: naval rivalry, East Asian stability and the road to Pearl Harbor*, a special issue of *Diplomacy and Statecraft*, E. Goldstein & J. Maurer (eds), **4**(3), 1993.
8. S. Howarth, "Isoroku Yamamoto", in *Men of war: great naval leaders of World War Two*, S. Howarth (ed.) (London: Weidenfeld & Nicolson, 1992), pp. 108–15.
9. See Ikuhiko Hata "Admiral Yamamoto's surprise attack and the Japanese Navy's War Strategy" in *From Pearl Harbor to Hiroshima: the Second World War in Asia and the Pacific 1941–5*, S. Dockrill (ed.) (London: Macmillan, 1994).
10. *ibid.*, p. 68.
11. Belote & Belote, *Titans of the seas*, pp. 20–2.
12. R.J. Overy, *The air war 1939–45* (London: Macmillan, 1980), p. 95.
13. M.P. Parillo, *The Japanese Merchant Marine in World War Two* (Annapolis: Naval Institute Press, 1993), p. 244.
14. Source, *The war against Japanese transportation 1941–5 (The United States Strategic Bombing Survey)* (Washington: Government Printing Office, 1945–9).
15. M.P. Parillo, *Japanese Merchant Marine*, is the best account of this strategic blunder.
16. Overy, *Air War*, p. 92; I. Masanori with R. Pineau, *The end of the Imperial Japanese Navy* (New York: Secker and Warburg, 1956), p. 84.
17. J.B. Cohen, *Japan's economy in war and reconstruction* (Minneapolis: University of Minnesota Press, 1949), p. 233.
18. W.T. Y'Blood, *Red Sun setting: the Battle of the Philippine Sea* (Annapolis: Naval Institute Press, 1981) is the best account of this action.

19. R. Nagatsuka, *I was a Kamikaze: the Knights of the Divine Wind* (London: Abelard Schuman, 1972), pp. 205–12.

20. See I. Morris, *The nobility of failure: tragic heroes in the history of Japan* (New York: Secker & Warburg, 1975); R. Inoguchi, T. Nakajima, R. Pineau, *The Divine Wind: Japan's suicide squadrons in World War Two: the story of the Kamikaze pilots* (Annapolis: Naval Institute Press, 1958); Nagatsuka, *I was a Kamikaze*; R. Inoguchi & T. Nakajima, "The Kamikaze attack corps", in *The Japanese Navy in World War Two* (Annapolis: Naval Institute Press, 1969).

21. Y'Blood, *Red Sun setting*, pp. 138–9.

22. J.B. Cohen, *Japan's economy*, p. 212; W.F. Craven & J.L. Cate, *The army air forces in World War Two, Volume VI* (Washington: University of Chicago Press, 1983), pp. 353–4.

23. *USSBS, Report 63*, p. 3 (Washington: Government Printing Office, 1945–9).

24. R.J. Francillon, *Japanese aircraft*, p. 4.

25. Cohen, *Japan's economy*, p. 210.

26. Overy, *Air War*, p. 150.

27. Francillon, *Japanese aircraft*, p. 6.

28. Cohen, *Japan's economy*, p. 74.

29. Overy, *Air War*, p. 93.

30. "Japanese fighters assigned to the defence of Japan", *USSBS, report 62, exhibit D* (Washington: Government Printing Office, 1945–9).

31. E. Angelucci, *The world encyclopaedia of military aircraft* (London: Jane's, 1980), p. 240.

32. Cohen, *Japan's economy*, pp. 85–97.

33. Francillon, *Japanese aircraft*, p. 5.

34. Cohen, *Japan's economy*, pp. 220–6; pp. 296–302.

35. *ibid.*, p. 231.

36. Francillon, *Japanese aircraft*, p. 13.

37. Cohen, *Japan's economy*, pp. 210–27.

38. Quoted in Francillon, *Japanese aircraft*, p. 11.

39. *ibid.*, pp. 13–6.

40. *ibid.*, p. 10; Overy, *Air War*, pp. 150–1.

41. L. Allen, "The campaigns in Asia and the Pacific", in *Decisive campaigns of the Second World War*, J. Gooch (ed.) (London: Frank Cass, 1990), p. 165.

42. H. Probert, *The forgotten air force: the Royal Air Force in the war against Japan 1941–5* (London: Brassey's, 1995), pp. 303–5.

43. W. Koenig, *Over the hump: airlift to China* (London: Pan, 1972), pp. 153–8.

44. R. Weigley, *The American way of warfare: a history of United States military strategy and policy* (New York: Indiana University Press, 1973), pp. 92–5.

45. E.S. Miller, *War Plan Orange: the US strategy to defeat Japan 1897–1941* (Annapolis: Naval Institute Press, 1991).

46. R. Spector, *Eagle against the Sun: the American war with Japan* (New York: Viking, 1984), Chapter Three.

47. W.F. Craven & J.L. Cate, *The army air forces in World War Two – plans and early operations – Volume I* (Chicago: University of Chicago Press, 1948–58), p. 63.

48. S.W. Kirby, *The war against Japan – Volume V* (London: HMSO, 1969), p. 398.

49. Hallion, *Strike from the sky*, pp. 165–7.

50. The best account of this battle is still found in C. Reynolds *The fast carriers: the forging of an Air Navy*, 2nd edn (Annapolis: Naval Institute Press, 1992), especially Chapters Three, Four and Seven.

51. C.G. Reynolds, *Admiral John H. Towers: the struggle for naval air supremacy* (Annapolis: Naval Institute Press, 1991), Chapters 13 and 14.

52. W. Hays Park, " 'Precision' and 'area' bombing: who did which, and when?" in *Airpower: theory and practice*, J. Gooch (ed.) (London: Frank Cass, 1995).

53. C. Crane, *Bombs, cities and civilians: American airpower strategy in World War Two* (Kansas: University of Kansas Press, 1993); and M. Sherry, *The rise of American air power – the creation of Armageddon* (New Haven: Yale University Press, 1987) are the best examples of this trend.

54. Angelucci, *Encyclopaedia of military aircraft*, p. 296.

55. R. Spector, *Eagle against the Sun* (New York: Viking, 1984), pp. 488–9.

56. Crane, *Bombs, cities and civilians*, pp. 128–9; Spector, *Eagle against the Sun*, p. 493.

57. Crane, *Bombs, cities and civilians*, p. 131.

58. The best accounts of this can be found in L. Cortesi, *Target: Tokyo* (New York: Secker and Warburg, 1983), pp. 233–74; T.R. Havens, *Valley of darkness* (New York: University Press of America, 1978), pp. 178–81; and Crane, *Bombs, cities and civilians*, pp. 131–3.

59. G. Alperovitz, *Atomic diplomacy: Hiroshima and Potsdam: the use of the atomic bomb and the American confrontation with Soviet power* (London: Secker & Warburg, 1965).

60. R.C. Butow, *Japan's decision to surrender* (Palo Alto, California: Stanford University Press, 1954).

61. E.B. Potter, *Nimitz* (Annapolis: Naval Institute Press, 1976), p. 400; D. MacArthur, *Reminisces* (New York: Fawcett, 1964), p. 276.

62. B.J. Bernstein, "Compelling Japan's surrender without the A-bomb, Soviet entry, or invasion: reconsidering the US Bombing Survey's early-surrender conclusions", *Journal of Strategic Studies* **18**(2), 1995.

63. J. Vander Meulen, "Planning for VJ-Day by the US Army Air Forces and the atomic bomb controversy, *Journal of Strategic Studies* **16**(2), 1993, pp. 227–39.

Chapter Eight

1. General M. Dugan, *US News and World Report*, 11 February 1991.

2. W. Biddle, *Barons of the sky – from early flight to strategic warfare: the story of the American aerospace industry* (New York: Henry Holt, 1991), Chapter Ten.

3. An issue raised by Paul Kennedy in *Preparing for the twenty first century* (London: HarperCollins, 1993).

4. Congress of the United States, Office of Technology Assessment, *New technology for NATO* (Washington: Government Printing House, 1987), pp. 103–4.

5. See the quotes of Churchill and Lord Tedder in T. Mason, *Air power: a centennial appraisal* (London: Brassey's, 1994), p. 62.

6. For the work of Brodie see B. Brodie *The absolute weapon* (New York: Institute of International Studies, 1946); B. Brodie "The heritage of Douhet" in *Air University Quarterly Review* **6**(2); and B. Brodie *Strategy in the nuclear age* (Princeton: Princeton University Press, 1965).

7. Best example of Earle's pessimistic view is E. Earle "The influence of air power on history", *Yale Review*, June 1946.

8. See E. Beard, *Developing the ICBM: a study in bureaucratic politics* (New York: Columbia University Press, 1976).

9. Third report of H.H. Arnold to the Secretary of War, *Air power and the future*, 12 November 1945, quoted in W. Millis (ed.), *American military thought* (Bobbs Merrill Co., 1966), pp. 445–6; and C. Spaatz, quoted in R. Futrell, *Ideas, concepts, doctrine: basic thinking in the United States Air Force 1907–60* (Montgomery: Aerospace Studies Institute, Air University, 1989), p. 214.

10. D.A. Rosenberg, "The origins of overkill: nuclear weapons and American Strategy 1945–60", *International Security* **7**(4), 1983, pp. 12–3.

11. W.S. Borgiasz, *The Strategic Air Command: evolution and consolidation of nuclear forces 1945–55* (New York: Praeger Press, 1996), p. 143.

12. T. Mason, *Air power: a centennial appraisal* (London: Brassey's, 1994), p. 84.

13. JCS paper of May 1947 quoted in T.H. Etzold & J.L. Gaddis (eds), *Containment: documents on American policy and strategy 1945–50* (New York: Columbia University Press, 1978), p. 302.

14. H.R. Borowski, *A hollow threat: strategic air power and containment before Korea* (Westport: Greenwood, 1982).

15. D. Lilienthal, *The journals of David E. Lilienthal – Volume II – The atomic energy years 1945–50* (New York: Harper & Row, 1964), p. 391.

16. B. Blechman & R. Powell, "What in the name of God is strategic superiority?", *Political Science Quarterly* **97**(4), 1982/3; R. Dingman, "Atomic diplomacy during the Korean War" and R.J. Foot, "Nuclear coercion and the ending of the Korean Conflict", both in *International Security* **13**(3), 1988/9.

17. D.A. Rosenberg, "American atomic strategy and the Hydrogen Bomb decision", *Political Science Quarterly* **76**(1), 1976.

18. L. Freedman, "The first two generations of nuclear strategists", in *Makers of modern strategy from Machiavelli to the nuclear age*, P. Paret (ed.) (Oxford: Oxford University Press, 1986), p. 738.

19. Borowski, *Hollow threat*, p. 165.

20. H.R. Borowski, "A narrow victory", *USAF Air Force Magazine*, July–August 1981, pp. 18–27.

21. Borgiasz, *Strategic Air Command*, pp. 143–4.

22. See S.J. Ball, *The bomber in British strategy: doctrine, strategy and Britain's world role 1945–60* (Boulder: Westview, 1995).

23. Mason, *Air power*, p. 91.
24. Borgiasz, *Strategic Air Command*, Chapter Two; D.A. Rosenberg, "The origins of overkill: nuclear weapons and American strategy, 1945–60", *International Security* **7**(4), 1983.
25. Freedman, in Paret (ed.), *Makers of modern strategy*, p. 741.
26. Borgiasz, *Strategic Air Command*, p. 49.
27. J.F. Dulles, "The evolution of foreign policy", *Department of State Bulletin* **30**, 25 January 1954, quoted in Paret (ed.), *Makers of modern strategy*, p. 740.
28. The "trip-wire" analogy was actually coined in 1956 during discussions on NATO doctrine.
29. J.F. Dulles, "Policy for Security and Peace," *Foreign Affairs* **30**, April 1954.
30. The best single volume on the rise of Soviet nuclear capability is D. Holloway, *Stalin and the bomb* (London: Oxford University Press, 1994).
31. D. MacIssac, "Voices from the central blue: the air power theorists", in Paret (ed.), *Makers of modern strategy*, p. 642.
32. T. Greenwood, *Making the MIRV: a study in defense decision making* (Cambridge, Mass.: University Press of America, 1975) gives a full account of this development.
33. L. Freedman, in Paret (ed.), *Makers of modern strategy*, p. 760.
34. R. Overy, "Air power and the origins of deterrence theory before 1939", *Journal of Strategic Studies* **15**(1), 1992.
35. D. MacIssac, in Paret (ed.), *Makers of modern strategy*, p. 643.
36. R.F. Futrell, *The United States Air Force in Korea 1950–53* (Washington: Aerospace Studies Institute, Air University, 1983) is the revised official history, but see also M.J. Armitage & R.A. Mason, *Air power in the nuclear age* (Champaign, Illinois: Macmillan, 1983).
37. C.S. Maier, "Finance and defense: implications of military integration 1950–52", in *NATO: the founding of the Atlantic Alliance and the integration of Europe*, F.H. Heller & J.R. Gillingham (eds) (London: Macmillan, 1992), pp. 335–6.
38. R.A. Wampler, "Conventional goals and nuclear promises: the Truman administration and the roots of the NATO new look", in Heller & Gillingham (eds), *NATO*, pp. 353–5.
39. Mason, *Air power*, pp. 91–4.
40. *ibid.*, p. 97.
41. J.H. Hanson, "Development of Soviet aviation support", *International Defence Review* **5**, 1980.
42. General B. Rogers, "Greater flexibility for NATO's flexible response", *Strategic Review*, Spring, 1983; General D.A. Starry, "Extending the battlefield", *Military Review*, March 1981; Mason, *Air power*, pp. 97–104.
43. Armitage & Mason, *Air power in the nuclear age*, pp. 112–3.
44. C. Berger (ed.), *The United States Air Force in southeast Asia* (Washington: Office of Air Force History, 1977), p. 166.
45. A.L. Gropman, "The air war in Vietnam 1961–73", in *War in the third dimension: essays in contemporary air power*, R.A. Mason (ed.) (London: Bassey's, 1986).

46. S.R. McMichael, *Stumbling bear: Soviet military performance in Afghanistan* (London: Bassey's, 1991).
47. The carrier debate dominated discussion in journals such as the *US Naval Institute Proceedings* for many years, but also see G. Till, *Modern sea power* (London: Bassey's, 1988).
48. Mason, *Air power*, pp. 67–79.

Select bibliography

This is just a sample of what is available (and there is a vast amount) but most of the key sources are listed below. I have concentrated on readily available material in English where possible. Use the bibliographies in these books to lead on to other material.

Armitage, M.J. & R.A. Mason. *Air power in the nuclear age* (Champaign, Illinois: Macmillan, 1983).

Ball, S.J. *The bomber in British strategy: doctrine, strategy and Britain's world role 1945–60* (Boulder: Westview, 1995).

Barnett, C. *Engage the enemy more closely* (London: W.W. Norton, 1991).

Belote, J.H. & W.M. Belote. *Titans of the sea* (New York: Harper & Row, 1975).

Berger, C. (ed.). *The United States Air Force in southeast Asia* (Washington: Office of Air Force History, 1977).

Bernstein, B.J. Compelling Japan's surrender without the A-bomb, Soviet entry, or invasion: reconsidering the US bombing survey's early surrender conclusions. *Journal of Strategic Studies* **18**(2), 1995.

Best, G. *Humanity in warfare* (London: Weidenfeld and Nicolson, 1980).

Bialer, U. *The shadow of the bomber* (London: Royal Historical Society, 1980).

Biddle, W. *Barons of the sky – from early flight to strategic warfare: the story of the American aerospace industry* (New York: Henry Holt, 1991).

Bilstein, R. *Flight in America 1900–1983* (New York: Johns Hopkins University Press, 1984).

Boog, H. (ed.). *The conduct of the air war in the Second World War: an international comparison* (Oxford: Berg, 1992).

Borgiasz, W.S. *The Strategic Air Command: evolution and consolidation of nuclear forces 1945–55* (New York: Praeger, 1996).

Borowski, H. *A hollow threat: strategic air power and containment before Korea* (Connecticut: Greenwood, 1982).

Brodie, B. *Strategy in the nuclear age* (Princeton: Princeton University Press, 1965).

Buckley, J. *The RAF and trade defence 1919–45 – constant endeavour* (Keele: Keele University Press, 1995).

Calder, A. *The myth of the Blitz* (London: Jonathan Cape, 1991).

Christienne, C. (ed.). *Histoire de l'Aviation Militaire Francaise* (Paris: Charles Lavauzelle, 1980).

Clarke, I.F. *Voices prophesying war 1978–84* (Oxford: Oxford University Press, 1964).

Cohen, J.B. *Japan's economy in war and reconstruction* (Minnesota: Minnesota University Press, 1949).

Collier, B. *A history of air power* (London: HMSO, 1974).

Cooling, B.F. (ed.). *Case studies in the development of close air support* (Washington: Office of Air Force History, 1990).

Cooper, M. *The German air force 1933–45: an anatomy of failure* (London: Jane's, 1981).

Corum, J.S. From biplanes to Blitzkrieg: the development of German air doctrine between the wars. *War in History* **3**(1), 1996.

Corum, J.S. *The Luftwaffe: creating the operational air war, 1918–40* (Kansas: University Press of Kansas, 1997).

Corum, J.S. *The roots of blitzkrieg* (Kansas: University Press of Kansas, 1992).

Crane, C.C. *Bombs, cities and civilians: American airpower strategy in World War Two* (Kansas: University Press of Kansas, 1993).

Craven, W.F. & J.L. Cate. (eds). *The army air forces in World War Two* [6 vols] (Chicago: University of Chicago Press, 1948–55).

Crouch, T. *A dream of wings – Americans and the airplane 1875–1905* (Washington: Smithsonian Institution Press, 1981).

Deichmann, P. *Spearhead for blitzkrieg: Luftwaffe operations in support of the army 1939–45* (London: Greenhill, 1996).

Dockrill, S. (ed.). *From Pearl Harbor to Hiroshima: the Second World War in Asia and the Pacific 1941–45* (London: Macmillan, 1994).

Douhet, G. *Command of the air* (London: Faber & Faber, 1942).

Ellis, J. *Brute force: Allied strategy and tactics in the Second World War* (London: Andre Deutsch, 1990).

Ferris, J. The theory of a French air menace, Anglo-French relations and the British Home Defence Air Force programmes of 1921–25. *Journal of Strategic Studies* **10**(1), 1987.

Francillon, R.J. *Japanese aircraft of the Pacific War* (London: Putnam, 1970).

Franklin, H.B. *War stars: the superweapon and the American imagination* (Oxford: Oxford University Press, 1988).

Fritzche, P. *A nation of fliers: German aviation and the popular imagination* (Harvard: Harvard University Press, 1992).

Futrell, R. *Ideas, concepts, doctrine: a history of basic thinking in the USAF 1907–64* (Montgomery: Aerospace Studies Institute, Air University, 1971).

Garrett, S. *Ethics and airpower in World War Two* (New York: St. Martin's, 1993).

Gibbs-Smith, C.H. *Aviation: an historical survey* (London: HMSO, 1970).

Gooch, J. (ed.) *Decisive campaigns of the Second World War* (London: Frank Cass, 1990).

Gooch, J. (ed.) *Airpower: theory and practice* (London: Frank Cass, 1995).

Gooderson, I. *Air power at the battlefront: Allied close air support in Europe 1943–45* (London: Frank Cass, 1998).

Gooderson, I. Allied fighter-bombers versus German armour in North-West Europe 1944–45: myths and realities. *Journal of Strategic Studies* **14**(2), 1991.

Gooderson, I. Heavy and medium bombers: how successful were they in the tactical close air support role during World War Two? *Journal of Strategic Studies* **15**(3), 1992.

Greenhous, B. Close air support aircraft in World War One: the counter anti-tank role. *Aerospace Historian* **21**, 1974.

Greer, T. *The development of air doctrine in the army air arm 1917–41* (Washington: Office of Air Force History, 1985).

Hallion, R.P. *Strike from the sky: the history of battlefield air attack 1911–45* (Washington: Smithsonian Institution Press, 1989).

Hanson, J.H. Development of Soviet aviation support. *International Defence Review* **5**, 1980.

Hardesty, V. *Red Phoenix – the rise of Soviet air power 1941–45* (Washington: Smithsonian Institution Press, 1982).

Higham, R. & J.W. Kipp. *Soviet aviation and air power: a historical view* (Boulder: Westview, 1977).

Higham, R. *A concise history of air power* (London: St. Martin's, 1972).

Higham, R. *The military intellectuals in Britain 1918–39* (New Jersey: Rutgers University Press, 1966).

Holloway, D. *Stalin and the bomb* (London: Oxford University Press, 1994).

Homze, E.L. *Arming the Luftwaffe: the Reich Air Ministry and the German aircraft industry 1919–39* (Nebraska: University of Nebraska Press, 1976).

Howard, M. (ed.). *Restraints on war: studies in the limitation of armed conflict* (Oxford: Oxford University Press, 1979).

Kennett, L. *A history of strategic bombing* (New York: Scribner, 1982).

Kennett, L. *The first air war 1914–18* (New York: Free Press, 1991).

Killen, J. *A history of maritime air power* (London: Muller, 1969).

Kilmarx, R. The Russian Imperial Air Forces of World War One. *Airpower Historian* **10**, 1963.

Mason, R.A. *War in the third dimension – essays in contemporary air power* (London: Brassey's, 1986).

Mason, T. *Air power: a centennial appraisal* (London: Brassey's, 1994).

Maurer, M. *Aviation in the US Army 1919–39* (Washington: Office of Air Force History, 1987).

McFarland, S.L. & W.P. Newton. *To command the sky – the battle for air superiority – 1942–4* (Washington: Smithsonian Institution Press, 1991).

McInnes, C. & G.D. Sheffield. (eds.). *Warfare in the twentieth century: theory and practice* (London: Unwin Hyman, 1988).

McMichael, S.R. *Stumbling bear: Soviet military performance in Afghanistan* (London: Brassey's, 1991).

Mead, P. *The eye in the air* (London: HMSO, 1983).

Morrow, J.H. *Building German air power 1909–14* (Tennessee: University of Tennessee Press, 1976).

Morrow, J.H. *German air power in World War One* (Nebraska: University of Nebraska Press, 1982).

Morrow, J.H. *The Great War in the air – military aviation from 1909–21* (Washington: Smithsonian Institution Press, 1993).

Murray, W. & A.R. Millett. *Military innovation in the interwar period* (Cambridge: Cambridge University Press, 1996).

Murray, W. *Luftwaffe: strategy for defeat* (Washington: Allen and Unwin, 1985).

Noakes, J. (ed.). *The civilian in war: the Home Front in Europe, Japan and the USA in World War Two* (Exeter: Exeter University Press, 1992).

Omissi, D.E. *Air power and colonial control: the RAF 1919–39* (Manchester: Manchester University Press, 1990).

Overy, R. Air power and origins of deterrence theory before 1939. *Journal of Strategic Studies* **15**(1), 1992.

Overy, R. *The Air War 1939–45* (London: Macmillan, 1980).

Overy, R. *Why the Allies won* (London: Jonathan Cape, 1995).

Pape, R.A. *Bombing to win – air power and coercion in war* (New York: Cornell University Press, 1996).

Paret, P. (ed.). *The makers of modern strategy from Machiavelli to the nuclear strategy* (Oxford: Oxford University Press, 1986).

Parillo, M. *The Japanese merchant marine in World War Two* (Annapolis: Naval Institute Press, 1993).

Paris, M. *From the Wright brothers to Top Gun: aviation, nationalism and popular cinema* (Manchester: Manchester University Press, 1995).

Paris, M. *Winged Warfare – The Literature and theory of aerial warfare in Britain 1859–1917* (Manchester: Manchester University Press, 1991).

Pisano, D.A. *Legend, memory and the Great War in the air* (Washington: Smithsonian Institution Press, 1992).

Probert, H. *The forgotten air force: the RAF in the war against Japan 1941–45* (London: Brassey's, 1995).

Rae, J.B. *Climb to greatness: the American aircraft industry 1920–60* (London: MIT Press, 1968).

Raleigh, W. & H.A. Jones. *The war in the air* [6 vols] (Oxford: Oxford University Press, 1922–37).

Reynolds, C.G. *Admiral John H. Towers – the struggle for naval air supremacy* (Annapolis: Naval Institute Press, 1991).

Reynolds, C.G. *The fast carriers – the forging of an air navy* (New York: McGraw Hill, 1968).

Richards, D. & H. Saunders. *The Royal Air Force 1939–45* [3 vols] (London: HMSO, 1953).

Ritchie, S. *Industry and air power – the expansion of British aircraft production 1935–41* (London: Frank Cass, 1997).

Rogers, B. Greater flexibility for NATO's flexible response. *Strategic Review*, 1983.

Rosenberg, D.A. The origins of overkill: nuclear weapons and American strategy 1945–60. *International Security* **7**(4), 1983.

Segre, C.S. Guilio Douhet: strategist, theorist, prophet? *Journal of Strategic Studies* **15**(3), 1992.

Sherry, M. *The rise of American air power – the creation of Armageddon* (New Haven: Yale University Press, 1987).

Smith, M.S. *British air strategy between the wars* (Oxford: Oxford University Press, 1984).

Spector, R.H. *Eagle against the sun – the war against Japan 1941–45* (New York: Viking, 1985).

Starry, G.A. Extending the battlefield. *Military Review* March 1981.

Terraine, J. *The right of the line: the Royal Air Force in the European War 1939–45* (London: Hodder & Stoughton, 1985).

Till, G. *Air power and the Royal Navy 1914–45: a historical perspective* (London: Jane's, 1979).

Underwood, J.S. *Wings of democracy: the influence of air power on the Roosevelt administration 1933–41* (Texas: Texas University Press, 1991).

Webster, C. & N. Frankland. *The strategic air offensive against Germany* [4 vols] (London: HMSO, 1961).

Wells, H.G. *The war in the air* (London: George Bell and Sons, 1908).

Wood, D. & D. Dempster. *The narrow margin – the Battle of Britain and the rise of air power 1930–40* (London: Hutchinson, 1961).

Y'Blood, W.T. *Red sun setting: the Battle of the Philippine Sea* (Annapolis: Naval Institute Press, 1981).

Young, R.J. The use and abuse of fear: France and the air menace in the 1930s. *Intelligence and National Security* **2**(4), 1987.

Index